FUTURE VISIONS

Provides a useful round-up of the 'new' screen technologies and fills in some of the background.
The Guardian

Future Visions *offers not just a snapshot of where we are now but ... good short histories of how we got to this point.*
Journal of Media Law and Practice

(A) mixed collection of articles on various new media technologies, including ecial effects, HDTV, multimedia, video games and virtual reality. Histories of video games and large screen cinema systems are particularly good.
Screen Digest

Essentially the book summarises the state of technology for generating images, examining both the scientific developments and the cultural implications. The list of contributors is equally impressive ...
Film Ireland

hortlisted for the 1993 Kraszna-Krausz Awards for the best books on the moving image

Film format comparison

70mm

35mm

IMAX®

Screen comparison

IMAX® Screen, Jakarta, Indonesia
70.5 x 92.75 ft. (21.5 x 28.3m)

70mm Screen
29.5 x 64.75 ft. (9 x 19.7m)

35mm Screen
15 x 28 ft. (4.6 x 8.6 m)

35 mm, 70 mm and IMAX film frames and screens

FUTURE VISIONS

New Technologies of The Screen

EDITED BY PHILIP HAYWARD & TANA WOLLEN

THE **ARTS COUNCIL** OF GREAT BRITAIN

BFI Publishing

First published in 1993 by the
British Film Institute
21 Stephen Street
London W1P 1PL

Copyright © British Film Institute 1993

Individual contributions
copyright © author 1993

Reprinted 1994

British Library Cataloguing in Publication Data

Future Visions: Introduction and
Development of New Screen Technologies
 I. Hayward, Philip   II. Wollen, Tana
 791.43

ISBN 0–85170–384–4
    0–85170–400–x pbk

Cover design by David Hockin
Cover photograph from *Terminator 2: Judgement Day*
courtesy of Industrial Light and Magic © 1991

Set in 10/12 pt Garamond
by Fakenham Photosetting Ltd
Fakenham, Norfolk
and printed in Great Britain by
Page Bros, Norwich

To
Rosa
and to
the Blue Mountains

CONTENTS

ACKNOWLEDGMENTS

Among the many people who generously gave their time, advice and expertise in the preparation of this volume, the editors would like to thank the following especially: Manuel Alvarado, Edward Buscombe, Roma Gibson, Christine Gledhill, Stephen Herbert, Dawn King, David Meeker, Anita Miller, Richard Paterson, Michael Prescott, at the British Film Institute; Will Bell at the Arts Council of Great Britain; Rod Varley at the National Museum of Photography, Film and Television in Bradford; Captain George Lindman and Vern Cottee at Qantas Airways Ltd; Karen Hynes at Qantec Library; Augie Grant at the University of Texas at Austin; Juliane Brown and Lisa Pierce at the IMAX Corporation; Gary Warner at the Australian Film Commission; Kevin Robins, Susan Morris, Jon Weinbren, John Wyver, Kathleen Rogers, Catherine Richards, Paul Brown, Philip Bell, Jan Knapman, Kerry Lewis, Andrew Murphie and Rosa Coyle-Hayward. The BFI would like to acknowledge the Arts Council of Great Britain for its financial assistance in the publication of this volume.

NOTES ON CONTRIBUTORS

Philip Hayward lectures in Mass Communications at Macquarie University, Sydney. He has written and edited several books including *Culture, Technology and Creativity*. He is editor of *Perfect Beat* – a journal of research into contemporary music and popular culture.

Tana Wollen is Head of Television and Projects Unit at the British Film Institute.

Robin Baker is Director of Visual Computing at the Royal College of Art, London. He lectures in the USA and Europe and consults widely with industry on the strategic use of computing in design. His current projects include work with the Design Museum, the Design Council, Marks and Spencer plc, Courtaulds and Coats Viyella. His book *Visible Surfaces: Computing in Design and the Visual Arts* will be published in 1993.

Jean-Luc Renaud is the editor-in-chief of the international industry newsletter *ATM – Advanced Television Markets*. He is also president of London-based consultancy Globalcom Ltd. Over the past ten years he has conducted research into the media industries and lectured on communications technologies, economics and regulation in Europe and the United States. He is co-author of the book *The Future of the European Audio-Visual Industry*.

Frank Rickett is a Psychology graduate from Liverpool University with a Master's degree in Computer Science from Hatfield Polytechnic. He is a freelance producer of multimedia and a lecturer in Computer Science.

Timothy Binkley is Chair of the graduate programme in Computer Art and Director of the Institute for Computers in the Arts at the

School of Visual Arts, New York. He has created software for artists, designed interactive installations and is the author of *Wittgenstein's Language* and *Symmetry Studio* as well as numerous articles on aesthetics and computer art.

Leslie Haddon is currently a senior research fellow in the Media Studies Department, University of Sussex, investigating the consumption of information and communication technologies in the home.

Rebecca Coyle is a lecturer in Mass Communications at Macquarie University, Sydney. She writes and broadcasts on advanced technology and has recently completed a book on holography. She was an organiser of the Third International Symposium on Electronic Art held in Australia in 1992.

Sally Pryor is a computer artist, animator, programmer and writer. Her computer-generated prints, animations, videos and installations use both high and low-end systems. She is a lecturer in a wide range of computer-based topics at the University of Technology, Sydney.

Jill Scott is a video artist who makes both interactive installations and single channel works for television. She has been researching Virtual Reality applications for OTC Australia and the University of New South Wales, College of Fine Arts. She lectures in Computer Graphics and Video at the Holschüle der Bildenden Künste Saar in Germany.

INTRODUCTION
Surpassing the Real

Philip Hayward and Tana Wollen

Technologies have captured sounds and moving images for over a century. Once the early juddering blurs began to sharpen in the light, it became clear that not only could the camera frame a slice of life, it could restore past moments to the present and could show what one had seen to many. Sight and vision were no longer limited to the singular, the personal. Nor was the purchase of a few pictures reserved for the rich. In the mid-1990s the instant and constant proliferation of moving images makes it difficult for us to imagine the states of excitement, even awe, in which they were at first beheld. It is impossible to borrow the minds of those for whom cinema first invented new ways of seeing. The irony is that however much cinema and television archives are able to restore the past to us, the flow, clarity and speed of sounds and images have now become so habitual that those very processes of restoration make the past recede more rapidly into the distance and obscure whatever preservation has kept flickering in the light.

Sound and moving image technologies have not developed along a straight track, nor have they been fuelled by a singular motivation. Nevertheless, if any teleology draws their accumulated histories, it will show that attaining the real has been a forceful ambition, and for André Bazin this was the camera's greatest achievement. 'For the first time, between the originating object and its reproduction there intervenes only the instrumentality of a non-living agent. For the first time an image of the world is formed automatically, without the creative intervention of man ... The objective nature of photography confers on it a quality of credibility absent from all other picture making.'[1]

1

There have been many other firsts: since the early days of cinema, innovations in audiovisual technologies have aimed to provide a series of new, notionally improved experiences for audiences. The moving camera, synch sound, faster film stock, Technicolor, broadcast television, wraparound sound, digital tape; each 'upgrading' has enhanced sounds and images. Their improvements have always resulted in a more vivid capture of the real: greater clarity, firmer focus, richer hues.

It would be too tempting to see the development of audiovisual technologies as entirely driven by a realist project, however, to make realism the screen's grand narrative. That plot not only omits a rich heritage of the surreal and extraordinary which audiovisual technologies have brought forth, it allows the inconstancy of the real to get away. Trains coming into stations were not the only early images projected; screens were adorned with spectacle and fantasy too. The desire for magic has driven technological development as intensely as any quest for the real. The worn story of how the Lumières' audience gasped in fright as the train pulled into La Ciotat is worth remembering though. The 'real' spans the shocking to the banal and it can occasionally be both. The photographic realism of any age assumes quaintness or distance as soon as 'improvements' achieve fresh immediacy: our notions of the 'real' are changed by the 'realisms' which supersede each other to represent it.

Realism can express the gritty, the mundane, the horrific, the dramatic across a range of photographic, cinematic and televisual aesthetics. The development of audiovisual technologies has been driven not so much by a realist project as by an *illusionary* one. That is to say, the illusion of the real has had to be made more convincing and the spectacular has had to be made more 'realistic'. The second-hand has had to become first-hand, the vicarious has had to be made vivid. Audiovisual technologies have had to make illusions realities. 'The fundamental drive behind all these inventions seems to have been to make second-hand experience as 'authentic' as possible by either swamping one sense with stimuli or by giving as many senses as possible mutually confirming information.'[2]

Now, audiovisual technologies have apparently removed barriers between the real and the represented by their production of the hyperreal (the 'more perfect copy of the real'), and have ironically rendered problematic indexical relationships each time they have exceeded the latest *ne plus ultra* in their illusionary project. It would be wrong to continue considering these technologies as self-animated energies somehow independent of specific economic systems. New technolo-

2

gies do not simply emerge, but by virtue of their development the market promotes their use (sometimes to the point of insistence), creating needs which the new technologies serve to commercial advantage – as the firm grip CD audio has taken on the hi-fi market demonstrates. Volkov wrote of science being 'the helmsman of the modern industrial revolution' but in late capitalism it is market aspirations which determine product development and succession rather than any evolutionary instincts within technology.[3] Nevertheless, the introduction of each new technology to existing communication systems, however disruptive to media ecologies it may be, is based ostensibly on its right of succession to an older form deemed comparatively inefficient. This rationale for the production and marketing of new technologies can be characterised as *Techno-Futurism*. Over and above the relations between technological developments and their economic and industrial contexts prevails a progressive ideal: new technologies benefit culture and society. It works as a classic ideological paradigm, appearing simply as 'common sense', as any advertisement for a new car or computing system will show. Ironically, it was one of Futurism's most fervent proponents, the Italian Filippo Marinetti, whose oft-cited aphorism illustrates the principle's *reductio ad absurdum*, 'Progress is always right, even when it's wrong'.

All the systems discussed in this anthology are relatively new. They are each at different points part of a continuing dynamic, a drive towards product upgrading in order to retain and revive audiences. They share distinction in that they are instances in a process of convergence between old and new and in that by requiring interaction they transform audiences and consumers into users.

Convergence

Sounds and moving images are no longer fixed on celluloid or magnetic tape: the colonising, promiscuous computer has digitised them. As algorithmic composites they rely no longer on prints or tapes, projectors or recorders, but can be sent, copied, reassembled, refigured anyhow, anywhere. ... Having memory and storage the computer is archive; it is also editor, player and recorder. It can create sounds and images as easily as it plagiarises them.

> One of the nice things you can do with the technology as it's advanced now, on your own desk top, is you can take a videotape or a laser disk of a film, and you can send the signal to the computer and watch the film on the screen. You can stop it,

reverse it, put it in slow-motion and so on. . . . The computer gives you the power to shift everything around in the film. I can take a character from one scene, store the character in the attitude I've selected, and then I can move that character into any one of the other scenes.[4]

The stable characteristics of older media – photography, film, video – are collapsing as digital technologies spawn hybrid forms of protean capabilities. CD-I, for instance, carries sounds, still and moving images, text and graphics. What would Bazin have made of the computer whose algorithms model geometric forms and obviate any need for *a priori* objects or events to generate photographic images?

For the moment, these new media hybrids are not yet anchored to cultural institutions (in the same way film is to cinema, for instance), although this is not to deny their significant force in the contemporary commodification of culture. How computer games or virtual reality will generate new cultural institutions, or penetrate existing ones is difficult to say, but behind the technological convergences which characterise the new media hybrids lie new institutional alliances. Discernible tracks charted across some of the chapters in this anthology lead from instances of developments and applications of technologies by the military to their promotion and use in the entertainment industries. These institutional links are as distinctive a feature of the new audio-visual instruments as the intermarriage between their technologies. In the most accessible introduction to virtual reality published so far, Howard Rheingold remarks on these links when describing the NASA Ames Research Center at Mountain View: 'It was there that a human interface researcher, a cognitive scientist, an adventure game programmer and a small network of garage inventors put together the first affordable VR prototypes.[5] A recognisable cast of entrepreneurial, innovative characters moves between state and corporate funded R and D in communications or weapons design, to computer graphics and special effects facilities, or to toy manufacture.

For the purposes of cultural analysis, the digital breaches through old media boundaries will mean at least further disciplinary extensions to Film and Media Studies, if not upheavals in their epistemological foundations as well. Computing processes and their consequences will have to be considered alongside the distinct signifying systems, texts and institutions of film and television, video and photography. This anthology provides no more than a tentative starting point. Through its descriptive histories of new screen technologies it charts some of the gulfs lying between computing and cultural discourses but cannot pretend to bridge them. Its value lies in its indication of the inter-disciplinary challenges ahead.

In order to comprehend the changes and possibilities new technologies might generate, we need to shape new metaphors. As surrogate eye the camera lens has served well, as a mechanical medium between the real world and its analogical representations it has assumed the equivalence of sight merely by delivering what the eye can see. To sight, in Western culture, are attributed other virtues, namely knowledge and control. To see is to know, to survey, to control – now epitomised in the computing-speak WYSIWYG (what you see is what you get). The camera in reportage, in closed-circuit surveillance, in the nose of a smart missile, is sight–knowledge–control. It is outer vision, the external perspective which has become privileged in the now habitual camera/eye analogy, perhaps reinforcing the prevalent fixation in Film and Media Studies on realism as the dominant ideology in representation.

The camera lens as portal to inner vision, yielding access to the imaginary, is a less familiar construction. Nevertheless, the camera does offer dual entry to the outer world (sight) and to the inner world (vision): it documents *and* makes magic. If sight is associated with the rational and vision with the irrational, how are the analogies with the camera lens stretched when our access is obtained through computer interfaces, data gloves, goggles or sensor helmets? How are objectivity and subjectivity skewed?

Interactivity

There are more means to vicarious experience now than ever before. Adding CD-I, HDTV, computer games and virtual reality to books, audiotapes, radio, video, TV and cinema seems to indicate unlimited appetites for fictional pleasure. Are the effects of the illusionary project striving to impress images upon us, to immerse us until we are all but lost, so different from that time-honoured activity 'getting into a really good book'? The hype would claim that they are, and a great deal is made of the active participation these technologies require. In order to move through the diegeses of video discs, arcade games or virtual reality programmes, audiences/players need to make decisions, react and even predict the nature of the rules and dimensions of their fictive systems. Unlike predetermined texts (a novel or feature film, for

5

instance) which demand at best active readings, or at least a degree of passive 'drift', intervention is claimed necessary for the new media and it is this which makes them distinctive from older forms.

The enhanced audiovisual experiences on offer promise to *immerse* us, not merely leave us listening in and looking on. This might belie the very promise of interactivity since the notion implies audience action/reaction from somewhere outside the text rather than from within it. Virtual reality, an audio-visual-haptic medium *par excellence*, is not so much a closed text but a responsive environment in which sensors react to movement and gesture by changing the sounds and images within the programme. This is a medium in the true sense of the term, linking human intelligence with an artificial one. This intelligence relationship works within simulations, reality substitutes, which stretch the term 'representation' to its limits.

Virtual reality programmes are multi-purpose. In biochemistry they make invisible molecular structures visible and manipulable; in architectural design they can make visible what is not yet realised; in coin-op arcades they construct fantasy war scenarios; in therapy they enable users to act as they never actually could. These programmes, computed texts, are model makers, responding to the mental models human beings make within the imaginary. Here sight and vision are superimposed. The simulation is a symbolic representation but once *seen*, it can be known and mastered, the more so if we are able to move around it and move it around too. Enveloping us, the simulation appears as the realisation of images in the inner mind, a kind of audiovisual Walkman which forces plenitude by blocking out everything else but itself.

Virtual reality is oxymoronic not only in self-description, but also in what it does, embodying the disembodied. Within these intelligence relationships human bodies become part of the machine; the machine is personalised and becomes a personal agent. This machine-body has of course had a long life mutating from Frankenstein to the Terminator, but if science fiction/horror narratives are necessary and welcome expressions of the latent fears about the lack of control human beings can exert over their own creations, what are the expressions, where is the language to name what is being created now, to describe it, to bring it into our ken?

Paradoxically, it would seem as though language was returning us to a pre-mirror phase relationship with the great mother machine. Separation and recognition of an Other are past, our future is in fusion. The brain and cognition are described as 'wetware', the spinal column as 'the ultimate co-axial cable'.[6]

The cyberspace experience is destined to transform us in other ways because it is an undeniable reminder of a fact we are hypnotized since birth to ignore and deny – that our normal state of consciousness is itself a hyperrealistic simulation. We build models of the world in our minds using the data from our sense organs and the information-processing capabilities of our brain. We habitually think of the world we see as 'out there', but what we are seeing is really a mental model, a perceptual simulation that exists only in our brain. That simulation capability is where human minds and digital computers share a potential for synergy.[7]

This has a satisfying, self-fulfilling prophetic ring about it. Minds and machines have always had a 'potential for synergy', after all. Descriptions like these are in danger of relegating human and artificial intelligences to a purely formal symbiosis abstracted from culture, history or nature. As new technologies are developed and used, how they are thought of, spoken and written about will be important, although it would be naive to suppose that 'artists' using technologies will automatically make them beneficial. As Donna Harraway,[8] Catherine Richards, Nell Tenhaaf[9] and Jill Scott and Sally Pryor (in this volume) show, the mind-machine couplet is a particularly male fantasy and talk of liberation through new technologies is tempered (even within the same commentaries) with fears of their inhuman, militaristic capabilities.

The technologies discussed in this anthology are being developed in particular cultural, economic and political contexts. The digitisation of the photographic has renewed debates about the (un)reliability of the indexical relationships between the represented and its representation. Digitisation has made the malleability of sounds and images seem like something new and has rekindled anxieties about the ability to communicate truthfully; in an era when communications technologies proliferate, the irony is painful.

There is another irony at work in the tension between the lack of verity or significance which signification overload has produced on the one hand and the pressing, urgent realities on the other. The video evidence submitted in Rodney King's defence, the jury's acquittal of the policemen who attacked him and the riots which erupted in Los Angeles in 1992 as a result, are symptomatic of this increasingly troubled relationship. Once doubt has been cast on photographic truth how, when the need for justice arises, can it be appealed to? The more

7

disturbing reality is that even if and when the arguments can be made, they are often of no account. As Martha Rosler, writing about photographic misrepresentation puts it:

> A more general cultural delegitimisation than the questioning of photographic truth is at work in the industrial societies. This delegitimisation is as much a product of political failure as of image societies, and it entails the declining faith in the project of modernity and its religion of *progress*. (her italics)[10]

In this data commodification age, the technologically poor have new levels of disenfranchisement to plumb. As our planet burns will the new grey goods help to confront and halt destruction? How will necessary information compete with everything else zipping around the global mind-machine networks? Perhaps conscience and consciousness, at least in the technologically rich societies, are now too finely laminated between the different stages, purposes and levels of representation of which so many different kinds of technology are now capable.

This anthology leaves unanswered as many questions as it raises. In compiling it our aim has been modest: to gather and disseminate information about new technologies for those whose engagement with older media leads them to expect changes. This diverse collection starts with chapters about image-enhancing technologies (IMAX, HDTV and computer-generated special effects), moves on to consider digital processes and some of their cultural forms (computer games) and then introduces some of the latest composite technologies (CD-I and Virtual Reality). We hope it will be one of the first of many publications to stimulate inter-disciplinary work in a range of cultural and scientific studies to ensure that new technologies are not developed outside critical and constructive commentary. We hope it will interest and encourage rather than threaten readers who, like us, are only just beginning to emerge somewhere between dire warnings and new dawns, still blinking . . .

NOTES

1. André Bazin, 'The Ontology of the Photographic Image', *What is Cinema?*, vol. 1 (Berkeley: University of California Press, 1967), p. 13.
2. Andrew Higgens, 'Symptoms of Wider Issues', *Artlink*, vol. 2 no. 5, July 1985, p. 5.

3. G. Volkov, *Era of Man or Robot? The Sociological Problems of the Technological Revolution* (Moscow: Progress Publishers, 1967), p. 162.
4. Victor Burgin, 'Realising the Reverie', *Digital Dialogues, Ten-8*, vol. 2 no. 2, 1991, p. 8.
5. Howard Rheingold, *Virtual Reality* (London: Secker and Warburg, 1991), p. 128.
6. The latter phrase, attributed to Marvin Minsky, was quoted by Catherine Richards in her talk at the 'Culture, Technology and Creativity' conference at the ICA, London, April 1991.
7. Rheingold, *Virtual Reality*, p. 387–8.
8. Donna Harraway, 'A Manifesto for Cyborgs: Science, Technology and Socialist Feminism in the 1980s', *Socialist Review* 80, 1985.
9. Catherine Richards and Nell Tenhaaf explored mind-machine hybridity in the 'Bioapparatus Seminar' they led in Banff, Canada during the autumn of 1991.
10. Martha Rosler, 'Image Simulations, Computer Manipulations', *Digital Dialogues, Ten-8*, vol. 2 no. 2, 1991, p. 63.

THE BIGGER THE BETTER
From CinemaScope to Imax

Tana Wollen

I wish I were as in the years of old
While yet the blessed daylight made itself
Ruddy thro' both the roofs of sight, and woke
These eyes, now dull, but then so keen to seek
The meanings ambush'd under all they saw ...

Tennyson: Tiresias, published 1885

In 1953, publicity for *Bwana Devil*, Hollywood's first 3-D feature, promised any viewer intrepid enough to buy a ticket 'a lion in your lap, a lover in your arms'. By 1990 Bill Breukelman, Chairman of Imax Corporation, was making a more dramatic offer. 'We sell involvement ... When you see our movie about mountain gorillas you are not a human being watching a gorilla. You *are* a gorilla.[1] Both these assertions were signposts on a route to future forms of cinema but they also pointed to the future of our experience more generally since cinema, as the dream palace of modern technology, has often indexed the possible shape of things to come.

From its deepest roots in the films of the Lumières and of Méliès, cinema has brought a double shock, a mixed pleasure to the optical palate. Audiences' recognition of the real in cinema's now plentiful representations of the world is mingled with their delight or horror at its capacity to make realistic not only what is actually impossible but what was previously unimaginable. Rendering the real and the magical is by no means peculiar to cinema – literature, painting and radio can induce senses of both recognition and awe – but it is of course cinema's visual opulence, immediacy and amplitude which make this duality so captivating. As cultural forms particularly indebted to technology and to capital, cinema and later television have had their developments fuelled by the aspiration to attain degrees of realism each more convincing than the last. However, technological developments have not only rendered the real more colourful, more luminous, more clearly defined. The quest for audiences in order to recoup capital investment has meant that achieving the real has tended to privilege the more real than real, the 'realistic', in the most startling and dramatic of guises. If capturing the real has been the teleological project of photographic moving images, then making the real marvellous would also seem to be part of that project. As Kevin Robins puts it, 'the photograph has always promised to take us beyond vision'.[2]

If anything distinguishes this century from others it must be the ways in which technology has supplemented, illuminated and now almost replaced our sight. Oppressed as he was by the gift of prophecy, Tennyson's Tiresias could have neither foreseen nor described the camera's ceaseless progeniture. Nevertheless, the connection he made between 'meanings ambush'd' and the very fact of their elucidation has a contemporary sting. There are countless ways in which the improved clarity and power of film have enhanced our vision; countless ways in which audience identification with characters, stars and narratives has been mobilised. Enlarging the screen from Edison's 1:1.38 ratio has been one of them. It is the purpose of this chapter to explore the audiovisual range wide-screens have opened, to consider the commercial and cultural imperatives which have made wide-screens signify the future for cinema and to assess their aesthetic consequences.

In the 1950s Hollywood was an industry intent on attracting audiences through innovation and for a while 3-D became its Holy Grail. However, although *Bwana Devil* (1953) and *House of Wax* (1953) made good box office, their exhibition was sometimes disappointing. There were often problems in aligning projection and in cheaper productions some of the scenes were badly shot. Audiences tended to blame the resulting eyestrain and headaches on the special glasses that had to be worn which in turn caused problems for the cinema managers. It was wide-screen rather than 3-D which very quickly gave Hollywood its new lease of life. With other formats such as TODD-AO and 70 mm, CinemaScope and Cinerama were also part of Tinseltown's defence against the onslaughts of television. In addition to their size they were also able to exploit the slight illusion of depth their screen's curved shapes suggested. 'Cinerama is better than CinemaScope and CinemaScope is better than 2-D pictures projected

11

on wide-screens but 3-D films projected on wide-screens will be the best of all' was one critic's opinion.[3] Nevertheless, it was the wide-screen rather than 3-D which very quickly gave Hollywood its new lease of life. Spyros Skouras, President of 20th Century–Fox heralded CinemaScope with the claim that it would restore the public's interest in the 'greatest entertainment in the world'. The *Daily Film Renter's* 'Commentator', reporting on the test reels of *The Robe*, wrote 'Today I have seen the entertainment of the future'.[4] Television's threatened dominance had been held at bay.

The first experiments in wide-screen relied on multi-projector systems requiring intricate shooting and alignment. Cinerama was the first commercially successful wide-screen process. Film was shot on three cameras bridled together and projected by three projectors onto a concave screen at a depth of 7.5 m at its centre arc. A fourth projector carried the soundtrack while the other three cross-projected distinct reels which, if aligned correctly, made a panoramic spectacle. Although the seams could never be completely effaced, maximum colour and luminosity were thrown onto the screen since each frame passed through a single projector. Cinerama spectacles had many precedents. The more ambitious magic lantern shows had used multiple projection in the late 1880s. The Lumières used ten projectors to throw aerial views of Paris and Brussels onto a circular screen more than 91 m in circumference and projected images onto both sides of a 21 m by 16 m screen at the Paris World Exposition in 1900. By 1905 they had experimented with 70 mm film.[5] Abel Gance's *Napoleon*, first shown in 1927, included sequences which were projected onto three screens. The film had taken two years to produce and the specially designed camera lenses meant that images could appear on different planes within the panoramic view. Much later, Roman Kroitor (who, with Graeme Ferguson, was a founder director of IMAX) devised their film *Labyrinth* on principles similar to Cinerama's. If their five-projector screening at Expo '67 in Montreal seemed avant-garde at the time it must partly have been because these early antecedents had been forgotten.

Cinerama's projection arrangements were complicated enough to limit it to special roadshow presentations. An additional disadvantage was that the screen's deep curve meant that the optimum viewpoint was restricted to seats in central positions leaving either wasted space or parts of the audience dissatisfied. Several features were shot in Cinerama during the early 1960s, but its technological specifications were so unwieldy that the more flexible CinemaScope soon forced its demise.

CinemaScope must be one of the most illustrious examples in the history of audacious marketing. Combining technological and financial panache it enabled 20th Century–Fox to raise very high stakes and win. The respiratory effect it had on Hollywood is worth brief consideration here, if only to serve as a comparison with the development and marketing of IMAX later. It compressed the image onto a conventional 35 mm film strip through an anamorphic lens fitted to a single camera. A corresponding lens on the single projector then unsqueezed the image, expanding it over a wide screen. Apart from its single camera and projection system, which permitted greater versatility and therefore more opportunities to experiment with different subjects than Cinerama, CinemaScope had a further advantage. Its screen required a less severe curve (1.5 m at its deepest) and its effects could be appreciated from any seat in the house. Henri Chrétien had in fact developed the lens (the hypergonaar lens as he called it) to permit an expanded field of vision through tank sights.[6] Having bought the manufacturing rights to the lens, in 1953 Fox declared with gauntlet-throwing bravura that all its films would be made in CinemaScope. 'The 20th Century–Fox company has gone all out on CinemaScope with the conviction that it brings to theatre-goers a new type of entertainment unavailable in any other medium, and so startling in effect that it truly brings a new dimension to the motion picture theatre. We believe it will supplant all other types of films.'[7]

Although Scope required less dramatic alterations to existing theatres than Cinerama, exhibitors were daunted by the expense of converting to Scope, especially since in the early days at least 20th Century–Fox insisted on the installations of stereosound systems. The company took great pains to reassure exhibitors through the trade journals that there was no need to worry unduly but in any event the razzmatazz surrounding CinemaScope's showcase presentations in Hollywood, Paris and London left exhibitors with little choice. 'Whether or not cinemas can afford it, once you have seen Cinema-Scope, seems curiously beside the point. They may have to afford it. For the medium is more than entertaining, it is engulfing.'[8] By 1956, only three years after its launch, CinemaScope had become *the* film format. In the USA and Canada, 17,408 theatres (of a total of 22,000) and 3,656 drive-ins (of a total of 4,500) were equipped to show Scope films. Not only was box office decline sharply reversed but the number of new theatres increased in order to meet audience demand. Skouras could proclaim 'Not only has the pace of CinemaScope theatre installations exceeded our greatest expectations but the number and variety

13

of CinemaScope productions which have been filmed for these exhibitions are far beyond anything we originally dared to hope. Every major Hollywood studio, except one, is currently filming its principal product in CinemaScope'.[9]

The exception Skouras referred to was Paramount which, not to be outdone, was developing VistaVision, its own widescreen format. VistaVision widened the image, not through an anamorphic lens but by increasing the size of the film negative frame in the camera, running it horizontally, exposing a frame with eight sprocket holes. VistaVision's horizontal shooting and projection heralded the IMAX system.

In the USA CinemaScope's success not only forestalled television's threat, it enabled the film industry to transform it into a new market for its product. Less than three months after Scope's Hollywood launch, 20th Century–Fox was reported to be considering the sale of its entire back catalogue (worth $30 million) to television, thereby accentuating its own revitalisation as an entertainment for the future while relegating the more recent medium to a second-hand past: 'ultimately all product which is not third-dimensional or made for panoramic showing will be sold to TV stations throughout the world'.[10] At the beginning of 1953 exhibitors had pleaded for some intervention to standardise new 3-D and wide-screen formats, but within two years CinemaScope had become the standard since it had almost completely eclipsed other formats. Its success was certainly due to the technical and economic advantages it held over other systems such as Cinerama, Natural Vision's 3-D and Stereotechniques Ltd, but eyewitness reports in the trade journals helped enormously.

The Robe is commonly accepted to be Hollywood's first Cinema-Scope film. In fact *How to Marry a Millionaire* was completed in CinemaScope first and had to wait to be released after *The Robe*. Extracts from both these films were included at the end of 20th Century–Fox's showcase reel which began with a sequence from a car race, shots of New York's harbour and a clip from *Gentlemen Prefer Blondes*. The *Daily Film Renter*'s 'Commentator' was transported with awe: 'The shots produced a complete sense of audience participation, particularly in interior scenes with Betty Grable, Lauren Bacall and Marilyn Monroe skilfully distributed over the screen's full width and indulging in sparkling conversation in which I felt myself almost taking part.'[11] No doubt the 'skilful distribution' of three of Hollywood's most glamorous female stars across the screen's new expanse had a lot to do with 'Commentator's' warm glow but it will be pertinent to compare his (surely his) response with the responses courted

14

by IMAX later. CinemaScope's showcase reel demonstrated a fair range of the format's possibilities: speed, panoramic views, sharp light and rich colour, epic *mise-en-scène*. It is interesting that in his response 'Commentator' isolated for praise the more conventional elements of film – interiors, the stars and 'sparkling conversation' – all key elements binding an audience into narrativity. By 1956, Skouras understood that size did not mean everything. '... CinemaScope alone is not enough. We believe that first and foremost must come the story, then the men and women who can translate that story into great screen entertainment no matter what the dimension.'[12]

As wide-screen technologies have evolved, the films' content and aesthetics have changed. Different aspects of their attraction have been emphasised, accentuating particular expectations and reactions. The ingredients which make up a gripping story, which provoke jaw-dropped, white-knuckled reactions have changed. It is now appropriate to consider why some of those changes have occurred and why particular kinds of audience involvement with wide-screen films have been privileged over others by making special reference to IMAX, the most innovative wide-screen format to be developed after Cinema-Scope and the first to be designed as a totally integrated system – from camera to film stock, from projector to the screen, to the cinema itself.

At the time of writing there are almost ninety IMAX theatres worldwide. The IMAX Systems Corporation (ISC) is developing another forty in major cities and intends to have a hundred theatres dedicated to showing feature films by the end of the 20th century, claiming that both George Lucas and Steven Spielberg want to work in the format. As a proportion of the world's total number of cinemas, even of the total number of cinemas equipped to show the range of wide-screen formats now available (VistaVision, Todd AO, 70 mm, Showscan, etc.), ISC's figures seem less than dramatic. Nevertheless, were such a comparison actually possible, it might at least demonstrate the intensity with which any new audiovisual format now has to compete. The wide-screen did not forestall television's dominance in the entertainment and leisure industries and since the mid-70s cinema has had to face additional competition from video and cable TV. Audiences have become accustomed to adapting to, and expecting, different kinds of narratives and generic inflections depending on what and where they are watching. So many mainstream films now have their first releases on 70 mm that the wide-screen can no longer claim novelty value. Any new format venturing into this highly competitive field will therefore require heavy initial investment and persistent marketing and will need to offer audiences something distinctly new and different. 'A good colour TV image isn't that different from what you see on the usual movie screen. Soon product is going to be available in cartridge form. So, when the public wants to go out to a movie, it better be better. Technically it will have to be eyeball-filling high-fidelity. Artistically it will have to be breaking through new frontiers, not the millionth re-hash of the same old clichés.'[13]

ISC now faces competition from companies such as Iwerks Entertainment, World Odyssey and OmniFilms International Inc., which suggests that there is still room for more in the big screen business. Although basic IMAX patents expired between 1988 and 1990, significant improvement patents have lives beyond 1996 and, moreover, ISC would argue that it has itself created a market capable of sustaining the competition. If this is a credible argument, how has IMAX created an audience demand which others are now able and ready to supply? From what beginnings has it sprung? There are very few written accounts of IMAX films which do not refer to the system's origins and development. It is as iff the IMAX experience is still (after nearly twenty-five years) held to be so extraordinary that, rather like the creation of the world itself, an answer to the expected question has to be given: how did all this come about? The repetition suggests that, like most creation stories, it holds a certain fascination in itself.[14]

Roman Kroitor's *Labyrinth*, the multiple projection screening at Expo '67 in Montreal, has already been mentioned. It used a 2-screen 70 mm system but its exhibition at Montreal was not unlike an extended version of Cinerama. The five screens were assembled vertically and horizontally in the shape of a cross and the film was shot on five cameras yoked in the same fashion and then projected in various arrangements within the cross form. Members of the public visiting Expo '67 compared the show's startling effects to the first screenings at the turn of the century but Japanese visitors who were already preparing Expo '70 kept extensive records. They invited Roman Kroitor and Colin Low to collaborate with Fuji's Keiichi Ichikawa to develop a cinematic exhibition for the Fuji Group Pavilion in Osaka. Graeme Ferguson and Robert Kerr who had formed MultiScreen Corporation in 1967 joined them to produce *Tiger Child* for Expo '70 in Osaka. In less than three years a completely original film system had been developed in almost cottage industry conditions.

If the expense and the mechanical difficulties of *Labyrinth*'s shooting and projection (Kroitor remembers it as a 'technological octopus') were to be overcome a single film format had to be devised. This was

16

achieved by developing a 70 mm frame which would pass horizontally, rather than vertically, through camera and projector. The camera was designed and built in Denmark by Jan Jacobsen and then maintained by Pierre Abelos. Paramount's VistaVision, developed in response to Fox's CinemaScope, had also run horizontally, but its substantial changes required new non-compatible projectors, so it never became established as a major production system. IMAX film is shot on 65 mm stock and printed on 70 mm for projection. There are 15 perforations per frame which measures 49 mm by 70 mm giving three times more exposed surface area than a conventional 70 mm frame. This means that IMAX film has a ratio of 1.435:1 (as opposed to CinemaScope's 2.35:1 or the academy ratio of 1.33:1) and can be projected on a flat or a slightly curved screen as large as 33.5 m wide and 24.3 m high without any depreciating granularity (see frontispiece). The IMAX image can occupy 60–120 degrees of the lateral and 40–80 degrees of the vertical fields of human vision.

To take optimum advantage of the luminosity that frame size would allow meant adapting a special xenon projection lamp. The first lamps used were 20,000 w and 25,000 w; later 12,000 w and 15,000 w ones were developed. The film's large format, its horizontal movement and the heat generated from the lamp all meant that a completely new projection system compatible with the camera had to be designed from scratch. William Shaw, a mechanical engineer, was engaged for the job. The lamp's heat was dissipated through water-cooled metalled mirrors in the lamphouse and by using a quartz reflecting mirror. Apart from the lamp heat the main problem was moving the large film strip with its fifteen perforations per frame through the projector at the right speed without its tearing.

A breakthrough came from Brisbane, Australia in the form of Ron Jones's famous 'Rolling Loop' system. MultiScreen bought the patent rights to his loop mechanism and from it William Shaw devised the IMAX projector. There were long trials and errors but the Rolling Loop avoids the problem of tangling sprockets with unwieldy film stock by using air pressure to push the strip gently along a roller so that each frame is looped and laid down over the projection aperture. This means there is very low wear on the film and high registration accuracy which gives a rock steady image. Since its early days airjets and vacuum suction have streamlined this process and further improved the film handling. The film stock has to have a polyester (rather than acetate) base to minimise shrinkage and allow durable splices, bound sonically because Butt splicing will not hold up in the projector. This relatively stressless projection system means that IMAX film prints enjoy a long life and, given the elaborate soundtrack system, this is of no little significance. Losing frames on damaged prints would require very complicated re-edits to recapture correct synchronisation.

Sound in an IMAX film runs not on a single strip on the film print but on a separate 35 mm magnetic film carrying six sound channels, or more recently on a system of CDs. This strip is run synchronously with the picture. It allows six channels through which sound, music and effects can be mixed and then fed to speakers placed behind the screen and at the back of the theatre. Some have as many as 57 speakers and the OMNIMAX in Caesar's Palace has 'sensaround' sound boasting 16 speakers behind the domed screen and another 82 speakers throughout the theatre. This means the sound can be positioned as much as the visual image and since the image extends beyond the audience's effective field of vision, sound cues can be deployed to move the viewer's focus onto action in different spaces on the screen.

IMAX film stock is expensive. The camera magazines generally carry 1,000 feet although for some filming situations 2,700 feet is also possible, but in either case the IMAX camera needs time to reach full speed and the stock runs faster through it. The 1,000-feet loads give about three and a half minutes and the larger 2,700 loads 8 minutes. IMAX 65 mm stock (such as 5247 Eastman camera negative) is more expensive to shoot than 35 mm film stock. The IMAX 65 mm camera negative film stock costs $0.80 per foot, or about $269.00 per minute of screen time. Conventional 35 mm camera negative film stock costs $0.45 per foot or about $40.00 per minute of screen time. If both are calculated at 24 frames-per-second (FPS), IMAX is 6.7 times more expensive than 35 mm per minute of screen time.

However, the costings are different when the release prints are considered. These are about 30 per cent less than it costs to maintain a 70 mm, 5-perforation print and in fact, a single 70 mm IMAX print with Photogard protection coating, run on the IMAX Rolling Loop projector, will cost about the same as it would to maintain a number of 35 mm prints over the same number of screenings.

The audience's sense of being surrounded, indeed engulfed by the IMAX experience, is due not only to the screen size and to the intensity and mobility of sound, but also to its position in relation to the screen. IMAX auditoria are specially built (the ISC recommends 'an enter-low, exit-high audience flow') so that viewers are seated in sharply raked rows relatively close to the screen. Few theatres can be converted to accommodate IMAX (Bradford, in England, is one exception) and the architecture of IMAX cinemas is itself an important feature in ISC's publicity. *Tiger Child*, the film MultiScreen produced for Expo '70, was screened in the Fuji Pavilion in Osaka, an extraordinary structure of huge inflated tubes designed by Yukata Murata; the IMAX cinema at Futuroscope outside Poitiers is a vast glass structure shaped like a gigantic rock crystal jabbing the sky. (Illus. 1)

OMNIMAX films, originally produced for screening in planetaria, also depend for their effects on placing the audience in a particular relation to the screen and projector. OMNIMAX films are shot through a fish-eye lens and projected onto hemispheric screens angled above and below rather than in front of the audience, extending the image beyond the field of human vision (180 degrees lateral, 125 degrees vertical), effectively immersing the audience in the image. Seats are raked more steeply than in IMAX auditoria but they recline at a slight angle so that the audience looks up and around at the screen, as though it were a kind of heaven. Projection in this system comes from a rear-of-centre point in the auditorium. To prevent wasting any seat space the projection machinery would occupy in this position, an ingenious two-storey system has been designed so that the projector itself is elevated into a small box in the auditorium and the film runs into it from the projection room below (illus. 2).

The expense of developing, producing and exhibiting an IMAX film has meant that ISC's catalogue consists almost entirely of films financed or co-sponsored by large corporations or institutions: Lockheed, NASA, Chubu Electric, National Film Board of Canada, Johnson Wax, Smithsonian Institution, NTT, Conoco Inc., Fujitsu Ltd. Sanwa Midori. IMAX cinemas are generally located within exhibition contexts such as museums, trade fairs or science centres where the IMAX is display at its apogee. These conditions of funding, commissioning and exhibition have so far produced films in a relatively limited generic range – one, incidentally, which closely resembles the range produced in cinema's early years:

- **natural history** films such as *Ring of Fire* (1991), *Blue Planet* (1990), *The Deepest Garden* (1989), *Only The Earth* (1989), *Beavers* (1988), *Water and Man* (1985), *Energy, Energy* (1982);
- films which celebrate **technology** such as *I Write in Space* (1989), *A Freedom to Move* (1985), *The Dream is Alive* (1985), *Hail Columbia!* (1982);
- **tourism or destination** films such as *Switzerland* (1991), *Polynesian*

19

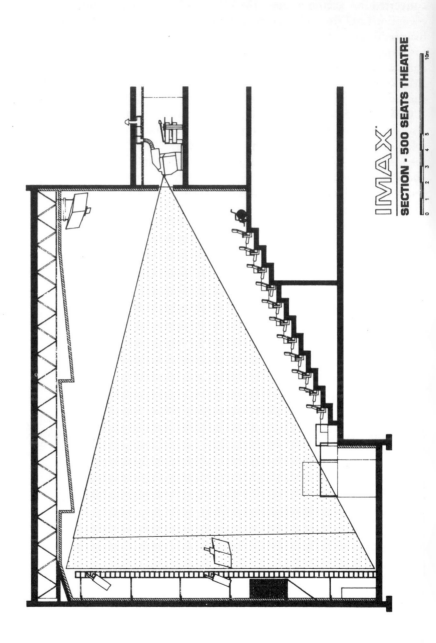

IMAX®

SECTION · 500 SEATS THEATRE

0 1 2 3 4 5   10m

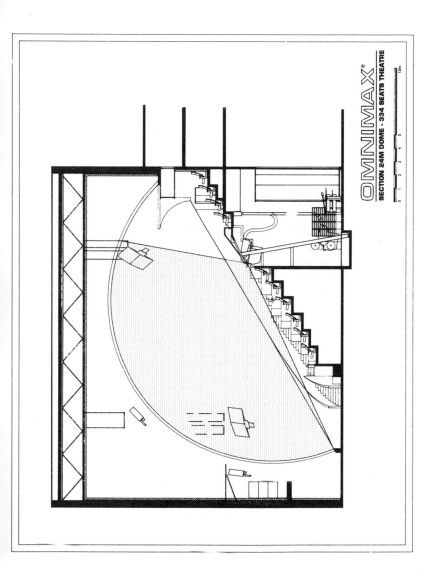

OMNIMAX®

SECTION 24M DOME - 334 SEATS THEATRE

Odyssey (1990), *Niagara: Miracles, Myths and Magic* (1987), *Picture Holland* (1986), *Faces of Japan* (1984), *Grand Canyon: the Hidden Secrets* (1984), *El Pueblo del Sol* (1983), *Behold Hawaii* (1983), *The Great Barrier Reef* (1981), *Ontario/Summertide* (1976);

- **adventure** films (although ISC would doubtless classify the experience of seeing any IMAX film as an adventure) such as *Race the Wind* (1989), *Flyers* (1982), *An American Adventure* (1981), *Circus World* (1974);
- **civilisation** films which celebrate the 'great' moments of human achievement such as *The First Emperor of China* (1989), *Alamo ... The Price of Freedom* (1988), *Chronos* (1985), *Journey of Discovery* (1984), *Darwin on the Galapagos* (1983).

There are few dramatic narrative films (that is to say films motivated by character action, dialogue or relationships) and only one experimental film, a three-minute sound poem called *Primiti Too Taa* (1988).

IMAX films are like the early CinemaScope pictures which concentrated on spectacular adventures in exotic locations. 'In telling the story, we utilized the entire range of American scenery, from Vermont to Florida, from the coast of California to the coast of Hawaii, from the lowland heat of the great deserts and canyons to the snow-capped mountains of the Sierras.'[15] Reporting on Ron Fricke's approach to directing *Chronos, American Cinematographer* stated 'Ron knew very little of Europe's history and aimed his camera at what appealed to him aesthetically. Though thousands of years separate them, the builders of Luxor and Los Angeles draw their inspiration and their technology from the same creative well. This planet has always had some phenomenal force playing architect and wet nurse. We're not spinning out of control.'[16] In IMAX the world might as well be the size of an oyster.

No geography, time or distance can impede. Icelandic geysers, the Taj Mahal, the Great Barrier Reef, the Great Wall of China, a stamping herd of wildebeests, the ocean's abysmal depths, the great globe itself is opened out to a vast spectatorship. Production accounts of IMAX films are eulogies to the technical mastery of what appear to be impossible shots and to the supremacy of the film crew over environmental adversity. Greg MacGillivray, a veteran IMAX film maker, exemplifies this stance. In *Flyers* he includes 'one of the most dangerous aerial stunts ever attempted for film, in which a wing walker makes a mid-air transfer between two planes while freefalling over the Grand Canyon'.[17]

In *Behold Hawaii*, MacGillivray-Freeman Films fix a special cable dolly rig, a minicrane and a waterbox to hold an IMAX camera 'on the nose of a surfboard, or the bow of a Hobie catamaran, from the outboard bow mount on the Hokule'a canoe'. A gyro stabiliser is built to eliminate 'the yaw and pitch of a normal boat camera platform keeping both the horizon and the viewers' stomachs on an even keel'.[18] Filming in the Grand Canyon, Keith Merrill had to commission a waterbox to protect the camera which had been designed to film rapids on the Colorado River and special filters to accommodate the sharp contrasts of light that rockfaces threw across the frame. IMAX filming is machismo filming. It requires strength, jaw-clenched grit and technical know-how to defy extremely hazardous conditions. As Stephen Low, director of *Skyward* (1985) put it, 'there's no use having an "artiste" running around with the light meter and not able to really tackle the problems of beam splitters and lenses'.[19]

The IMAX format imposes particular possibilities and limitations. Since the viewer sits lower in relation to the IMAX screen than in a conventional theatre, the frame's centre lies about a third of the way up from the bottom of the screen. Close-ups therefore need plenty of headroom. While long shots can be framed wider than usual, the movement from extreme long shot to medium close-up can be very condensed and the screen's enormity cannot tolerate grainy or irresolute images. It is interesting to note that some of the difficulties (or challenges) the IMAX format poses have provoked reactions very similar to those expressed by directors working in early CinemaScope. 'IMAX is not a very forgiving format. Lighting that might be quite acceptable under television conditions or borderline for theatrical release could be totally unacceptable for IMAX. All the flaws and unpleasantness of a situation are magnified tenfold.'[20]

Since screen size can be used to direct viewers' focus to different points of its surface, IMAX edits have to be paced at longer intervals, giving the audience time to assimilate the images and sounds coming from left, right, below and behind and forcing 'a whole mental house-clearing of all previously engrained ideas concerning visual psychology'.[21] Longer pacing and the large frame are ideal for the wide-world films IMAX produces but they send acting, dialogue and emotional scenes into the wrong orbit. Camera set-ups closer than twenty feet are almost impossible. 'It's much harder to maintain an intense interaction with an actor under these conditions. Often times you need headphones just to hear what they're saying. It takes away some of the intimate contact you need. Plus, all the extra light and accompanying heat tends more quickly to make actors irritable.'[22] Never mind the make-up it would take to make a close-up of a human face acceptable at 26 m × 36.5 m. Quick cuts are a rarity in IMAX because they would subject the audience to severe jolts and probably, violent nausea. Snappy dialogue, reactions and stunts all have to happen within the duration of a longer shot and, at over twenty feet away, these common enough ingredients in a gripping film narrative are entirely wasted. *My Strange Uncle* (1981) is the first IMAX narrative feature and is supposed to be 'an entertaining mix of adventure, humour and action' but these fall flat and have to be compensated by scenic New Zealand where the film was shot.

Perhaps it befits the film format which so blazons the triumph of technology to return to the quest for the third dimension. *Echoes of the Sun*, produced for the Fujitsu Pavilion at Expo '90 (again in Osaka) is the first IMAX SOLIDO film. Directed by Fumio Sumi who produced the first complete OMNIMAX film composed of 3-D computer graphics, *We are Born of Stars*, for Fujitsu's Pavilion at Expo '85 in Tsukaba, Japan, *Echoes of The Sun* tells 'the story of photosynthesis'. Molecular structures fly straight towards, pass by and through the viewer who is sucked up and along the capillary roots and the veins of leaves. The effect is achieved by a hi-tech return to goggles and to a dual shooting and projection system. Like OMNIMAX, the SOLIDO screen is domed. Film is shot on two cameras. One shoots the right, the other the left-eye view and the film is projected through two lenses which alternate left-eye, right-eye images on the screen at the rate of 96 times a second. The audience wears liquid crystal display (LCD) glasses which are cued by infra-red signals on the screen to clear and darken in synchronicity with the projectors. Thus, the right-eye lens clears and darkens 48 times a second, alternating exactly with the left-eye lens. Photosynthesis, a process invisible to the naked eye, assails the sight in gigantic, computer-generated three dimensions.

Wide-screen formats seem set for expansion in the 1990s as cinema-going becomes more closely woven into one of the most pervasive activities of modern urban life – shopping. To continue embellishing the attractions of retailing and consumption has meant, especially in North America, the development of malls where shopping can be combined with other activities – visiting a museum, a library or a cinema – to make a day's expedition special. A large-screen cinema with a programme running for about an hour suits this kind of leisure/expenditure pattern. ISC is currently developing cinemas in US and Canadian shopping centres in close conjunction with their developers.

The erstwhile President and Chief Executive of IMAX, Fred T. Klink-hammer declared that ISC's priority in the 1990s was 'to build a chain of highly specialised commercial theatres in which to show SOLIDO films'.[23] The company has also targeted 200 zoos, aquaria and natural history museums as potential sites for new theatres where its film library can be exhibited but it has been prompted into developing feature films for a number of reasons. OmniFilms claimed its business tripled in 1990. With competition from other big screen companies ISC will have to differentiate its product. Since it pioneered the field, its reputation and established network of theatres and international co-productions mean IMAX features will have comparatively safe exhibition.

The 'IMAX experience' currently enjoys a double marketing advantage. It is still a novelty for most people but is becoming more widespread. Those for whom IMAX means exhilarating, speedy aerial shots of the natural world will need films of a different kind if the attraction is to be sustained. Audiences have an immensely sophisticated range of audiovisual experience and appreciation and the kind of derision *Cahiers du Cinéma* poured on *Water and Man* (1985) should make ISC wary: 'On ingurgite ce brouet sans trop de problèmes' ('This pap can be gulped down without any problem').[24] Spectacle will have to be stiffened with material provoking more varied emotional and intellectual responses. Anticipating HDTV must also have spurred the widescreen industries into action. Once HDTV is successful its effects on cinemas could be devastating. The direct transmission of films in HDTV to cinemas will eliminate the distributors' need for hundreds of individual prints and for payment of freight charges. In 1984 it was estimated that these savings would amount to over $2 million for each major film release.[25] However, HDTV's main impact will be on the home entertainment market and cinema will have to offer bigger and better to draw audiences out of doors.

One of the formats which could challenge IMAX successfully is Dynavision, produced by Mobile Vision Technology Inc. (New York). It is another system which seems to have taken a cue from VistaVision, having the advantage of shooting 35 mm film in 35 mm cameras and converting this to a horizontal 70 mm frame with only 8 sprockets. This allows versatile shooting to give a wide-screen result with relatively trouble-free conversion required of the projection hardware or cinema architecture. Dynavision films can also be exploited in their 35 mm format. *We Will Rock You*, a concert film of the rock band Queen was the first Dynavision film produced for commercial release in 1985 and may have provoked ISC to launch its first IMAX rock concert film, *Rolling Stones AT THE MAX* (1991).

Rock concerts are so obvious a subject for IMAX the surprise is this is the ISC's first. Relatively safe from competition until 1988, the company had no pressing need to diversify and to justify the expense of filming rock concerts meant finding a band which enjoyed international and inter-generational popularity and one whose sound could take the big IMAX treatment. The Rolling Stones fitted the bill. *AT THE MAX* is financed by IMAX and the BCL Group in the hope that it will recoup quickly at the box office, bringing those for whom IMAX might have become a bit of a yawn, right back.

This new stage in the format's development does not necessarily guarantee its long and healthy life but it is worth considering the qualitatively different kinds of interactivity between audiences and screens which have been, are now and might be available, so that the relative value of the particular experience IMAX offers can be assessed. To this end some of the debates provoked by earlier wide-screen formats are pertinent.

A decade after the launch of CinemaScope Charles Barr continued fighting its critical quarter in his seminal 'CinemaScope: Before and After'.[26] Defending the format against attacks from film purists of a peculiarly British sensibility, Barr's essay charted the changes in the film frame's aesthetic which had emerged since early Russian cinema. Another of his essays in the same period cites examples of how Scope can be used artistically by auteur directors such as Otto Preminger, Nicholas Ray, François Truffaut, Don Siegel and Stanley Kubrick. Barr saw these directors making the wide-screen format work to their creative advantage, their composition within the frame rather than their sequential juxtaposition striking him as being as significant to the development of cinema as the achievement of deep focus.

Wide-screen offered new possibilities of 'montage within the shot' and Barr argued (with the moral outlook a critic in the early sixties would have been expected to have), that 'the widening of the screen, at first condemned for submerging the director, in fact gives him, as the interpreter of reality, more responsibility than ever before'.[27] The viewer too had more to do. Whereas meanings and nuances achieved through montage were more visibly in the director's control, viewers had to select their own points of focus on the wide-screen, they had to make juxtapositions, and connections within the frame for themselves. Howard Hawks in an interview with Peter Bogdanovich (which Barr quotes) argued against the use of CinemaScope for precisely that reason. 'I don't think CinemaScope is a good medium. It's good only for showing great masses of movement. For other things, it's distracting, it's hard to focus attention, and it's very difficult to cut. Some people just go ahead and cut it and let people's eyes jump around and find out what they want to find. It's very hard for an audience to focus – they have too much to look at – they can't see the whole thing.'[28]

Hawks may have had a valid point since Scope proved unworkable for many directors, but Barr's argument demonstrated that it could be used creatively too. Later, very similar criticisms were (and continue to be) levelled at IMAX. CinemaScope's ratio and its rectangularity match the human field of vision more closely than the IMAX format which forces the head to move up, down and around if all the screen information is to be gathered. In the intervening years however, as Georges DuFaux, Director of Photography on *Tiger Child*, indicates, film audiences have developed a remarkably versatile spectatorship. 'The motion picture medium has freed itself from the linear convention of "doorhandle" continuity. With TV, the spectator has become still more used to grasping and understanding a mixture of a variety of images (actuality, fiction, news, commercials) freed from the psychological preconception of the theatrical experience. The visual sensibility of the audience has reached a new threshold of perception.'[29] The question is whether, having stretched our eyes, IMAX (or any of the new wide-screen film formats about to take off) can be used creatively rather than developed technically. Are they as capable of compelling audience identification, of tickling curiosity and provoking interpretation as their predecessors?

The IMAX narrative, such as it is, could be said to conform to an explanatory or celebratory mode, and sometimes to both. They are the stories of success. See how 'man' has conquered space, understand the awesome work of nature, celebrate the progress made through civilisation. IMAX has traditionally shown the upside of achievement. *Blue Planet* (1990) is a new IMAX film which begins to recognise the limitations of this message. 'Taken 330 miles above the Caribbean, through the huge pillars of a space shuttle, it reveals the vast blue ball of Earth, flecked with pearly, swirling clouds in dizzying sharp focus far, far below us. This is a deep-focus shot that might have made Orson Welles drool...'[30] The film shows gaping holes in the ozone layer over Antarctica and red soil eroded from deforested Madagascar swirling into the Indian ocean. From this vantage point the visible fragility of the globe's ecosystem shocks.

IMAX relies heavily for its effects on point-of-view shots and thus dramatically shifts our perceptions of the world we inhabit but, ironically, given the impact of the IMAX point of view, the format cannot construct identification with character nor implicate the viewer in action motivating the narrative. The films position their audiences emphatically, drastically, and move them at speeds they would never really experience: in the nose of a space rocket, hovering over Niagara, zipping down a ski-run, crawling down a human lung, inching up the vertical rock in Yosemite National Park. The format represents the real so extraordinarily that its effect marries the imperative to the conditional. Just look! Feel! This is what it *would be like if* you were really there! As the ISC publicity says, 'IMAX films bring distant, exciting worlds within your grasp. ... It's the next best thing to being there'. Publicity stills from IMAX films inevitably lose their gigantic presence when reproduced in print, so a distinguishing feature of the marketing is to include the audience in the picture as well. This is not just going to the movies, it is going in order to react and feel just like these people whose eyes send wonder directly to their jaws and panic racing to the gut.

How has IMAX changed our ways of seeing, our cinema-going experience, our interaction with the screen? Its magnitude certainly gives the viewer a sense of being involved, of being where the action is but very little sense of interactivity. Engulfed, almost pinned down by image and sound, the viewer has neither the time nor the distance to forge an emotional or thoughtful relationship with what appears on the screen and is forced through spectacularity into a world view that is dominantly North American. Through the corporate sources of their funding and commissions and through their filmic strategies IMAX films align our gaze with the conquerors' omniscient view, while their impact positions us as an almost victimised audience. IMAX exploits contemporary appetites for visual tourism to such extremes that it may well extinguish the desire to go anywhere else: the real places are so much less exciting than the IMAX. It is, according to *Newsweek*, 'the ultimate trip'.

Screen audiences today have plenty of visual trips to go on. There is the variety of film narratives on 70 mm, on video, on TV and even on HDTV to look forward to. As users or as players of many roles they can pit themselves against the computer's speed and intelligence, they can enter and manipulate virtual worlds. One day there may be a case for writing a chapter about the changes IMAX has wrought on our interpretive focus, a chapter which, like Charles Barr's early articles on CinemaScope, can assess how the format has developed cinema's aesthetics, how striking talents have opened new sights for new ways of thinking, how new narratives have organised new meanings for our times. On the other hand, the technical particularities and the levels of investment IMAX requires firmly lodge its exhibition in the science centres, trade fairs and museums, where it may have to remain. Whether there will be the funding for making and marketing a more varied use of big screens, it is not yet possible to say.

NOTES

1. *The Globe and Mail Magazine* (Toronto), July 1990, p. 57.
2. Kevin Robins, 'The Virtual Unconscious', *Science and Culture*, no. 14, 1991.
3. Henry Hart, *Films in Review*, vol. 4, no. 6, June/July, 1953.
4. *Daily Film Renter*, no. 6,467, 19 March 1953.
5. A fascinating, comprehensive history of wide-screens can be read in Robert E. Carr and R.M. Hayes, *Wide Screen Movies* (Jefferson, N.C.: McFarland and Company, 1988).
6. Some references say Chrétien developed the lens in 1918 while others give 1927 as the date of his invention.
7. Darryl F. Zanuck quoted in *Today's Cinema*, vol. 80, no. 6713, 10 March 1953.
8. *Picturegoer*, vol. 25, no. 932, 18 April 1953.
9. *Kinematograph Weekly*, no. 2,564, 4 October 1956.
10. *Kinematograph Weekly*, no. 2,390, 16 April 1953.
11. *Daily Film Renter*, no. 6,467, 19 March 1953.
12. *Kinematograph Weekly*, no. 2,564, 4 October 1956.
13. *American Cinematographer*, vol. 51, August 1970.
14. The best accounts of IMAX's origins are to be found in Gerald G. Graham, *Canadian Film Technology, 1896–1986*, (Cranbury, N.J. and London: Associated University Presses, Inc., 1989) and in *American Cinematographer*, vol. 51, August 1970. Since that issue, *American Cinematographer* has repeated various aspects of the IMAX history and reported on developments in the format in almost annual articles about the latest IMAX film to have been shot.
15. *American Cinematographer*, vol. 57, no. 7, July 1976.
16. *American Cinematographer*, vol. 66, no. 9, September 1985.
17. *American Cinematographer*, vol. 64, no. 12, December 1983.
18. Ibid.
19. *American Cinematographer*, vol. 68, no. 2, February 1987.
20. *American Cinematographer*, vol. 65, no. 11, December 1984.
21. *American Cinematographer*, vol. 57, no. 7, July 1976.
22. *American Cinematographer*, vol. 64, no. 12, December 1983.
23. *The Financial Post*, (Toronto), 3 October 1990.
24. *Cahiers du Cinéma*, no. 375, September 1985.
25. *Journal of Film and Video*, vol. 36, no. 2, Spring 1984.

26. *Film Quarterly*, vol. XVI, no. 4, Summer 1963.
27. 'Wider Still and Wider', *Motion*, no. 2, Winter 1961/62.
28. *Film Quarterly*, vol. XVI, no. 4, Summer 1963.
29. *American Cinematographer*, vol. 51, no. 7, July 1970.
30. *Los Angeles Times*, 23 November 1990.

COMPUTER TECHNOLOGY AND SPECIAL EFFECTS IN CONTEMPORARY CINEMA

Robin Baker

The computer is now a ubiquitous machine and most areas of the creative and performing arts have fallen under its influence in one way or another. The cinema is no exception and this chapter will look at the ways in which computer-generated effects have been used in films. It will also try to establish a framework to assist in interpreting different uses of the computer, placing computer technology not only within the context of contemporary cinema but also in the broader creative development of the visual arts. Although the history of computer graphics spans only three decades it is possible to look back at how computers have been used in the creative arts and to construct theoretical models. This is important because any emerging discipline needs some theoretical framework if its provenance and new directions are to be understood. It is also important to be able to learn from the experience of using such machines for creative work, however brief, and to chart that experience in a systematic way. However, they are only initial working interpretations of how computers have been used in visual design and are not to be seen as restrictive classifications incapable of modification. In the visual design arena, this framework is based upon theories of personal creative evolution and shows the stages through which users pass when working with computer technology. These theories are now being developed into simple models from which it is possible to understand more about the creative application of computing to the arts.

Three writers who have looked at how computing can be categorised within the visual art and design fields are Robin King, John Lansdown and Irving Taylor. If their various models are compared, there appears to be an interesting similarity in the different stages of use in each schema. This could indicate that there are areas of common experience that are applicable across different art and design disciplines, so if we examine how a computer is used in graphic design, architecture or film it is likely that similar stages will appear.

King suggests four stages: **mimetic, derivative, innovative** and **emergent**. The first stage of **mimetic** work is characterised by the 'replication of works of art originally produced in other media, e.g. paint, silk-screen, film, photography etc. This is probably the most common result of initial experimentation with the technology.'[1] The next, **derivative** stage is marked by artists trying to establish their own stylistic conceptions on the computer-generated work. 'It is perhaps to be expected that an artist will try to extend his or her working methods and stylistic preferences to new technology or to work in an established stylistic framework.'[2] Then, the **innovative** class of computer artworks which 'demonstrates novel techniques, content or imagery through alterations or changes to the existing computer graphics paradigm' (my emphasis)[3] may involve programming techniques capable of converting the underlying structure of the software or indeed of creating software for a particular task. In King's last category, **emergent**, he suggests that the artwork is 'characterised by the unique properties of the media' and goes on to suggest that these are 'interactivity, simulation and intelligence'.[4]

Lansdown takes only three categories, **tool, medium** and **intelligent apprentice** to describe the process of using computers in art and design; and compresses the distinction between King's derivative and innovative into a slightly broader and comprehensive category of medium. The computer is used as a **tool** for the artist or designer to continue what they have already been doing but to enhance the efficiency, reliability, speed and accuracy of the work. In this way the content remains largely the same but how the work is performed undergoes some changes. This **medium** category is very similar to that of King's **innovative** stage and it looks at what computers can do that could not have been done before. This includes tasks that are basically tool usage but which have undergone such a significant transformation that they cannot now be executed without the aid of a computer. Such instances would be the design and construction of an aeroplane or a motor car. Lansdown's final category, that of the **intelligent apprentice**, takes the symbiosis of man and machine to a further level where one aids the other interactively.

In Taylor's model there are five stages, or transactions as he calls them: **Expressive, Technical, Inventive, Innovative** and **Emergent**.[5] They do not map exactly onto Lansdown's and King's but, although the three writers suggest slightly different categories there does appear to be a fundamental agreement on the distinction between differing stages of use. One problem with these interpretations is that there is very little research being carried out that would provide corroboration of these views, so they must remain for the moment as detailed observations.

If these observations are relevant and help in the understanding of computer-generated work in the arts, then how do they apply to film? If, as has been suggested, these categories of use are some form of common experience, not bound to particular artistic disciplines, then it should be possible to apply these models to the role of computers in film and see a similar pattern emerge. This chapter is not the place to develop the nuances of interpretation and meaning between the frameworks laid down by Lansdown, King and Taylor, but as there is an extensive horizontal overlap between their interpretations of computer usage, Lansdown's categories will be used to represent them as the basis of this brief examination of the computer in film.

Looking for Recognition: Computing as a Tool

It is quite difficult to establish just where and when the first computer-generated sequence was used in a movie, but *Alien* (USA, 1979) directed by Ridley Scott, was certainly among the first to use computer-generated images within the main body of the movie as opposed to the title sequence. In the late 1970s in Great Britain, computer graphics was an emergent discipline mainly based within academic institutions. These were the only organisations that could allow access to mainframe or mini computers for the rather 'subversive' purpose of generating images. Scott selected a small London-based company, System Simulation, to provide the computer work for the movie. Much of the work was carried out at the Royal College of Art, including the screen readouts seen on the bridge of the spacecraft. As the computer graphics in this context were restricted to computer screens, most of the displays were textual with information being typed in on a keyboard and the computer apparently answering. The only computer-generated image was a wireframe contour map of the surface of a planet on which the spaceship was going to land.

Many lines of Fortran code were written to provide a convincing display which, by perspective, gave the impression of the movement of the spaceship as it manoeuvred for landing. This sequence was the longest in the movie and gave a very persuasive impression of the position of the spaceship and of the detailed surface of the planet, even in wireframe. Since the director needed sound to reinforce the images, 'pings' and other computer-related sounds were recorded to provide a convincing aural representation of an advanced computer system. The stylistic impression of technology was very important since it represented what film directors felt audiences expected computers should be able to do. The sounds, colours (mostly green) and images were very contrived in the sequence from *Alien* and this characterisation of computing was to be exploited further in later movies. Computing was used to represent itself and therefore could only appear on a computer screen because this was the way computing was generally understood in the early 80s. Because of its high-tech image it also became a major feature in science fiction movies – it was a convenient hook upon which to hang the image of the future.

Tron (USA 1982) was the movie that was intended to prove the full range of creative visual effects computers could produce. Based on an idea by Steve Lisberger, the film's narrative is about a computer programmer called Flynn who suspects his boss is a crook. He attempts to prove his suspicions by actually entering a computer system populated by a group of electronic characters including a transformed version of his old boss, now called Sark. The film centres around many fights which use electronic gadgets such as light cycles. The idea was to be able to make use of the latest computer techniques combined with backlit animation in a seamless production that would have the look and feel of a computer arcade game.

> The technique was simple enough. The actors are dressed in white costumes overlaid with a pattern of black lines, representing computer circuits, and filmed in black limbo. Each frame is blown up into a large black and white transparency that can be reshot on an animation stand. The faces remain human but the figures are reduced to an almost cartoon-like web of lines. Lit from behind they can be made to glow as if illuminated from within ... against a computer generated background.[6]

There were only four US-based companies which had some experience in the use of computer graphics and were able to produce work of this kind: Triple-I, MAGI/SynthaVision, Digital Effects and Robert Able Associates and each produced a segment of the film. Robert Taylor, who had recently left Able's, was responsible for much of the initial research into the feasibility of computer graphics for the project. Lisberger's original intention was to raise independent funding but when this was unavailable, Disney was approached and, after some changes, agreed to back the movie. When it was finished the movie contained sixteen minutes of completely computer-generated work (which was considerably less than originally intended) and many of the backgrounds for live action were also produced by computer. MAGI and Triple-I were largely responsible for the work and Robert Able Associates designed and executed the title sequence. The film was a commercial disaster mainly because of the poor script but the backlit animation sequence also cost much more than expected and the final budget for the movie was well over the estimated $13 million that had been set aside for the project.

Looking back at the movie now it is interesting to see how limited computer graphics were in the early 80s and the extent to which simulated graphics had to be introduced to give the look and feel of a computer arcade game. The visual quality expected of computer graphics was way beyond its practical realisation and had to be synthesised with traditional techniques. Although *Tron* was not a great success it established the glowing green grid as the symbolic representation of computer graphics and computer-generated images for the next decade, a representation subsequently reinforced by its repetition in television commercials. However, after the failure of *Tron*, computer graphics were effectively exiled since few producers or directors had sufficient faith in this type of work to commission other projects.

Computing became an acceptable technique and re-established its role within the movies once it became used to help in cel animation where it could remove some of the tedium of the repetitive work of the hand animator. *Who Framed Roger Rabbit* (USA 1988) was a movie where computer techniques were used to provide backgrounds for both the cartoon and live action sequences. In this movie the computer was not used to express or represent its own particular aesthetic but used to imitate hand animation techniques in such a manner that they became indistinguishable from the traditional techniques. The animated characters fitted so seamlessly into the live action that the audience could temporarily suspend their disbelief about the relationship between the rabbit and the man. The computer work was so 'invisible' to the audience that many computer artists and designers argued that *Who Framed Roger Rabbit* put computer animation back a decade. Others maintained that computer-generated work had found its proper role and that it was just another tool to be used in as transparent a way as possible.

Computer graphics during this first period was looking for recognition as a serious and cost effective way of producing screen images equal to more traditional means of image production. However, the software was cumbersome and lacked the necessary finesse; the hardware was also very expensive and expertise was not readily available. After all, the computer had not been designed as an artistic tool and developing it into one was going to require money and time which is why *Tron* had to use traditional techniques to give the look and feel of computer technology.

Referring to the models of computer usage discussed earlier, this first period of computer-generated work represents the use of computing *as a tool* in the movies. The sequence in *Alien* could well have been produced by traditional techniques, as could many other similar uses of computing during this period. What was being done with the computer was sometimes cheaper and quicker but it was essentially the same type of work that had traditionally been done in animation departments. The movie *Who Framed Roger Rabbit* was the apotheosis of techniques which made computer animation indistinguishable from traditional animation. As Roger Malina comments:

> Computer animation films are not competitive with films made with traditional animation techniques; the recent winning of an Academy of Motion Picture Arts and Sciences Award by a computer animation short (*Tin Boy* by Pixar) is an example. Although these kinds of artworks are still often classified, exhibited and juried as computer artworks, it would be more appropriate to include them within more traditional art venues.[7]

Film makers had limited their use of the computer to generate the kind of work that they already knew and understood, perhaps because of concerns about finance but also because there was little understanding about how it could be used to enlarge cinema's scope. It was not until the late 1980s that alternative uses began to emerge which looked at how the new technology could be incorporated in a more radical manner.

The Medium of Computer Graphics in the Movies

During the early 80s, many computer animation and computer graphics companies collapsed. Costs were too high, deadlines were often over-run and because neither the software nor the hardware was sophisticated enough for the demands being made of them, many commissioning agencies were 'burned'. Until this point computer graphics had made no more than a short-lived and technically limited contribution to advertising or entertainment. The slow resurgence of computer-generated work in the late 1980s was based upon renewed confidence. The technological advances which had occurred in the mid-80s proved sufficiently strong to yield an entirely different product. This revival of computer graphics and computer-generated character animation in the Hollywood film industry stemmed from the remarkable, dedicated and creative work of many companies based on the west coast of the US and equipped with the latest computer products. These new computer animation companies were better tuned to survival than their predecessors. They were better managed and capable of demonstrating how computer animation could be accomplished within reasonable budgets and time-scales. Computer animation's acceptance was accelerated by TV advertising agencies which started using computer-generated character animation again because the more sophisticated software was able to meet their challenging demands for new imagery. Another bonus was that computer techniques now had the capacity to make graphics machine-generated and this, combined with new, exciting talent in the industry meant that the business of computer animation (as distinct from computer graphics) began to flourish.

One of the foremost companies was deGraf/Wahrman (now disbanded). Since its work was dedicated to the long-form of computer animation for the entertainment industry it provided an alternative to the advertising/broadcast computer animation sector. deGraf/Wahrman believed the use of computers in entertainment was at a watershed. They believed that new developments in computer systems, changes in production structure and integration with other media would propel computer-generated animation into a highly influential role in communications of all kinds. deGraf/Wahrman was one company to recognise that early computer-generated character animation had failed because it was too distant, lacked real 'feeling' and was unable to show convincing emotions and expression. To counter this they used actors from the performing arts, especially puppeteers, (rather than technicians or designers), to control character animation. The use of puppeteers was a master-stroke enabling them to use these professionals' considerable animation experience, learnt after many years of performance, to extend their hand and eye co-ordination in the new electronic world. The puppeteers just had to learn how to operate the mechanism used to control the various actions and expressions of the computer puppet. This mechanism was called a Waldo; one was built for each project and if the characterisations were complex, more than one puppeteer would operate the controls. This proved successful, providing just the additional realism character animation needed by allowing it to become much more expressive. From this point the company felt that it could really offer something attractive to the movie industry. Michael Wahrman once described this use of the Waldo as 'building a new kind of piano for all those pianists out there'.[8]

An early project for Michael Wahrman was *Star Trek V: The Final Frontier* (USA 1989). He did the work on the graphics for the Enterprise's flight bridge and the company also helped in the film's pre-production. Three projects were then to follow in quick succession, *Jetsons: The Movie* (USA, 1990), *RoboCop 2* (USA 1990) and *The Funtastic World of Hanna-Barbera* (USA 1990). MCA/Universal Studios and Hanna-Barbera Productions used deGraf/Wahrman to create the opening sequence and computer-generated backgrounds for *Jetsons: The Movie*. To make it possible to match the painted backgrounds, the shading and cartoon realism were kept very simple and the major sequences of the film were split between two companies: deGraf/Wahrman providing the background sequences where shading was paramount and Kroyer films producing the scenes requiring integral two-dimensional character animation. All the modelling, animation and rendering was done using a Symbolics computer system – hardly surprising as Michael Wahrman, when free-lancing, led the production of the now famous *Stanley and Stella: Breaking the Ice* sequence using symbolics, which had been one of the landmark productions at the SIGGRAPH show of 1987. The puppeteering approach to this sequence for Orion Pictures showed what the potential was for driving computer systems in such a manner. 'Puppeteers are real animators. They just come from another world. Two different cultures, but they share a common goal, creation of characterisation.'[9]

One of the latest and most interesting developments has been the interest in the use of computer-generated characters and situations for theme parks. Universal Studios recently opened such a park in Orlando, Florida. Strapped to their seats, visitors can enjoy a fantastic ride around different cartoon environments. Universal Studios' simulator ride called *The Funtastic World of Hanna-Barbera* is a massive project taking the viewer on a story ride with the Flintstones, Scooby-Doo, Yogi Bear and Boo-Boo. One section of the simulated town,

38

Downtown Bedrock, consists of a computer model containing the detail of ten streets. deGraf/Wahrman was involved in the Orlando project from design consultation to modelling, choreography, lighting, rendering and the final film recording on 35 mm VistaVision. Rhythm and Hughes, another Los Angeles-based computer graphics company executed the final work on the *Jetsons* section with the cel animation produced by Sullivan-Bluth. The most interesting and testing work for deGraf/Wahrman to date has been the computer-generated facial animation for *RoboCop 2*. A very special effect for Orion Pictures' sequel to *RoboCop* had to be created. To get the range of facial expressions that was necessary, Tom Noonan's head was three-dimensionally scanned by laser and some forty expressions were captured to form the cyber monster's face. The animation was then transferred to videodisc and displayed – one frame at a time – when the model cybernetic monster was filmed. In the second half of the film the cybernetic head is displayed on a small monitor which is part of Noonan's costume.

The major contribution to the development of computer animation in the movies has undoubtedly been the role of a company called Industrial Light and Magic (ILM). Founded by George Lucas, ILM first came to the attention of movie-goers with its work on the Star War series. *Star Wars* (USA 1977) demonstrated the potential use of new technology in the movies with sophisticated computer-controlled models and computer-controlled cameras providing very accurate shots. ILM has worked on countless commercials since and on about sixty films, many of which have a high proportion of special effects. These include *The Terminator* (USA, 1984), *The Abyss* (USA, 1989), *Total Recall* (USA, 1990) and the latest and most sophisticated use of computer animation, *Terminator 2: Judgment Day* (USA, 1991), *Hook* (USA 1991) and *Star Trek 6: The Undiscovered Country* (USA 1992). The director James Cameron was almost single-handedly responsible for the resurgence of the computer-generated work at ILM by including a significant and pivotal segment of special effects in both *The Abyss* and *Terminator 2*. Persuading the director that computer animation could be brought in on time and within budget in *The Abyss* took considerable effort as Cameron, like many other Hollywood directors, was still somewhat suspicious about the claims made for this kind of technique. 'It was a great leap of faith to use computer graphics', admitted Cameron. 'But it was a unique scene. We were trying to create something that had never been seen before.'[10]

It took ILM six months of intensive work and constant checking with the director on the form and realism he required for *The Abyss* before its magnificent pod became a convincing animated object, reflecting the interior of the rig through which it passed. Cameron wanted the surface of the pod to be constantly undulating like the surface of a swimming pool. This was achieved by specially written software that allowed the animating and timing to be controlled highly accurately. 'What finally worked was a blend of things. Playing with the scale and speed of the ripples, determining the right mix of reflection and refraction. If the ripples weren't the right scale and speed, the surface looked like jello or molten glass. With too much reflection, it looked like chrome.'[11] In the scene where the pod imitates an actor's face the design team used a three-dimensional digitiser to make a separate scan of the actor's expression. This information was fed into the computer system and then applied to the end of the pod to give the impression of the actor's reflection. 'The exciting thing is that we discovered we can get computer graphics to do things that were once thought impossible. Computer graphics used to have a reputation for being slow, expensive, not looking real. Now we have the tools for high-quality effects with a fast turnaround and realistic, even organic results. Almost anything can be modelled and brought to life.'[12]

In James Cameron's latest movie – *Terminator 2: Judgment Day* (Tri-Star Pictures) the challenge was to create a convincing character that would blend into the live action seamlessly, as no scene in the movie was completely computer generated. ILM produced a very successful characterisation for T-1000, the humanoid, as he metamorphoses between his incarnation as a silvery robot and as an American police officer. This transition is highly convincing and accounts for the character's survival of many horrendous events and his emergence from very surprising places – rising through a chequered floor behind an unsuspecting security guard, for instance. To achieve this effect, a new software technique called 'morph' was used which allows a very smooth transition between one form and another so that it looks continuous, making it impossible to detect where the boundary of one character finishes and the other begins. It was necessary to keep the transition realistic so that when the human actor took over, and T-1000 became the police officer, it appeared convincing. To do this the morph software provides a cross dissolve allowing the key features – nose, eyes and ears – to stay in the same location as the transformation takes place. This technique was first used by software engineer and animator Doug Smythe in the movie *Willow* where it was used to provide a smooth transformation between one animal and another. Anthony Lane recently remarked:

Terminator 2 beckons the art of special effects into alarming and beautiful new territory, and forces you to reconsider their place in cinema. Because they involve surface manipulation – anything from a rubber nose to computer yanking of 3D images – it's assumed the effect is correspondingly shallow. Certainly, in the hands of a dullard they are little more than million-dollar graffiti, scrawled across a crumbling film in the hope of keeping it upright. James Cameron, however, who directs both Terminators, is something else. He doesn't just play with all those swanky toys; they actually excite him into his most fertile and expressive work.[13]

Another movie, this time not from the ILM stable but from Dream Quest, which also very successfully managed a seamless move from computer-generated work to live action, is *Total Recall*, directed by Paul Verhoeven. When the hero passes behind a weapon-detecting X-ray screen, the shot begins with him moving toward the screen in live action but as he passes behind it the computer animation takes over and we see his skeleton moving at the same walking pace. He then emerges from behind the other end of the screen and continues, convincingly, into the live action. Although these movies have had some critical success they depend upon the use of computer animation for their spectacular effects. It is as if the quest for technological magic, exceeding the effects in previous movies, becomes the paramount concern. This has been termed 'impact aesthetics' and can be seen as a 'preoccupation with the use of the new technologies for novel image effects'.[14] While the impact can only be sustained by increasing the technological wizardry (which is certainly possible), is it desirable?

The second period of the late 80s and early 90s, represented primarily by the *Terminator* movies, *The Abyss* and *RoboCop 2*, saw movies beginning to exploit computer animation as a medium in its own right. This corresponds to Lansdown's second category, where artists, designers and directors begin to create things that have never been done before. The results achieved by the computer-generated techniques used in these movies would have been very difficult, if not impossible, with traditional techniques.

Cinema's 'Intelligent Apprentices'

With movies such as *Terminator 2* it is perhaps easy to imagine the move from partial computer generation of a character integrated into live action to that of the entirely synthetic movie character which functions in its own right or which emulates a real actor. While this

41

seems a perfectly acceptable approach in the context of cartoon characters, when simulation assumes the role of 'real' actors, controversies arise. To make a completely synthetic movie, including synthetic actors, it is crucial to generate a model of a human head with convincing facial expressions and speech. The human body must then be modelled with animated postural and translocational movements – no mean task even for advanced computer graphics techniques. Realistic reconstruction and animation of the human head is a daunting challenge for computer graphics people but one many have tried. Facial expressions are the most direct expression of our feelings and making them is a skill that we all develop from our early years. If the new digital movie is to be at all convincing then this is a problem that will have to be solved. The task is extensive, complicated by the fact that the slightest muscular movements can communicate intentions and that very small changes in facial expression can imply quite different meanings.

For the last decade creating imaginary people has been a goal for many in computer graphics. Underlying this project is an ambition: if reality could be conquered (and what is more real than a person?) the supremacy of the synthetic over the real would be established. In Europe the work of Daniel Thalmann and Magnenat-Thalmann has focused on this goal and their seven-minute movie *Rendez-vous à Montreal* (Switzerland 1987) showed the state of the art in an entirely computer-generated movie. Attempting to recreate Marilyn Monroe and Humphrey Bogart as synthetic characters who embark upon a romance, the movie begins in an imaginary hereafter with Bogart wishing to live again and begging Marilyn to return to earth with him. Eventually she agrees and, now much older, she sets up a rendezvous for the next day in Montreal and the romance begins. The computer techniques used ushered in a completely new idea of a computer-generated movie by digitally recreating dead actors and then making them perform a drama against a digital background. As an early attempt the film had many faults, the characters lacked personality and the movements were stiff and unconvincing. Critics found such an approach very disturbing. 'Some people are talking about computer-generated images replacing actors. I don't think that will happen because the personality is in the performer, and that's what you want … people are talking about scanning in pictures of Cary Grant, and then manipulating the images digitally, but I think that would be an actor without emotions.'[15]

However, *Rendez-vous à Montreal* does set out the possibility of a completely synthetic production becoming technically feasible within a very short time. If some degree of artificial intelligence were incorporated it would be possible to achieve not only visual realism but behavioural realism too. This prospect opens a completely new set of digital allusions that could have both disturbing and creative consequences. In this drive for realism on as many levels as possible, computer software companies find this a challenging arena in which to demonstrate their products. Matt Elson from the computer company Symbolics has produced a series of computer animations that seek to show what can be achieved within the computer graphics community. His latest project, submitted to SIGGRAPH 1991, was based on a development of his 1989 star Lotta Desire. This leopard-skinned woman has a major role in a short piece of animation, called *Virtually Yours*, showing Lotta waiting for a love who takes so long to arrive that she begins to age. Her image transforms from a young, beautiful female to a woman in her old age, still recognisably the same person, but with a rather sad look. Matt Elson has now spent a considerable time in developing synthetic characters and each entry he has made to SIGGRAPH shows an increasingly 'real' feel. Moving nearer his goal of making virtual and real action indistinguishable, he comments in the SIGGRAPH daily newspaper, 'I wanted characters that would fully and uniquely revel in being computer characters. We're getting closer ...[16]

Although the work of Matt Elson is still far short of bringing a truly synthetic actor into existence, it would be possible even now to include such an actor in the middle distance or background of a movie and at this range they would probably be indistinguishable from human actors. With ever more realistic representation of the human form and its behaviour it is possible to expect an almost independent character perhaps learning from situations and responding to others in a way that is indistinguishable from 'real' actors. There seem to be two ways in which digital technology and the cinema are converging which represent Lansdown's third category of computer usage, suggesting the application of intelligence to computing. The first part of this representation is solving the problem of achieving intelligent characterisation of the human form: contributors to this field include Daniel Thalmann and Magnenat-Thalmann in Europe and Matt Elson in the United States. These are not the only people working in this field but they are cited here as examples of how the fully synthetic movie might develop and how it could impinge upon the traditional cinema. The second part of the application of intelligence to computing could be seen as the development of the interactivity between the movie and an audience able to participate with it.

The traditional delivery of information as a book or a film has been linear, controlled by the author or producer. Their linear sequence meant that you started at the beginning and worked your way through – in the movie frame by frame and in the book page by page – until it was finished. It may be that the constraints imposed by linear narrative structures will be broken. As John Sayles elaborated in a recent BBC interview:

> It would be wonderful to be able to write on film – to write with the production, to say, let's try this angle, or let's keep the scene running and let's see where you people go. And then we'll cover it if it's any good. We would like to do that but we can't just afford to. If you want to think of it this way, there are two basic ways to make a film. One is to be like a sculptor who takes a huge stack of marble and chisels (out) this little statue, but he doesn't see it until he has chiselled away half the marble then it gets to take shape (*sic*). And you can get wonderful stuff this way. ... I assume that in *Apocalypse Now* there is a lot of great stuff on the cutting room floor. The other way is to say I can't afford all that marble, give me enough pieces to make the statue. I am going to draw it to scale, give me just enough concrete and I am going to make a mould and pour it in . . .[17]

New moulds may be made through the convergence of new and old screen technologies, i.e. cinema and television, HDTV and virtual reality. Massive computational potential means that higher resolution images, wider screens, improved sound and colour could combine with immersive and interactive texts which will change both computers and the cinematic experiences they will have created.

As participants, audiences could become part of the movie itself, almost as Flynn was, when he penetrated the world of the computer in the movie *Tron*. With sensory feedback, wide field-of-view screens, and wearable interactive devices, movies in the twenty-first century may become the 'imaginative displacements' that Joseph Weizenbaum talks about:

> To say that the computer was initially used mainly to do things pretty much as they had always done, except to do them more rapidly or, by some criteria, more efficiently, is not to distinguish

it from other tools. Only rarely, if indeed ever, are a tool and an altogether original job it is to do, invented together. Tools as symbols, however, invite their imaginative displacements into other than their original contexts. In their new frames of reference, that is, as new symbols in an already established imaginative calculus, they may themselves be transformed, and may even transform the original prescriptive calculus. These transformations may, in turn, create entirely new problems that then engender the invention of hitherto literally unimaginable tools.[18]

NOTES

1. Robin King, *Computer Graphics and Animation as Agents of Personal Evolution in the Arts: Leonardo* Supplement Issue (Oxford: Pergamon Press, 1988).
2. Ibid.
3. Ibid.
4. Ibid.
5. Irving Taylor, 'An Emerging View of Creative Actions' in Irving Taylor and JW Getzels (eds.), *Perspectives in Creativity* (Chicago: Aldine Press, 1975).
6. Christopher Finch, *Special Effects, Creating Movie Magic* (New York: Abbeville Press, 1984).
7. Roger Malina, *Digital Image – Digital Cinema: The Work of Art in the Age of Post-Mechanical Reproduction: Leonardo* Supplement Issue 1990, (Oxford: Pergamon Press, 1990).
8. Michael deGraf, SIGGRAPH Panel, 1990.
9. Michael deGraf, SIGGRAPH Panel, 1990.
10. James Cameron, from an interview by Kodak Eastman Co. on 11 November 1991, *Celebrating Innovation in the Arts.*
11. Ibid.
12. Ibid.
13. Anthony Lane, 'Really Special Effects' in *The Independent on Sunday*, 21 September 1991.
14. Philip Hayward, 'Industrial Light and Magic: Style, Technology and Special Effects in the Music Video and Music Television', in Philip Hayward (ed.), *Culture, Technology and Creativity* (London: John Libbey 1990).
15. Cameron, *Celebrating Innovation.*
16. Barbara Robertson, 'The Electronic Theatre' in *SIGGRAPH Show Daily*, Tuesday 30 July 1991.
17. John Sayles, in an interview on *Naked Hollywood*, tx BBC 2, 31 March 1991.
18. Joseph Weizenbaum, *Computer Power and Human Reason* (Harmondsworth: Penguin Books, 1976).

TOWARDS HIGHER DEFINITION TELEVISION

Jean-Luc Renaud

Proponents of high definition television (HDTV) point to a worldwide market of 750 million TV sets which will eventually have to be replaced. This is a formidable battleground for consumer electronics manufacturers, a sector whose growth rate has dropped dramatically over the last ten years. The Japanese see HDTV as a hit product to re-ignite the market. For the European consumer electronics and semiconductor producers, who have lost considerable ground to Pacific Rim competitors, the mastery of HDTV is seen as a matter of survival. For the Americans, control over HDTV would ensure the existence of a strong semiconductor sector, but the absence of a domestic consumer electronics manufacturing sector limits their international ambitions.

If a vast market beckons manufacturers, what does HDTV offer broadcasters, producers, directors and consumers? The route to fully-fledged HDTV is plagued with difficulties. Historical parallels are often drawn between the move from conventional to HD television and the transition from black and white to colour. However, it is difficult to know whether consumers will consider better picture resolution worth a very substantial investment in new equipment. In Europe and Japan, work is currently being carried out on less costly technologies, under the generic label of enhanced definition television (EDTV), which aims to improve existing television systems. The single main feature on which proponents of the various EDTV and HDTV systems worldwide have reached agreement is the new wide-screen 16:9 aspect ratio. This format presents producers and directors with as many constraints as it does opportunities.

Will broadcasters and consumers settle for EDTV and so further delay the implementation of HDTV? Will HDTV be the hit product of the end of this century, the saviour of an entire electronics industry? Investigating these questions becomes all the more interesting when consideration is given to the widely different strategies that Europe, Japan and the US have chosen to introduce HDTV.

Historical Perspective

With an ever widening range of technologies aimed at improving the existing TV picture, the term HDTV is getting confused. In fact, 'high definition' has been widely used throughout the history of broadcasting to define a number of advances in television's picture quality. RCA first used the term in its 1934 Annual Report, identifying the role HDTV would play in the commercialisation of television. Also in 1934, Vladimir Zworykin, a pioneer in the development of electronic television, defined the parameters for HDTV 'regarding 240 scanning lines as a minimum'. A British engineering report from the Royal Television Committee in London offered a similar definition. A commemorating plate reminds passers-by that from the BBC studio at Alexandra Palace in North London was launched 'the world's first regular television service in high definition'. That was in 1936, and the TV picture consisted of 405 lines!

In its modern usage, the term refers to technological developments which started in the 1960s in Japan. It is in 1968, within ten years of the introduction of television in Japan and only two years after Japan adopted NTSC as its colour standard, that public broadcaster Nippon Hoso Kyokai (NHK) began research on an HDTV system that would use projected 35 mm film as a technical benchmark. A research team led by Dr Fujio examined the psychophysical attributes of human vision as well as the technical foundation for such a system. It reached the conclusion that HDTV – to be called 'Hi-Vision' – was to have a vertical picture resolution of at least 1,000 lines. NHK settled on 1125 lines, based on a mathematical correlation to both 525-line NTSC (Japan/US) and 625-line PAL/SECAM (Europe) colour standards. In 1972, NHK drafted a programme of study for HDTV to present at the International Radio Consultative Committee (CCIR) of the International Telecommunication Union (ITU). Based upon the parameters of the NHK system that included 1125 lines, a 60 Hz field rate and a 5:3 aspect ratio, the CCIR set up an internal committee in 1974 to study the possible standardisation of HDTV.

By the end of the 1970s, HDTV research in Japan began to be disseminated through many of the technical journals and conferences held by the International Electrical and Electronics Engineers (IEEE) and the Society of Motion Picture and Television Engineers (SMPTE). In 1977, SMPTE formed its first study group on HDTV. In 1978, the BBC entered into discussions on high definition by publishing a report on a system of satellite broadcasting for HDTV. In 1979, NHK began its first experimental satellite transmission in HDTV, and two years later, US network CBS demonstrated the Japanese system in North America for the first time at an SMPTE winter conference. In 1989, NHK began a daily one-hour HDTV service which was increased to eight hours daily on 25 November 1991.

An HDTV picture is made up of four to five times the amount of information necessary for a conventional PAL, SECAM or NTSC picture, so the transmission of an HDTV signal requires a much larger bandwidth than the 6 MHz frequency band allocated to terrestrial television in the United States, or 8 MHz in Europe. In 1984, the Japanese government and industry had agreed on a 1125/50 Hz transmission standard called Multiple Sub-Nyquist Encoding (MUSE). MUSE is a bandwidth compression technique that made it possible for HDTV signals to be accommodated within a 27 MHz bandwidth located within the 12 GHz frequency band allocated to broadcast satellite services by the World Administrative Radio Conference (WARC) in 1977.

The principal parameters of the Japanese HDTV system were adopted at an interim Working Party meeting of the International Telecommunication Union (ITU) in Tokyo in January 1985 and were submitted for adoption as the world standard at the ITU International Radio Consultative Committee (CCIR) held in Dubrovnik the following year. The proposals were rejected by the Europeans on the ground that the Japanese 60 Hz-based HDTV system was incompatible with the 50 Hz refresh rate (50 frames per second) used in Europe. More fundamentally, the Europeans feared that a green light from the ITU would allow Japanese manufacturers to strengthen further their hold on the consumer electronics industry worldwide and in Europe in particular.

The European Commission's IT Task Force had alerted the European industries to the potential threat posed by the Japanese HDTV technology in the mid-1980s. In the wake of the Dubrovnik meeting, a pan-European strategic alliance called the EUREKA Programme was set up in 1986 to co-ordinate, amongst other things, European HDTV research. From 1986 to 1989, the EUREKA 95 industrial consortium succeeded, at the price of a $350 million investment, in developing in record time all the component equipment necessary in the HDTV chain. The European system, called HD-MAC, uses the multiplexed analogue components (MAC) transmission method. This standard provides for the progressive implementation of HDTV through an interim stage, D2-MAC, which ensures full compatibility with existing TV sets. HD-MAC offers a 1250-line image resolution in the 16:9 format at a 50 Hz scanning rate. HD-MAC is to be broadcast via satellite.

After initial moves towards adopting the Japanese HDTV system, the US decided to choose its own route to HDTV. In March 1990, the Federal Communications Commission (FCC) defined the parameters for the implementation of an HDTV transmission standard. It will be a simulcast system terrestrially transmitted. The simulcast approach allows existing television channels to keep their existing channel allocations (6 MHz). However, each station would also be given an additional 6 MHz channel to transmit a bandwidth-compressed HDTV signal. Existing NTSC receivers would take the NTSC signals, while new HDTV sets would pick up the HDTV signals. There are five contenders developing HDTV in the United States:

- Advanced Digital Television (ADTV) – from the Advanced Television Research Consortium (ATRC), comprising North American Philips, Thomson Consumer Electronics, NBC, the David Sarnoff Research Center, and Compression Labs, Inc.
- Alliance Interlace – from the American Television Alliance, comprising General Instrument Corporation (GI) and the Massachusetts Institute of Technology (MIT). This is the successor to GI's DigiCipher system submitted to the FCC in June 1990.
- Alliance Progressive – also from the American Television Alliance, this replaces MIT's Channel Compatible hybrid system submitted earlier to the FCC.
- Digital Spectrum Compatible – a joint venture between Zenith and AT&T.
- Narrow MUSE – from Japan Broadcasting Corporation (NHK).

Introducing HDTV to the Market
The different technological routes Europe, Japan and the United States are taking towards HDTV mean different strategies are being considered for its implementation:

- Europeans have chosen the backward/forward compatibility

49

approach. Those owners of 4:3 TV sets now equipped with a Scart, connected to a D2-MAC decoder and a satellite dish for the reception of D2-MAC broadcasts, will be able to receive, albeit in the 625-line format, future HD-MAC transmissions in addition to existing PAL/SECAM broadcasts. For their part, HDTV set owners will be able to pick up HD-MAC/PAL/SECAM signals. The successful implementation of HD-MAC is predicated on the initial development of a large installed base of D2-MAC receivers, especially 16:9 D2-MAC sets, on which HD-MAC will be piggybacked.

- In the United States, a non-compatible simulcast approach has been chosen. Under that scheme, TV stations broadcasting will be allocated an additional terrestrial 6 MHz channel to transmit a bandwidth-compressed digital HDTV broadcast. While existing NTSC receivers pick up the NTSC signal, new 16:9 HDTV sets will be needed to pick up the HDTV signal.
- In Japan, it is the backward-only compatible route which has been chosen. HDTV broadcasts were not designed to be received on existing NTSC sets. To receive Hi-Vision programmes requires the purchase of a 16:9 HDTV set plus a satellite dish. These sets can also pick up conventional NTSC broadcasts. However, the arrival on the market of MUSE-to-NTSC decoders is making things more complicated. More about that later.

In summary, Europe, the United States and Japan are approaching the question of how to implement fully-fledged HDTV in different ways:

- Europe is taking the 'progressive path' – terrestrially-broadcast 625-line 4:3 PAL/SECAM→satellite-broadcast 625-line 4:3 D2-MAC→625-line 16:9 D2-MAC→1250-line 16:9 HD-MAC
- USA is taking the 'big jump' – terrestrially-broadcast 525-line 4:3 NTSC→terrestrially-broadcast 787–1125-line (depending on system selected) 16:9 HDTV
- Japan is taking the 'quantum leap' – terrestrially-broadcast 525-line 4:3 NTSC→satellite-broadcast 1125-line 16:9 HDTV

If these are the different plans, what are their prospects?

Enhanced Definition Television
Because HDTV broadcasts require the transmission of vast amounts of data, thus necessitating large bandwidth requirements, the HDTV

systems designed by the Europeans and Japanese can only be delivered via satellite where such bandwidth exists. This makes HDTV out of reach of terrestrial broadcasters, and would compel viewers to purchase satellite receivers to pick up the HDTV signal. Not to be left behind, terrestrial broadcasters are developing technical solutions to enhance the existing television signals (in particular, providing the wide-screen format). These developments, known under the generic term of EDTV (for 'enhanced definition television') are important because they could drastically affect the market take-up of true HDTV systems.

Europe

European terrestrial broadcasters and consumer electronics manufacturers are looking to enhance the existing PAL standard. With the recent emphasis on wide-screen display as the selling point for MAC, terrestrial broadcasters, not to be left behind, went back to work. Their efforts culminated in the development of PALplus.

PALplus is properly speaking the name of a strategy group formed in 1989 by the German public broadcasters ARD and ZDF, together with their Munich-based Institut für Rundfunktechnik (IRT) as well as ORF and ZDF, the Austrian and Swiss public broadcasters. The BBC and the Independent Television Commission (ITC) came on board in January 1991. These organisations work together with consumer electronics firms Philips, Thomson, Grundig and Nokia to develop an enhanced terrestrial transmission system compatible with conventional PAL. It was thought that a significant improvement in terrestrial distribution would be needed in the future in order to compete with commercial satellite broadcasters for whom the MAC standard was designed. The PALplus Strategy Group set itself the task of enhancing the PAL signal by

- developing the 16:9 letterbox aspect ratio
- increasing the usable luminance bandwidth
- reducing cross-colour artefacts
- working on echo cancellation
- improving sound

The provision of a wide-screen 16:9 format is the most notable feature of PALplus – by now a generic name. But its 'trade mark' is also the display, on conventional 4:3 receivers, of pictures in the so-called letterbox format with black bands at the top and bottom of the TV screen.

In the approach towards wide-screen PAL, the letterbox format was not the system originally favoured by UK broadcasters. They believe that, unlike continental viewers, their audiences will be resistant to programmes broadcast with 'disruptive' thick black bands at the top and bottom of the screen. However, recent surveys do not paint such a bleak picture. The letterbox format has rarely been used on British television. UK viewers have been watching truncated images. The pan/scan techniques employed to fill up the 4:3 TV screen with wide-screen picture sources are not always successful. Nevertheless, although both the ITC and BBC have now joined the PALplus Strategy Group, they have not conceded defeat without a fight.

Now-privatised National Transcommunications Ltd (NTL), which carries out work for the UK's Independent Television Commission (ITC), had been studying an alternative 'side panel' approach whereby a standard 625-line 4:3 picture, or a 4:3 portion of a 16:9 picture is transmitted in the normal manner. In this way receivers display normal 625 PAL vertical and horizontal resolution. For 16:9 sources and displays, side panel information is transmitted as 'buried' transparent data within the normal signal. This information is recovered by the wide-screen receiver and the side panels 'stitched' back on to the main signal prior to line doubling for final display. The difficulty is finding capacity within the main signal because this information must be 'stitched' back on to the existing 4:3 picture without the 'join' becoming visible. Also the side panel method requires more pre- and post-transmission processing than the letterbox method. Given that the time-frame foreseen for the introduction of wide-screen PAL is 1995 onwards, the 'side panel' approach is no longer considered to be a viable option.

Another method for wide-screen PAL developed by NTL is the 14:9 aspect ratio 'window' option. With this technique the number of active lines making up the picture is increased from 432 to 494, leaving at the top and bottom of the screen smaller bands half the width of those generated by the letterbox method. The ITC believes that the 14:9 'window' format may be a useful stepping-stone which could ease the introduction of fully-fledged 16:9 PALplus letterbox in the UK.

It appears that the techniques used in PALplus could equally well be applied to SECAM signals and the French are reviewing options to enhance their domestic SECAM system. Indeed, Thomson Consumer

Electronics declared at the Berlin Fair in October 1991 that it would be possible to create an extended SECAM transmission format on the back of the development of PALplus. Work is currently under way on a so-called SECAM-plus.

It is worth noting that East European broadcasters are also looking at enhancing SECAM. They met in November 1991 to set up working parties to begin research into SECAM-plus. The chief engineer of the Czechoslovak state broadcaster said the decision to press ahead with research into SECAM-plus was taken after a series of abortive attempts to ditch SECAM altogether and switch to PAL. It would appear that research has already begun in Bulgaria, Hungary, Poland and the former Soviet Union. However, the deteriorating economic conditions in Eastern Europe and the former Soviet Union in particular are unlikely to put those countries at the forefront of SECAM-plus development.

Japan

In Japan, the implementation of Hi-Vision is facing cheaper alternative technologies, namely, the arrival of TV sets with MUSE-to-NTSC down-converters and the development of wide-screen Clearvision or EDTV-2.

Japan's public broadcaster and originator of the Hi-Vision system, NHK, began to transmit eight hours a day of HDTV programming to 160 locations across the country. NTV schedules about fifteen hours of EDTV programming a day which, except for films, is virtually its entire daytime and evening lineup. And the shows are beamed to nearly all of the nation's 39 million TV households. Of course, few of those households can see those shows in Clearvision, as EDTV is known in Japan.

Clearvision is the result of a crash research project started in September 1985, led by Japan's commercial broadcasters under the auspices of the Broadcasting Technology Association (BTA) and the Japanese government. In January 1986, the BTA began research on a system that could operate within the terrestrial 6 MHz bandwidth, be compatible with NTSC, and offer an improved picture based on progressive scanning. Ten of the twenty-five proposed EDTV systems were selected by the BTA for testing by the Ministry of Posts and Telecommunications (MPT). But this first-generation Clearvision system (EDTV-1) features the same 4:3 aspect ratio as the current NTSC, and is generally not perceived by consumers to be a significant enough technological improvement. According to the Electronic

Industries Association of Japan, approximately 6,000 Clearvision sets were sold in the first nine months of 1991.

Work is proceeding on the second-generation Clearvision system, EDTV-2, which offers not only a wide-screen 16:9 format – the same aspect ratio as HDTV – but superior picture and sound quality compared with the first-generation Clearvision. Regular EDTV-2 broadcasts are scheduled to begin in early 1995.

Major Japanese consumer electronics companies are not waiting for the finalisation of EDTV-2 to get into the wide-screen TV business. Over the last year, 16:9 NTSC sets with MUSE-to-NTSC down-converters have appeared on the market. These receivers, also categorised under the EDTV label, could pose a real threat to genuine Hi-Vision equipment. With the quality of the down-converters ever improving, consumers are unlikely to notice much difference between MUSE-transmitted pictures displayed on a Hi-Vision HDTV set and the same pictures down-converted to NTSC. Manufacturers are not trying to develop anything radically new. Instead, they are concentrating on added functions and making incremental improvements. In short, what the Japanese have always done best.

At the Japan Electronics Show in October 1991, EDTV systems grabbed the industry's attention. Manufacturers are worried that the price of HDTV sets will not drop fast enough to make the sets a mass-market product until the end of the decade. Wide-screen Clearvision could well be what they need to generate sales of TV sets in a market already saturated. Demonstrations given at the show left pundits wondering whether EDTV-2 might, in fact, turn out to be so good that it will kill Japan's version of HDTV, which although more technically advanced, will offer consumers only a marginally better picture. The government gave EDTV an unexpected break by granting permission for half a dozen new satellite-TV channels in 1992. These will be broadcast on conventional communications satellites, which are not powerful enough for HDTV.

The United States

One group promoting EDTV has been associated with the work of Yves Faroudja, a pioneer in NTSC enhancements. In early 1991, Faroudja, working with his broadcast and cable supporters, undertook a series of SuperNTSC demonstrations. These field tests involved satellite, broadcast and cable transmission, and used both 35-inch size cathode ray tube (CRT) displays and 12-foot size projection systems. Demonstrations took place in three cities over a four-month period.

The tests included broadcast programmes as well as segments from cable networks, including Showtime, The Movie Channel, The Discovery Channel and ESPN. Though not rigorously controlled, they suggested the vast majority of viewers would be willing to pay a $300 premium for a projection system equipped with SuperNTSC capability. The tests did not, however, consider whether viewers prefer a 16:9 wide-aspect ratio to the 4:3 displays used in the SuperNTSC demonstrations.

The second group of EDTV advocates is the Advanced Television Research Consortium (ATRC), comprised of NBC, the David Sarnoff Research Center, Philips and Thomson, and its most recent member, Compression Labs, Inc. ATRC has proposed two ATV systems to the FCC. One, known as Advanced Compatible Television (ACTV) is an NTSC-compatible wide-screen 16:9 EDTV system that uses some of the same enhancements as Faroudja's SuperNTSC. However, in March 1992 the ATRC withdrew its ACTV proposal from consideration following FCC chairman Al Sikes's insistence that broadcasters move directly to a fully-fledged HDTV system.

Since HDTV is already designed to be delivered terrestrially in the US, Sikes expressed impatience with those who want the US to 'lower its horizons and concentrate on half-steps, systems that trade under the heading of EDTV'. 'Pursue a great leap forward', he told broadcasters, 'and the FCC will almost certainly find the way to make a significant frequency allocation [for HDTV]. Opt for gradualism, however, and the premise disappears.'[1] Unless all the HDTV system candidates fail on the test bench, it is unlikely that enhanced definition TV will be resurrected in the US.

Strategies for implementing HDTV

At its inception in the mid-1980s, Europe's MAC had a lot going for it: absence of cross-colour artefacts, digital stereo sound, a secure conditional access system, compatibility with future HDTV transmissions and support for the 16:9 format. If everything had gone according to plan, Europe would have had by now a respectable number of satellite-delivered D2-MAC channels serving a substantial base of installed D2-MAC receivers. So, what went wrong?

A 1986 European Community Directive which had mandated the use of the MAC standard for all high-power direct broadcast satellites (i.e. TDF1/2, TV-Sat2, Marco Polo, Tele X) had not anticipated the possibility that medium-power telecommunication satellites (i.e. Astra, Eutelsat, DFS Kopernikus) would deliver TV signals strong

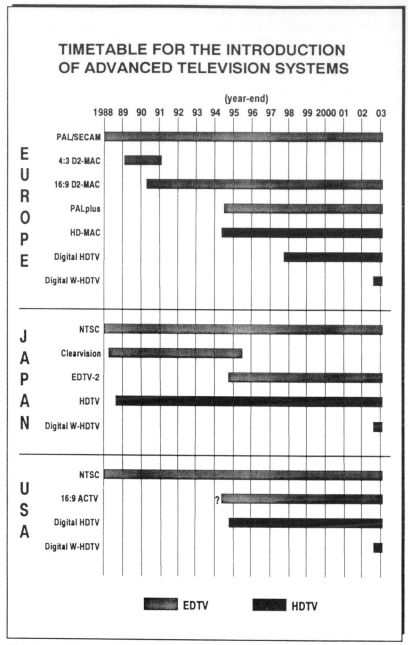

Fig. 1

enough to be received on small individual satellite dishes. The first satellite broadcasters, guided by commercial considerations, went on Astra and used the conventional PAL standard. The rest is history. There are today in Europe over 5 million PAL Astra receivers, and PAL became the de facto satellite broadcast standard.

The new Directive, which was issued in December 1991, was originally intended to close the loop-holes. But, given the market dynamism, interventionism was no longer in fashion, and it was only a considerably watered-down version of the Directive which could be agreed by all parties.

What disturbed in no small measure the 'technological tranquillity' surrounding MAC as an advanced TV system, was the claim that the analogue technology no longer had a future. Proponents of the all-digital HDTV route point to the United States where the FCC will certainly choose a digital standard. It also emerged that European researchers are well advanced on the digital front. It is also certain that some commercial broadcasters, who probably could not see the difference between a computer chip and a potato chip, joined the digital bandwagon in order to defeat a Directive they perceived to be inimical to their business. Suffice it to say that the Directive leaves the door open to all-digital HDTV. Incidentally, the digital HDTV technology is also seducing a growing number of those Japanese engineers who have a dim view of the market prospects of their country's HDTV Hi-Vision system.

By now everybody recognises that the television of the future will be based on digital technologies. But how far away is the future? Proponents of the MAC route argue that it takes about ten years for a technology to move from the lab to the consumer home, and therefore MAC has a 'window of opportunity' wide enough to justify its introduction to the market in the interim.

The latest developments suggest that the announcement of the death of MAC has been exaggerated. Ironically, it could well be that what the EC interventionism could not achieve, market forces might. Observers will have noted that the MAC proponents have of late shifted their 'strategy of seduction' by focusing primarily, if not exclusively, on the wide-screen advantage of their technology. Some would say it may be the only redeeming value of MAC, but it is a potent one, and MAC proponents are now capitalising on it. Simply put, MAC is the only standard that can offer today a feature likely to be very attractive to the consumer, namely, the 16:9 picture format. In a highly competitive environment, where product differentiation is essential, offering wide-screen broadcast services could become an attractive proposition for satellite broadcasters, conditional, it is true, upon some financial help from the European Commission or elsewhere. And 1992 looked promising in that respect.

TV Plus has started a four hour a day 16:9 D2-MAC service. Film-Net is planning to offer programming in that format. BSkyB says it hopes to be offering one channel in 16:9 by the end of 1992. TV1000-Succé already transmits six movies a month in wide-screen. This will surely resolve the chicken-and-egg problem: consumers buy programming, not technology. Meanwhile, the price of 16:9 D2-MAC receivers is coming down. After exhibiting Rolls-Royces at over $6,000, manufacturers will soon market more affordable Renaults. Philips launched in May 1992 a 28-inch wide-screen set for $2,400. Nokia will offer similar size sets for $1,800.

But, this is EDTV. How will HDTV come about? MAC proponents are quick to point out the superiority of their 'progressive path' approach towards fully-fledged HDTV as opposed to the Japanese 'quantum leap' approach. The question from the point of view of the equipment manufacturers, is whether backward/forward compatibility is the right way to ensure market penetration of a new technology and whether an interim stage is indispensable.

A new technology is likely to be successfully introduced into the market not only if it offers a much improved home viewing experience of attractive programmes, but also if it is the exclusive way of accessing these programmes. The wide-screen EDTV sets are likely to offer this improved TV viewing experience. It may be that, after disbursing a substantial sum for the purchase of such a set, consumers will be unlikely to spend even more to acquire a 1250-line HDTV set proper, in view of the marginal benefit it will procure. It could well be the case that the successful adoption of wide-screen 625-line D2-MAC will slow down the development of 1250-line HD-MAC. Ironically, compatibility could even stop the path towards HD-MAC halfway through.

However, if HDTV is the ultimate goal, the Americans and Japanese might be on to something by breaking completely with the existing standard, namely, moving from NTSC directly to a non-compatible HDTV standard. Or are they?

Simulcasting the same programmes, if it is what is intended, could make sense with the US approach, designed to move from NTSC directly to a non-compatible HDTV standard without going through what some might consider a wasteful interim standard on the European model. Initially, music studios have been releasing the same titles in both vinyl and CD formats to cater to two non-compatible types of audio equipment – the record player and the CD player. As the penetration of CD players grows and their prices decrease correspondingly, music titles will be made available exclusively in the CD format which will further boost the CD equipment market.

The Japanese approach is even more radical. The Hi-Vision HDTV channel broadcasts a different programme lineup than the one on their terrestrial network. But the Japanese route to HDTV has two important stumbling blocks. First, the MUSE transmission system combined with the manufacturing process of high definition cathode ray tubes at this point in time have made HDTV equipment extremely heavy. Second, perhaps more damaging, is the arrival of wide-screen NTSC sets equipped with MUSE-to-NTSC down-converters for a fifth of the price of a true HDTV Hi-Vision set. As the quality of down-converters improves, consumers may not see the difference between a MUSE broadcast image received on a genuine Hi-Vision set and the MUSE pictures down-converted to NTSC.

The Americans are very optimistic about the price the consumers will pay for their digital HDTV but many observers suspect there is a lot of hype. If cathode ray tubes are to be the prime home display devices for HDTV broadcasts, manufacturing such HDTV tubes is still a very expensive undertaking.

The Future for HDTV or CRT?

The view is now spreading fast that for the consumers to enjoy the benefits offered by the technology, high definition pictures will have to be displayed on large screens. This cannot be satisfactorily accommodated by CRTs. The solution is flat-panel displays. Philips has announced the first HDTV CRT set for 1994–95, but recent discussions with company officials reveal that Philips is of the view that ultimately HDTV is a business for flat-screen, and no significant market penetration will occur before the turn of the century when the manufacture of large flat-screens will make economic sense. In October 1991, the company announced a $100 million commitment to liquid crystal display (LCD) production.

Japan leads the flat-screen sector for the same reasons that ensure that country's dominant position in the memory and semiconductor sectors. In Europe, HDTV is mostly associated with the broadcast delivery of TV programming to residential homes, but in Japan, HDTV is an integral part of the so-called Information Society. It merges the function of TV broadcasting, cinematography, photography, printing, graphic design, CAD, telecommunications and computer processing. Therefore LCD development is governed by a long-term vision committed to considerable investment. The Japanese strategy, unlike the European, is also based on the mastery and exploitation of the flat-screen technology across a wide range of applications. Toshiba, for example, manufactures TV sets and computers as well as spare parts for other manufacturers. Research and production of flat-screens are common to both markets and synergies and resulting economies of scale can therefore be achieved.

Shooting in HDTV

It had generally been assumed that to shoot in HDTV would be considerably more expensive than in the conventional 625-line format. Experience tends to prove otherwise. Paul Kafno, Thames TV senior producer and Europe's doyen of HDTV programme makers says: 'We were told HDTV requires two to three times the lighting needed for conventional TV. In reality, results are excellent with only an additional 50 per cent. HDTV production does not necessitate more personnel, though editing might take about 20 per cent longer because of the slower HD VTRs currently available.'[2]

Also HDTV, with its wide-screen 16:9 format, makes it possible to shoot longer sequences and with fewer cameras. A case in point is the recording of Marius Petitpas's ballet *La Bayadère*, which Kafno filmed at the Royal Opera House in Covent Garden, in both conventional 4:3 PAL and 1250-line HDTV. Edited, the 2h 10min production was made up of 600 shots using 6 cameras in the PAL version, and of 400 shots using 3 cameras in the HDTV version. By capturing the entire width of the stage, wide-screen shooting gives a truer rendering of the set designer's intentions. That HDTV also means more sophisticated sound is usually overlooked. HDTV provides for surround sound. Although standards have yet to be agreed as to the number of audio channels – the Germans have suggested eight – all parties will probably settle on a 5-channel system – three front speakers (left-centre-right) and two rear speakers (left-right).

Essentially, HDTV requires more pre-planning than conventional television (choosing the right fabrics, deciding on more precise set detail, etc.), but it does not result in the huge cost increase initially expected. Of course, the capital investment in HDTV equipment is another matter. So far, at this early stage in the game, the equipment

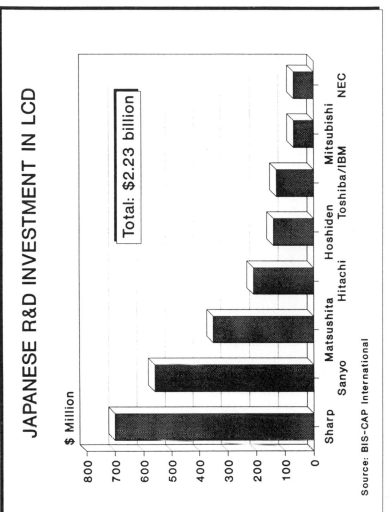

JAPANESE R&D INVESTMENT IN LCD

$ Million

Total: $2.23 billion

800
700
600
500
400
300
200
100
0

Sharp Sanyo Matsushita Hitachi Hoshiden Toshiba/IBM Mitsubishi NEC

Source: BIS-CAP International

Fig. 2

61

used by most people involved in HDTV is 'on loan' by manufacturers who are anxious to get feedback from users.

Kafno believes that, for the industry to develop, HDTV production should be handled no differently from ordinary TV production. It must not be considered 'experimental'. 'No special skill should be needed', he says. He wants to prove that by doing so HDTV production costs can be kept more or less on a par with that of ordinary TV production. Why shoot in high definition when no consumer HDTV set is yet available? Kafno believes it is important to build up a catalogue of HDTV programmes now. Moreover, this material can already be shown. 1250-line HDTV programmes down-converted to the 625-line format provide a better picture quality on existing PAL TV sets than productions originally made in the conventional format.

It remains the case that independent television producers who want to shoot their programmes in HDTV are effectively being forced to use Japanese-standard (1125/60) equipment, because the costs of direct access to European-standard (1250/50) equipment are too high, and there is not enough of it to go round. This, despite the fact that Vision 1250, a body which is the main source of European-standard equipment and into which the European Commission will have sunk around ECU 20 million ($24 million) by the end of 1992, has the encouragement of producers to make TV programmes in the EC-approved HDTV format as its principal aim. Vision 1250's high entry fee would appear to all but exclude independent producers from using its facilities. Although it is theoretically possible under Vision 1250 rules to set up a consortium of production houses and pay one subscription, the greater the number of consortium members, the more restricted their access to that equipment will be.

At present, however, the only real alternatives faced by European producers committed to shooting in HDTV are either to set up a co-production agreement with one of Vision 1250's members, or to opt for Japanese HDTV equipment. The latter choice generally means that the production has to be suitable for the Japanese market, of course, although 1125/60 programmes can be down-converted into European standard-definition formats, thus ensuring that the programme is not excluded from European transmission.

The most obvious source of 1125/60 equipment is the Japanese public broadcaster NHK, which has pursued a policy in Europe (and in the United States) of entering into HDTV co-production agreements under which they provide the equipment in lieu of cash. Shooting in 1125/60 brings another advantage with it: Japan's head start in developing HDTV technology means that there is a wider range of 1125/60 standard post-production equipment available – an important consideration where a producer is concerned to use special effects to exploit the new medium to its limits. Since one of the chief attractions of opting for Japanese-standard equipment is the existence of 1125/60 facilities houses in Europe, prospective users do not have to go via NHK.

As confusion grows around the profusion of competing advanced television standards – HDTV and EDTV – television companies have been hedging their bets by using a common standard in existence since the early 1970s – Super 16 film. In the UK, John Rogers, Head of Engineering at Yorkshire TV, firmly believes that Super 16 is the emerging format. His company has made two further six-part series of *The Darling Buds of May* in Super 16. Other executives at Yorkshire TV are equally enthusiastic about this ingenious short-cut into the new area of broadcasting. John Surtees, Yorkshire TV's Manager of Post Production Operations, regards shooting in Super 16 as an investment for the future so that when HDTV comes along in its final form, the company will have already established a substantial catalogue suitable for conversion to practically any 16:9 high definition format.[3]

Like all compromises, shooting in Super 16 for later transfer to one or other form of HDTV creates its own problems. But its overriding advantage is considerable cost-saving, together with the bonus of providing camera operators and others in the production team with hands-on experience of working in the wide-screen form. Super 16 has limited resolving power, so no one expects it to be fully capable of exploring the capabilities offered by all these systems, and there may well be a powerful case for shooting future wide-screen productions in 35 mm. As a matter of fact, the European Broadcasting Union concluded, in April 1991, that Super 16 is not suitable for high definition TV 'for reasons of resolution, film graininess, picture stability and problems with dirt and scratches'. Rogers, however, is working to a personal time frame of five years ahead, and one senses him echoing the feeling of many people at the sharp end of programme-making when he says that those in the past who tried to see twenty years ahead have usually failed.

One of the most troubling current dilemmas to emerge from dual-standard productions is whether to transmit in letterbox or regular 4:3. Channel Four was amongst the first to exploit Super 16 with its 1982 film *The Draughtsman's Contract*. This had both TV and cinema exhibitions, and was shown on TV in letterbox format. The debate over 4:3

versus letterbox screenings has raged ever since. Channel Four has screened other movies in letterbox format since then, chiefly to gauge public reaction. The UK public, however, has not taken to letterbox movies on TV in the same way as viewers in other European countries.

Some of the problems occur in the editing suite: working to dual standards creates problems, for example, of where to cut action moving left to right (or right to left) across the screen. This makes it essential for the camera operator to know at the shooting stage which format to work in. The shooting of *The Darling Buds of May* was divided roughly 50–50 between studio and location. There was basically no difference in approach between the two, according to Surtees, and the main thing was to make sure that all the important action was inside the 4:3 frame, and that there was plenty of 'dressing' for the side windows.

The irony now is that many people are talking about going into electronic production, just when producers themselves are seeing the benefit of developments in film technique such as T-grain film stock and high speed small grain stock, and are opting to continue using film because they like the look film gives to their productions. Those in television who see themselves at the cutting edge of technology may find it both unfashionable and unpalatable, but there is a powerful group which maintains that film will remain the main medium for the foreseeable future, providing the industry with a *de facto* unified TV standard.

The Industrial Context
In Europe as well as in the United States, the spectre of Japanese domination of the HDTV market has guided the policy *vis-à-vis* HDTV to a large extent. HDTV technology is perceived to be directly related to the following:

- the future of the consumer electronics industry, in terms of which companies and which nations will take the lead (and capture the market) in the manufacture and sales of HDTV television sets, VCRs, and related gear;
- the future of the computer industry, based on the fact that HDTV in any manifestation will require extensive data processing in its production, transmission, and display products, and will therefore need a heavy dose of semiconductors;
- the trade balance and economic strength – many people believe the development and control of HDTV by domestic companies will

help a country overcome its apparent weakness in the electronics field, especially in relation to Japanese strength.

A critical facet of the economic stake connected to the battle for HDTV is the electronic components sector, which includes optical components, tubes for cameras and receivers, and above all, semiconductors. It must be remembered that as the content of semiconductors in current television receivers has risen to 30 per cent, it will rise to 50 per cent for enhanced television receivers, and to 70 per cent for high definition television receivers. HDTV could become a significant new market for dynamic random access memory (DRAM) chips. Assuming a rapid growth of the HDTV market in terms of memory capacity, the use of DRAM in HDTV sets alone in fifteen years' time could be five times the total 1987 world demand. Over the past ten years, the capacity of leading-edge memory chips (DRAM) has increased 250 times, while the cost per unit memory has decreased nearly 100 times. Each generation of advanced TVs will use increasingly complex digital semiconductors to provide a better-quality picture at a lower cost. In turn, HDTV will directly push the state of the art in various aspects of digital signal processing (DSP), display, data storage, and possibly semiconductor packaging technologies, amongst others. The DSP market is growing rapidly and is expected to increase from about $650 million per year to $1.6 billion in 1992.

In 1988, Philips and Thomson joined Siemens within the framework of a programme called JESSI (Joint European Submicron Silicon), whose objective is to allow Europe to attain a technological level comparable to that of the United States and Japan within the next ten years. It is argued that the manufacture of HDTV receivers offers the European components industry a massive opening, which would generate financial resources to pay for the research and development effort needed for professional and defence electronics. In other words, the maintenance of a healthy and strong consumer electronics industry is, for Europe, a condition for maintaining its strategic freedom in an essential area: microelectronics. One of the few studies investigating the nature of this linkage is that undertaken by the Congressional Budget Office (CBO) in the United States.[4] It has analysed the extent to which the fate of that nation's semiconductors industry is dependent upon HDTV. Although Europe has constraints of its own, the analysis remains generally valid.

Reviewing various studies, the CBO report notes that, compared with the potential market for HDTV, the market for computers, communication equipment, and other electronic equipment is forecast to be much larger. While the American Electronics Association (AEA) report forecasts a $28.5 billion world market for HDTV receivers and VCRs by 2010, other US electronic industries are already much larger and are likely to continue to grow at a significant pace over the next two decades. Taken together, the world electronic equipment sector grew by $54 billion in 1989 to reach $461 billion by 2010. Thus, not only is this sector more than fifteen times larger than the HDTV market, but also its annual growth is almost double that projected for the HDTV market. The AEA figures also suggest that television receivers sold in the United States, including HDTV, will use a declining share of semiconductors over the forecast period, saying that TV receivers sold in the US will have consumed 1.4 per cent of the world's semiconductor production in 1990 and this will fall to just 0.4 per cent in 2010.

It has been argued that, although the absolute size of the HDTV semiconductor market might be small, the integrated circuits required are so sophisticated that HDTV technology will drive engineering innovation. However, the CBO contends that this seems highly unlikely. The US semiconductor industry spends over $2 billion each year on R&D and federal agencies spend another $500 million, independent of HDTV. The level of HDTV R&D specifically devoted to integrated circuit R&D is likely to be lower than this. So, assuming all R&D is equally productive, most semiconductor engineering innovations are more likely to come from the semiconductor rather than HDTV R&D programmes.

The other component technology increasingly mentioned in connection with HDTV is the flat-screen display. All forecasts generally assume that cathode ray tubes would be used for most HDTV receivers; flat-screen displays are currently much smaller and much more expensive than tubes. But HDTV engineers ultimately want to make the receiver displays using flat screens, which would then permit consumers to fit large, but relatively light receivers into their homes. Since the visual difference between HDTV and conventional colour television is more noticeable with larger screens, flat-screen television will help create the demand and therefore the opportunity for the HDTV market to grow. Since the large-screen segment of the television market is growing, linking HDTV to large-screen technology should improve its chances of success.

The Japanese government, in conjunction with several large electronics firms, has begun a $75 million joint research effort to develop large flat-screen displays for potential use in HDTV. This highly publicised, multiyear effort has further spurred concern that both US and European-based firms will find themselves at a technological disadvantage in this market unless they initiate similarly large research projects. If flat-screen colour television becomes a reality, it will be a major step forward in consumer electronics and could affect other parts of the electronic sector. Last year, nearly 900,000 laptop computers were sold in the US, most at premium prices. Most of these had some form of flat screen. The screens for colour television need to be better in several ways than the screens for personal computers. Television receivers need full-motion video whereas computer monitors do not need this level of quality. Consequently, any firm that masters the technology sufficient to produce flat-screen colour television receivers will be well positioned in the market for flat-screen computer monitors.

However, if quality flat-screen displays can be made at reasonable cost, their use will be widespread whether HDTV becomes a reality or not. They could be substitutes for television tubes of any format and, being less voluminous than cathode ray tubes of the same size, flat screens are more likely to be imported from Japan (if it maintains its lead in this technology) than produced in Europe or the United States. In most cases the CBO found that success or failure in the HDTV market would not determine the ability of potential suppliers of semiconductors, flat-panel displays, and computers to compete in international markets. Changes in market share in most of the supplier markets are more likely to result from actions of firms and the development of technologies within those markets than from pressures or advantages created by HDTV.

HDTV in the Global Context

High definition television is generally associated, and definitely in Europe, with the broadcast delivery of TV programming to residential homes. Such a view, for the Japanese, is very narrow. There, HDTV is an integral part of the so-called *Johoka Shokai*, the 'Information Society', an all-encompassing concept in which integrated information and communication systems contribute to industrial productivity and even to the solution of social problems. Many technical achievements for HDTV transcend their applications in the television industry and at the Telecom 91 exhibition in Geneva, many Japanese electronics companies were displaying wide ranging applications for technological convergences in a variety of signal compression, codec, HDTV full

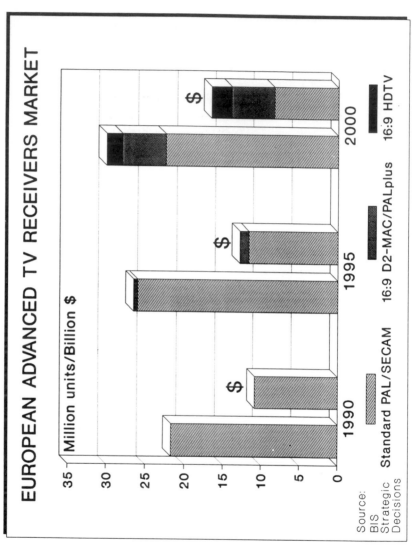

EUROPEAN ADVANCED TV RECEIVERS MARKET

Million units/Billion $

Source:
BIS
Strategic
Decisions

Standard PAL/SECAM   16:9 D2-MAC/PALplus   16:9 HDTV

Fig. 3

68

Price and Market Share of HDTV Sets

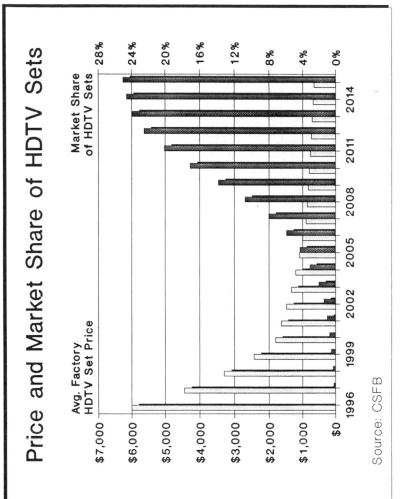

Source: CSFB

Fig. 4

69

colour printers, HD video database systems and other equipment for use in conjunction with broadband ISDN in particular.

If the application of HDTV crosses the boundaries defining the various industry sectors in which the Japanese excel on the world markets (such as electronics and semiconductors), it is no surprise that HDTV has become a bone of contention in international trade. The Europeans, for whom the HDTV concept is generally restricted to the broadcasting of TV programmes, go to great lengths to keep the Japanese HDTV technology at bay by imposing in their home market a proprietary broadcast transmission standard, HD-MAC, which is incompatible with Japan's MUSE.

Japan's international pursuit of involvement in advanced television technologies is taking various forms. Toshiba will team up with US firm Applied Materials Inc. to produce manufacturing equipment for active matrix liquid crystal displays. Texas Instruments has joined forces with Fujitsu, Sony and Hitachi to develop integrated circuits for digital signal processing for the Japanese MUSE standard. Sanyo and LSI Logic KK, a Japanese affiliate of LSI Logic Corp. of the US, will work together on the development of semiconductors for HDTV. Mitsubishi has signed an agreement with SkyPix, the world's first digital video compression DBS service, to finance manufacture of its satellite receivers. Hitachi America has opened its Advanced TV and Systems Laboratories in Princeton, New Jersey to develop HDTV technology. Hitachi follows Matsushita, Sony and Toshiba who operate similar R&D centres in the US. In Europe, Matsushita has opened its Panasonic European R&D Centre in Germany. Sony has chosen the United Kingdom to locate its own centre. The Ministry of Posts and Telecommunications and its French counterpart have agreed to jointly develop HDTV specification conversion technology.

The Japanese are also anxious to establish a foothold in Eastern Europe, following the opening up of those markets. Fifteen broadcasters and engineers from Bulgaria, Czechoslovakia, Hungary, Poland, Romania and Yugoslavia were invited to a two-week course sponsored by the Japanese government Ministry of International Trade and Industry (MITI), 'Training in New Technologies', at the European headquarters of Sony at Basingstoke, UK in October 1991. A remarkable feature of these strategic developments in HDTV is the Europeans' apparent lack of interest in building alliances with the Japanese (or with the Americans for that matter). After all, Philips teamed up with Sony for the development of the Compact Disc, and now Matsushita is working with both those companies on the Compact Disc Interactive (CD-I). Also Philips requested, and obtained, the support of several Japanese hardware and software companies for its Digital Compact Cassette standard, against Sony's Mini-Disc. Is the reluctance to team up with the Japanese on HDTV due to a European conviction that, with HD-MAC, they have the winning formula and need not learn from others? Is it because it is the best way to shield themselves from the perceived threat Japanese technology poses? One thing is certain. If the Europeans spurn Japanese overtures today, they will face more formidable competition tomorrow: powerful American–Japanese alliances working on the next generation digital HDTV technologies.

NOTES

1. Quotes from a speech to the Association for Maximum Service Television conference, New York, 7 November 1991.
2. Interview with the author, 2 December 1991.
3. Based on an interview published in *Advanced Television Markets* newsletter, Dec/Jan 1992.
4. 'The Scope of the High Definition Television Market and its Implications for Competitiveness', staff working paper prepared by the US Congressional Budget Office and published in July 1989.

MULTIMEDIA

Frank Rickett

As we look into the future of moving images and the media by which they are delivered, we cannot ignore the part played by changing technologies in shaping the pictures we see. In the 1960s, the arrival of video brought a new immediacy to programme production, and extended the programme makers' vocabulary of visual effects by several orders of magnitude. In the 1980s, the Video 8 format redefined the scope of news and documentary reporting by enabling the non-professional to make video recordings. In the 1990s, a new technology will be approaching its maturity, one which treats human activity not so much as a stimulus to be recorded for later interpretation but as a dynamic agent which provokes and incites reaction, participation and communication. In short, interaction.

In this context the term 'interactive' is quite specific. When it was first adopted by computer scientists, it was used to describe the two-way communication process which takes place between a computer and its human user. The more interactive a programme is, the more two-way communication there is between user and computer. A word processing package, for example, is highly interactive: it waits for and responds to every key-press. A programme which prints out a screen image is less interactive: once the filename and parameters are specified, the processor is left to get on with it.

Once this concept of interactivity is applied to the moving image, we have 'interactive video', a programme which can be controlled or affected by its viewing audience. In most cases, the viewing audience consists of one person, maximising the extent to which the programme is seen to be an individual experience. The video programme itself is stored on some 'random access' medium such as a compact disc or laser

72

disc, and the means of control is via a computer. Disc-based storage simply means that the sound and pictures it contains can be located and displayed in any sequence with a negligible delay between selected sequences. This circumvents the time-lag involved in rewind/fast forward operations associated with tape. It also means that sequences can be located with frame accurate precision, avoiding the approximations of all but the most expensive tape-based systems.

The types of interactive video which stimulate the most interest from the uninitiated are based on simple narratives. A story unfolds on the screen like a piece of conventional television drama, but at particular points in the story the viewer is allowed to make decisions which will affect how the story progresses. The brave knight stalks the dragon through its labyrinth. Should he take the left or the right turn at the junction ahead, or continue straight on? Moments later, the ground below his feet begins to collapse, he has a moment in which to dive for one of the adjacent doorways, but are they within reach? Which one conceals his nemesis? At its most sophisticated, interactive video becomes a vast game with photographic-quality moving images and a story where the finale depends on how well you perform; a movie in which the protagonist's fate is in the hands of the viewer. The parallel with amusement arcade games is irresistible, but to see interactive programme making simply as an adjunct to the computer leisure industry would be a serious mistake.

The Impact of Digital Media

Interactive video represents an enormous range of possibilities and shootouts are just one example from a vast array of vicarious experiences made safe: negotiating a contract, driving a heavy goods vehicle, performing an autopsy or defusing an unexploded bomb. However, there are certain limitations imposed by technical constraints, if not by subject matter. The first step in the medium's liberation is metamorphosis from analogue to digital format.

Video is conventionally an analogue rather than a digital medium. The technical details are less important than the implications, namely that the images and sounds which are retrieved and displayed cannot be changed or manipulated by the system. In other words the user interaction is effectively restricted to a selection process, and even though it may be disguised to give the user an impression of an apparently infinite freedom of choice, there is only a finite set of possibilities based on whatever video material the programme designer decided to include. Digital video achieves greater flexibility.

73

The transition from analogue to digital media is already taking place, with a succession of new hardware systems and a change in terminology. In fact, today the term 'interactive video' is rarely used, as it has for the most part been replaced by the term 'multimedia'. This is a more general description of any computer-based information delivery system that can combine text, graphics, still and moving photographic image, and sound, from a randomly accessible storage medium. Analogue technology is characterised by its dependence on recording variations in an electrical current. Digital techniques are based on the use of a more precise binary code which assigns precise values to momentary variations in signal (see chapter 5). One advantage of the digital method is the improvement in recording quality, the reduction of 'noise' compared to 'signal' which has made CD audio such a success. A more important advantage for multimedia is the flexibility it allows for the manipulation of information by the designer and the user of the system.

One instance of this type of manipulation is the resizeable video window. This allows the user to shrink or expand a moving image within its own 'window' and reposition this window anywhere on screen, perhaps to make other images 'underneath' more clearly visible. There would be complete freedom of scale available, not simply three or four fixed levels of magnification. Even the aspect ratio could be altered, producing fat or thin images in real time, i.e. without interrupting the programme flow. Digital video allows the user to take actors out of one scene and to place them in another, changing the context, perhaps mixing and matching the characters. This is possible because the actors and their backdrops can be defined by a set of digital values. Analogue technology by contrast could deal with the scene only as a unitary entity, unable to distinguish the elements that make up a scene as objects in their own right. Digital video is capable of such discriminations and can be made to treat these elements accordingly. Contrast this with interactive video whose analogue signals are permanently cast by the time the master tape leaves the online edit facility.

There is overwhelming evidence that all-digital media will predominate in the interactive technologies of the future. Being digital, the technology is capable of drawing on sources of data of all types (audio, visual, textual, numeric) and of presenting these disparate strands as a unified package within a single medium. The implications of this move away from analogue are enormous. Multimedia marketing suggests that there will be an explosion of cheap, high quality multimedia systems in a host of new and unexpected contexts, as well as the rejuvenation of existing markets, over the next ten years.

Interactive Video: Commercial Context

With the emergence of digital multimedia, interactive video is in many ways already a thing of the past. Although its roots can be traced back to the seventies, it was adopted in the 1980s by corporations and institutions, used in education and industrial training, in retailing and in marketing. To service these applications, there was a small interactive video 'industry', at least in Europe and the US, which existed as part of the corporate and non-broadcast film and video industry. Mainstream film and television producers tended to ignore it, although there have been one or two notable exceptions in the art world. So as a mainly industrial phenomenon, interactive video programmes were regarded less as audiovisual experiences and more as applications of technology. The nature of the industry dictated that each programme had to fulfil a need and serve a specific purpose for a carefully identified target audience: aesthetic merits or creative possibilities were never the medium's selling points.

Interactive video is essentially an industrial medium, a business or educational tool rather than a form of audiovisual entertainment or stimulation, and so it makes more sense to discuss interactive programmes in the context of the commercial or institutional environments in which they appear. Within the principal 'application areas', education, training, retailing and marketing, interactive video has been assessed according to how well the needs in each of these application areas have been addressed.

In 1986 the BBC's *Domesday Project*, a two-disc programme, made the ambitious claim of bringing the original Domesday Book (1086) up to date in an all embracing audiovisual tour of the English countryside. Schools were enlisted across the country to contribute factual and photographic information on their localities and all the information was assembled and delivered as a 'surrogate travel' experience. The intention was to allow the user to be free to make decisions and choices which would, for example, move the user around a gallery, or select any geographical area and permit successive magnification of that area from ordnance survey level, to street maps and down to photographs of the vicinity currently under scrutiny. Unfortunately, *Domesday* did not live up to its promise.

The practical considerations associated with managing a vast pictorial database gave way to implementation problems whose solution was a long line of compromise. The user either has complete freedom of movement within a restricted domain, or restricted movement within a complete domain. Consequently you can never quite 'go to' the place you thought you could choose. This type of constraint is, as we have seen, inherent in analogue video material but the mistake in this case was to suggest that greater freedom existed than was actually on offer. Manoeuvring around the informational terrain was not the smooth surrogate travel experience everyone had hoped for. The tracker ball, a kind of inverted mouse, was provided for user control, but it is not the most intuitively easy or ergonomically comfortable input device ever devised, and has since more or less disappeared as a computer interface. A far more severe failing lay neither in the implementation, nor in design, but in the underlying programme concept. Vast resources of information such as *Domesday* cannot be planned without a full consideration of how people might wish to use them. Will users want specific information on a single area? Will they want to cross-reference a number of themes? Will they be concerned with demographics? Will they want to find a particular street? There is little evidence to suggest that any of these questions were successfully resolved. Unfortunately the project never fulfilled the heightened expectations it had raised in the public imagination and this disappointment was to prejudice the public view of interactive technology as a whole. The *Domesday Project* was for many people their first experience of interactive video and unlike its predecessors it had a very high profile: it was the ambassador of interactive technology. The fact that it failed to achieve the goals it had set itself unfairly tarnished the reputation of many projects that followed by simple association. The damage extended beyond the educational market to generic and bespoke training.

Industrial training has always been the main application area of interactive video, with the large financial institutions being the principal commissioners. However, it was clear from the early 80s that there were more producers than commissioners. A mixture of enthusiasm and optimism seemed to keep the producers in business and some attempted to solve the problem by creating 'generic' training programmes. These would cover general business activities such as selling skills, business writing, negotiating, and so on. The commercial success or failure of these projects is beyond the scope of the discussion here, except to note that many potential commissioners bought the relatively inexpensive 'off the peg' titles as a testing ground for the technology – it was even possible to lease them in some circumstances. In this way the whole idea could be evaluated by an organisation before it took the plunge and commissioned specific titles to address specific training needs. However, rather like buying your first stereo system to play the LP you fell in love with, in the long run the tail begins to wag the dog. Once certain organisations had gone to the considerable expense of commissioning a bespoke interactive training programme and had installed the latest costly interactive video hardware, they then felt the need to collect as many programmes as possible to justify the investment in their hardware base.

Indivisible from an organisation's training needs is its corporate culture. In addition to providing specific training instruction, interactive programmes are invariably a vehicle for the expression and endorsement of these corporate ideologies and commissioning clients are seldom slow to recognise this fact. Frequently however, a problem arises when the ambitions of the corporate culture and the intentions of the training programme come into conflict. These two objectives seldom share a high level of congruence and it is often as much the designer's job to resolve contradictory corporate messages as it is to structure and deliver training material. There is a certain tension between a commissioning client and a programme producer in every field of corporate programme making. Managed well, this aspect of the relationship can lead to excellence, managed badly, to disaster. Since everyone is familiar with television, so everyone considers themselves an expert. In the interactive domain, this belief is particularly hazardous. Being technically more complex than a similar linear programme, interactive programmes are particularly vulnerable to falling foul of unscheduled modifications. Perhaps the best example of this can be seen in the general misapprehension of the nature of software. It is generally imagined that writing a computer programme is rather like writing a book or a script of some description, albeit of a more technical nature. In fact, a substantial piece of well-written software is a highly structured object whose parts presume a certain interrelationship in order that the whole should function as intended. From this perspective a piece of software is more like an architect's plan for a building or an engineer's blueprint for an aircraft than a novel or a script. It follows from this that client requests to 'change that bit slightly' can result in software that 'falls over' or 'crashes'.

As a mainstay of the industry, the arguments made for interactive training are economic. Personnel and administrative managers in large organisations are asked to compare the costs of training a workforce by conventional means (either on or off site) with training by interactive video systems. An interactive video which can be used unsupervised during quiet periods is argued to be much more 'efficient' than the process of sending people *en masse* to a training centre, with costs of accommodation and time off work. However, the most common form of industrial training, certainly in Britain, is learning on the spot from colleagues or workmates, or studying outside the company's time. Furthermore, interactive video was used by corporations to supplement rather than replace conventional training strategies – which nullifies the economic advantages justifying its use in the first place. Statistics on the efficacy of the technology are rarely convincing. Learning is an asymmetrical process: once something is learnt it cannot be truly 'unlearnt', which makes testing interactive systems against other methods difficult. How can a valid comparison be made between, say, one hour sitting through an interactive video programme and one hour with a human teacher? There might be ways of measuring the teacher's brilliance, the pupil's intelligence and the quality of the programme's design, and even ways of measuring how freely these three agents communicate with each other under experimental and control conditions but all such controls will be open to question. Questioning the statistics is not, however, something that ever happens. As students of cognitive dissonance know, when six figures have been spent on a training programme, a thorough check to find out how well it works will be avoided for fear of what might be discovered.

While training programmes abound, it is not clear why Point Of Sale (POS) and Point Of Information (POI) programmes are still uncommon in Britain, while they are gaining popularity in the US. Technophobia amongst the general public and the ugliness that typifies cabinet design doubtless hold some truth, but as an account of why these applications are so thin on the ground it seems suspiciously incomplete an explanation and more likely is the limited economic contribution that interactive video programmes like these have made to the businesses that commission them. Nevertheless, some useful and informative programmes appeared in the late 1980s and there is no hard evidence to suggest they would not be used if well situated within a retail outlet. One such programme, commissioned by a supplier of home decoration materials, enabled the user to choose, from a large pictorial database, a room which resembled the one they wished to decorate. Next, the user could 'colour the room' from the range of colours on offer and judge the colours' suitability and co-ordination with room furnishings for themselves. As a customer tool the programme offered an excellent opportunity to avoid expensive mistakes, or to hit on combinations which might otherwise have been overlooked.

As the technology evolves and prices drop, it seems reasonable to predict that POS/POI systems will become a more common feature of high street shopping. Meanwhile they enjoy popularity primarily as guides in museums and art galleries, domains in which providing a public service still takes priority over pure profit. One of the most ambitious examples in the UK is the *Micro Gallery* at the National Gallery. Essentially a catalogue of 2,000 paintings in the gallery's Western European collection, the twelve networked Mac IIfx-based touchscreen systems provide information indexed by the works or the painters' names. It can also generate a personalised tour, printing out a map locating points of special interest. With a focus on presenting high quality visuals, the system's dependency on keywords to access information means that the scope of its appeal is somewhat restricted. The system does not cater for users who cannot positively identify the painter or painting they seek because it fails to provide adequate support for serendipitous or directed browsing. Despite this drawback the system is popular with the National Gallery's visitors.

Interactive Video in an Artistic Context

Although interactive video has been developed predominantly in the context of 'corporate communications', it is not only found in large corporations and educational institutions. Artists have also experimented with interactive video even though their explorations of the new technologies are somewhat insular. One of the main problems was and still is the lack of a suitable forum, restricting the exchange of artistic ideas; hardware costs and software complexity also play their part in deterring greater artistic contributions.

One project which successfully flew in the face of these difficulties was *The Erl King*, completed in 1986 by Grahame Weinbren and Roberta Friedman. A customised hardware configuration was supported by a purpose-built authoring system which Weinbren devised to assist in programming the piece. Based on Schubert's *Erlkoenig* this installation embodied several strategies for interacting with the user. The first sequence of the piece, for example, begins with a soprano performance of the title theme. Touching the screen during the performance replaces the singer with related images while the music's seamless join allows it to continue without interruption. Other strategies allow the user to trigger supplementary events. For example, touching the lower right hand corner of the screen produces an English translation in text of the line in the song the user is currently hearing. It is via the use of these connecting edits that the user develops a sense of

79

moving through the piece, encountering numerous themes, stories and images related to the *Erlkoenig*.

Weinbren sees the relationship between the corporate and the artistic face of interactive video as essentially antagonistic, if not completely antithetical. 'Each technological advance brings along the idea that there is ... an enormous profit-potential if a "market" can be found. Businesses spend huge amounts of money "researching" these markets, and "developing" them when the research reveals they don't exist. One large wing of new technology business is the creation of new desires, or even better, new needs. Central to the vocabulary of the new tech salesman are terms like imagination, power, choice, freedom ... they are selling escape routes.'[1] Weinbren does not see the facility to make choices as in itself a sufficient condition to instil a sense of release in the user. On the contrary, he sees choice as a burden, and part of the shopper's mindset, rather than that of someone on the end of a communication line. Meanwhile the corporate entity continues to search for mass markets for artistic creations. This is not Weinbren's goal: 'I hope I can suggest some of the real potential of the new technology, which is in describing, expressing, reflecting some aspects of being human, not in exploiting the widespread bourgeois desire to shake off the ordinary.'[2]

Domesticating Multimedia

At present, the development of multimedia is beset by a standards war. Each technology has its particular strengths and weaknesses, but a repetition of the VHS versus Betamax situation is unlikely. These competing technologies will each find their own market niche in which they predominate, with only minor skirmishes across the borders.

From a strictly technical standpoint, the new multimedia technologies are merely formats or 'standards' for encoding digital information, usually on an optical disc. A more casual assessment might be to characterise consumer multimedia as a computer with a CD drive in a sleek box, packaged to look like a home video recorder. Both descriptions are correct, but while the first draws attention to the formal characteristics of the system, the second speaks volumes about technology and culture. Agreeing standards ensures a certain continuity which can encourage a market to develop. This is only part of the story, for without agreement on what these systems are expected to do, there can be no mass market. This implies making an unsuspecting public familiar with a new device and persuading it not only of its merit, but of its ease of operation. In this respect, the introduction of

80

multimedia products into the home is a 'technology driven' push, rather than a 'culturally led' pull.

The most neglected aspect of all computing systems has traditionally been the 'human interface', or the mechanism by which the machine does what the user wants it to do. Putting a keyboard in front of it immediately excludes those who feel they have no keyboard skills. Giving it a 'language' understood only by the voodoo technocrats effectively excludes ninety-nine per cent of the rest of us. 'User friendly' was a phrase invented to measure the extent to which the designer was responsible for the users' failure to understand the system. This gave a name but not a solution to the continuing problem.

The problem of 'unfriendly' systems cannot be overstated. In the UK the Department of Trade and Industry and the Design Council have mounted a joint initiative termed 'Usability Now'. This aims to highlight the damage done to UK industry through the development of systems with poor interface design and has reversing this trend as its goal. Fortunately, the situation is gradually improving. At research centres like the UK's National Physical Laboratory and in the MIT's Media Lab in the US, scientists are developing interfaces which link directly to the way humans communicate naturally, through eye contact, the use of gestures and, of course, speech. Human vision, for example, is being more usefully redefined as an output rather than an input phenomenon. Computers which follow eye activity can infer from the frequency and location of the human gaze which items on a screen are of most interest and adjust the display accordingly.

The emergent virtual reality technologies are just one part of this quest to humanise the 'coal face' of working with high technology systems. Virtual reality claims to solve the human interface problem by removing the interface. Users can 'step into' the system and manipulate digital information by physically 'taking hold' of it. This signifies the search for a paradigm shift in the way humans and computers interact, and these ambitious objectives are already beginning to be realised. Affordable, commercially exploitable products are still some years away. While the cost of the new technologies is certainly falling, the benefits of such systems have not yet had significant impact on the first wave of consumer multimedia systems.

Meanwhile, Philips, Sony and Matsushita, the developers of the Compact Disc Interactive (CD-I) system, have come up with a more immediate solution to the interface problem; the keyboard is removed and the system is no longer described as a computer. Whether this elegantly simple marketing manoeuvre will prove sufficient to banish technophobia, and hence resistance to the new products, remains to be seen. Nevertheless, the developers appear to have exchanged one difficulty for another. The problem appears to be the selection of an appropriate metaphor. If it's not really like a computer, what is it like? If it's a video then I can record on it, right? Wrong. Like all multimedia, CD-I resembles so many other more familiar formats without really behaving like any of them. This uncertainty can only be fully resolved through a technical assessment of the medium's capability.

Matsushita, the parent company behind more familiar names like Panasonic and JVC, has been co-operating with Philips and Sony on the development of CD-I. Philips and Sony are old collaborators when it comes to defining Compact Disc protocols, having defined CD Audio and CD Read Only Memory (CD-ROM) standards which have created enduring markets. This time, the story is likely to become more complex. Aside from the looming standards war, with companies like Commodore Business Machines launching CDTV, an entirely incompatible format, there is rumoured to be dissent within the ranks of the CD-I consortium themselves, with Philips eager to launch CD-I without waiting for it to include full-motion capability, a move which makes Sony a little uncomfortable. Sony would prefer to develop new products at least nine months before launch to allow time for full testing and debugging. This is to say nothing of the possibility of spoiling the market by having an under-specified product at launch which will need upgrading or replacing within a year. While CD-I is the current favourite to dominate the domestic multimedia market, it is not the only pretender.

The First Generation

First generation multimedia systems come in various forms and predictably enough each has its own distinct characteristics which make it more or less suitable in a given application. Included in this group are CD-I, DVI and CDTV.

CD-I is a superset of the more common CD audio disc. The CD-I standard puts not just 16 bit stereo sound on a disc, but three further levels of sound quality, still pictures, text, and eventually, full-screen full-motion video. Technical constraints bedevilled early attempts to squeeze video onto compact discs. The problem has now been solved by the Motion Pictures Expert Group (MPEG), a working party set up by the International Standards Organisation. As a result, 1993 should see the arrival of full-motion video of 'at least TV quality'.

The disc itself is essentially a stream of digital information which can be accessed in a random sequence. The layout of information on the disc and the behaviour of the disc player dictate which streams of data will be interpreted as pictorial, which as audio and which as text, according to the CD-I specification. The disc can store approximately 650 Megabytes of information, roughly the equivalent of all the telephone directories of a major European country or all its ordnance survey maps. CD is a large storage medium. Other members of the family, CD-ROM, CD-ROM XA and CD-Audio, differ only in the logical layout of this information on the disc's surface and consequently in the way this information is intended to be read.

Moving pictures in a multimedia system present a particular problem: a lot of information is required very quickly to update a screen image. CD-I can easily deliver the quantity of information required, but it has a major difficulty with speed. This is like being in the Sahara desert with a lifetime's supply of water which can only be sucked through a straw with the diameter of a pin. This difficulty has arisen because the system specification is based on the use of a CD-Audio drive mechanism, already mass produced and therefore relatively cheap. In CD-Audio, there is obviously no requirement for visual information, and therefore the relatively low data transfer rate is perfectly sufficient, but the saving in costs from using CD-Audio drives creates a huge information bottleneck when visual information is also required.

The solution has been to compress the video information stored on disc, so that the low transfer rate is then sufficient to deliver the picture information in its compressed form. The compression process takes the raw data which describes a picture and removes all the redundant information so that the image may be more succinctly described. Prior to compression, a picture is defined by noting the colour of every pixel at every position on the screen. Compression techniques abound, but a simple example would be to note only the first pixel colour and to add a note saying how many adjacent pixels can also be this colour before a new colour is encountered. To achieve the very high levels of compression required to fit motion picture sequences of some length onto a compact disc, the MPEG compression algorithm is applied not only to individual frames but also across sequences. Temporal compression makes use of the high degree of similarity between individual frames to interpolate a picture description, given the presence of uncompressed key frames before and after the predicted sequence. Compression is performed while the disc is in development, and decompressed 'in real time', at the moment of viewing. A complex decompression mechanism has to be called into action during playback, before the picture can hit the screen. For full-motion PAL video, all this needs to happen twenty-five times a second. Hardware decompression systems will be a feature of second generation CD-I players, but there is likely to be a trade-off between compression ratios employed and final image quality. The more tightly a picture is squeezed, the more 'crumpled' the result looks once it is unpacked. In practice, programmes which employ these features will need to balance the need for lengthy full-screen full-motion sequences against the need for high definition images. This is essentially a design decision and will be led by the specific requirements of individual programmes.

Digital Video Interactive (DVI) is a method for compressing or decompressing video in real time, embodied in a set of microprocessor chips. The storage medium on which the data resides is irrelevant, it could be a CD or it could be a computer's hard disc, but given the enormous storage requirements, a CD would generally be the best option, unless the capability of DVI to compress as well as decompress in real time is also borne in mind. This means that users can take their own videos and compact them into compressed digital format for later re-expansion and replay. DVI's data expansion capability is in principle what CD-I has so far lacked, but CD-I is a read only medium: what has been recorded on it cannot be changed, like a gramophone record and unlike a cassette tape. In theory, DVI allows the data to go in both directions. But if the storage device is a CD, the process of updating visual information can then quickly become prohibitively expensive, particularly since video compression is largely handled by Intel (developers of the system) rather than by the end user. The charge for and inconvenience of this service deter many would-be developers. A greater problem is the quality of the decompressed image. The quantisation process results in a somewhat 'over-pixelated' picture. As most of us now expect a high quality image on our television screens it is difficult to conceive of a situation where this limitation is unimportant.

Commodore Dynamic Total Vision (CDTV) is Commodore Business Machines' proprietary 'version' of CD-I, although not so highly specified. Based on their successful Amiga home computer, the CDTV is basically an Amiga with a CD-ROM in a single box. Commodore clearly intends to reformat a lot of its existing software, principally games, onto CD, which would give it an edge over Philips which needs to develop titles from scratch for its CD-I product. The response from

84

Philips has been to enter into an agreement with the Japanese games giant Nintendo to market their more popular games in CD-I format.

In addition, the Amiga, and hence CDTV, has always had a custom chip set which was designed to produce graphics at very high speeds. These custom chips access 'Chip' RAM without needing to notify the central processor (CPU). The CPU has its own memory store ('Fast' RAM) to which it has exclusive access. This arrangement is highly efficient and helps produce extremely fast graphics. While these chips are by no means state-of-the-art, they give CDTV a secure technical advantage over CD-I. On the other hand, CDTV is aiming to produce neither multiple audio standards nor full-screen full-motion video, because those endeavours are beyond the remit of its original design. Like CD-I, CDTV targets users likely to embrace the players and, more importantly, domestic users who might otherwise resist a technology which assumes computer literacy. Like CD-I, CDTV makes use of the semantic sleight-of-hand which suggests an altogether more approachable consumer item. A rose by any other name still has thorns, however – in this case, the growing library of games titles more clearly suggestive of amusement arcade action than of the respectability of a tool for growth and self-improvement. As with CD-I, CDTV lacks a metaphor which might otherwise have provided a convenient handle by which it may be understood by a slightly bewildered public. In Commodore marketing speak the claim is that CDTV will provide 'edutainment'. The apparent need to rely on neologisms confirms the difficulty manufacturers face when introducing the public to new media concepts.

Direct comparisons between DVI, CDTV and CD-I are difficult. DVI is not currently marketed as a consumer product in the same way as the others: CDTV is not capable of sustained full-screen full-motion video pictures, a feature which CD-I will soon be able to provide. CDTV is already available, at least one year before the projected release of CD-I. As with the VHS/Betamax story, it may not necessarily be the technically superior product that triumphs: availability is itself a persuasion. DVI looks set for specialist applications in industry where training requirements are subject to change and information needs to be updated on site on a regular basis. CD I V will undoubtedly be concentrated in the domestic computer games market, despite early attempts at more serious titles. However, it is difficult to see how this will be achieved since the Amiga itself sells in vast quantities, as a lower priced, more versatile machine than the CDTV, with its software costing about the same or less than the CDTV equivalent. Where CDTV's added value lies is not clear, particularly since most of the games so far developed for it are recycled versions of their Amiga equivalents. Nevertheless, history has shown that Commodore's marketing policy follows an obscure path and CDTV looks like being no exception.

As a domestic product, CD-I is even more of a wild card. Initial versions just fail to look good enough. People have become sophisticated enough through their experience of broadcast media to expect more than CD-I is delivering: unremarkable graphics without full-motion video capability (FMV). It is also a fearfully complex system and just getting a small dot to appear on the screen calls for applause among those who are starting up in the programme development cycle. Persuading the system to display a sequence of average complexity involves formidable levels of work, approximately equal to crafting every individual frame by hand. However, such achievements hold no interest for the viewing public, whose main concern is what happens on the screen rather than the labours that went into a programme's production. It is likely that the strength of CD-I will continue to stem from the corporate training market, the area currently using interactive video. Meanwhile the format is approaching a full specification with which to woo the domestic market: full-screen full-motion video, and even the development of small hand-held 'Walkman' style players featuring four inch colour LCD screens.

As CDTV and CD-I enter the high streets their software indicates both their target markets and the sources of their development. Three common categories are beginning to emerge in their titles: games, reference and educational, with a fourth category, 'professional' titles, belonging particularly to CD-I.

Commodore's CDTV beat a path to the shops well ahead of Philips' CD-I with a catalogue of familiar games titles. *Xenon 2 Megablast*, *Interceptor* and *Sim City*, like many others, had already existed as Amiga games. Since CDTV is really an Amiga with a CD-ROM drive, it has been relatively easy to kickstart a CDTV library by 'porting' existing software onto optical disc format by expanding or extending games originally developed for the Amiga so that they take advantage of the greater storage capacity offered by the CD format. In effect this usually means more screens, more 'levels', or enhanced image resolution.

The centrepiece of the CDTV reference catalogue is the *Grollier Encyclopedia* with 21 volumes, 9 million words and over 2000 images on disc. Other titles cover a wide if predictable range: the *Guinness CDTV Disc of Records*, *Garden Fax*, *Dr Wellman – Family Medical*

86

Advisor, Timetable of History, World Vista Atlas, the *Illustrated King James Bible* and the *Complete Works of Shakespeare*. The educational software, or 'early learning tools' in the new marketing speak, features a range of interactive storybooks such as *Scarey Poems for Rotten Kids*, *A Bun for Barney* and *The Hound of the Baskervilles*, as well as simple colouring book programmes like *My Paint*.

A wider range of software than games, reference and educational titles can be run on CDTV but this requires users to purchase additional hardware items such as floppy diskdrive and qwerty keyboard, thereby converting the CDTV into a full Amiga system, effectively transforming it from a consumer multimedia unit into a home computer.

Unlike Commodore, Philips had no ready-made software collection on which to draw, which meant that building a library of titles was slower and initially more expensive. Now expanding substantially, however, CD-I titles are beginning to offer CDTV ready competition. Its own 'professional' category addresses a variety of generic business needs from general management skills to specialist foreign language training programmes for the business traveller. The quality of these titles' content, design and execution varies enormously. The 'hand coding' essential to a good title is costly, so the retail pricing will reflect both development time and the small market which titles such as *Finance for Non-Financial Managers*, for instance, are expected to attract in their first year.

While it faces no real competition for 'professional' titles, CD-I is in a tough arena where games are concerned. Amiga-based CDTV not only has a tried and tested catalogue but it beats the CD-I system with custom co-processor chips which handle fast graphic manipulations in hardware (the 'blitter') and a number of established games houses are lined up behind what they see as the superior games machine. For CD-I to make real headway in this new market, talent will be needed to develop games which make the most of its strengths. A game like *Connect Four* makes the player long to return to pen and paper-based games, but *Palm Springs Golf* is one of the few engaging games which takes advantage of CD-I's high resolution and high storage capacity.

The flagship of CD-I reference titles is the high-budget *Smithsonian* disc featuring a large number of exhibits from the Smithsonian Museum with text and audiovisual support. Its development is rumoured to have run over $2 million which is typical of the kind of costs which early titles, intended to showcase the hardware, incurred.

As with CDTV, educational titles and software aimed at young children feature in abundance and are a crucial marketing strategy. The educational catalogue establishes multimedia as a benevolent domestic influence, with games for entertainment and relaxation coming in behind. After a few hours' hard study and cross-referencing, there can be a little 'kerpow splat' before bedtime: fun for all the family.

Predicting how multimedia can satisfy consumer demand is only half the story behind the software catalogues currently available. Copyright problems, which generally centre either on issues of alteration or on issues of reproduction, can attenuate titles to a significant degree.

A software developer might take a piece of copyrighted material (say, a photograph) and change it in some way. Once a photograph has been scanned or grabbed into a digital environment any number of transitions are possible – from the subtlest manipulation of a single pixel to a distortion so intense that the original image is no longer identifiable. At what point, then, does the new image cease to be sufficiently close to its original form as to continue being the property of the original copyright holder? When can it be judged to have changed so much that it is deemed a new creation, copyrighted by a new owner?

These 'boundary' cases can give rise to costly litigation, but the direct costs associated with acquiring rights to reproduce assets owned by third parties give developers even more severe headaches. For instance, the development of a pop music quiz could contain 2000 questions, each question requiring at least one photograph ('who is this?') and many more needing at least four ('which one of these ... ?'). Many would also require 10–20 seconds of sound extracts from copyrighted recordings ('identify the song from the opening bars'). Even if photographs and sound recordings are distorted to such an extent that their identification is made more challenging, and even if some kind of bulk deal could be made with picture libraries, the price would still make the project unacceptably high.

Developers are beginning to take one of three routes round the copyright problem. Rather than trying to negotiate the rights to a successful cartoon character, for instance, they will aim to set up a joint venture in which the copyright owner takes no fee for the use of his/her asset, in exchange for a proportion of the sales on the final product. This allows the developer to use a high profile name and the copyright owner to engage in a risk-free opportunity to make additional profits from his/her copyright material.

Originating new material avoids the copyright problem altogether.

It is often less expensive to commission the author of a highly success-ful children's book, for instance, to create a similar but new set of characters and situations specifically for multimedia application, than to purchase rights to existing copyright material. This approach also cuts the costs of converting a product created for other media into an interactive form.

Finally, anything on which copyright has lapsed, which is in the public domain, is fair game for multimedia adaptation. Thus the selec-tion and recirculation of 'classics' as new kinds of interactive texts may actually have more to do with their guaranteed freedom from copy-right than with their popularity or artistic merit.

Where Next?
Previously discrete technologies are beginning to converge. These new interactive digital multimedia signify the union of television with word processing, desktop publishing with high fidelity stereo, computer-based training with graphical arcade adventure. None of these is new when seen in isolation, but what is new is the synthesis, the 'all singing all dancing' appliance. So, what happens next?

Recent advances in biotechnology and biochemistry mean that there now exists engineering capability to create circuits and machinery not micro in nature (dealing in millionths of a metre), but nano, a thousand times smaller still. This is not simply the art of miniaturisation taken to its physical conclusion but the ability to create entirely new materials, to manipulate individual atoms, to create machines of molecular pro-portions. Nanotechnology will create computers with billions of bytes of memory which would fit in a space the size of a single bacterium. A storage unit six inches long could contain more information than the entire accumulated wealth of all human knowledge. Preposterous fan-tasy? The US National Science Foundation has recommended support for basic research aimed at developing molecular computers and motors. Japan has begun a multimillion dollar programme of research. NEC, Hitachi, Toshiba, Matsushita, Fujitsu, Sanyo-Deki and Sharp have begun full-scale research aimed at developing bio-chips for bio computers. The estimated time-scales put a mere ten to fifteen years between us now and the realisation of this prospect. Intelligent trans-ceivers and hardware decompression units built on this scale would make constantly updated personal multimedia units a reality. With such machines we could, for example, download vast amounts of information from a network of centralised databases. The information would be stored locally on a hand-held unit until no longer needed, then updated or replaced with another brief data transmission. Such a system would function as a mobile knowledge bank, presenting facts, opinions and interpretations of events or situations as they arise. The user might call up a travelogue of the town they're visiting, a shopping list with motion picture demonstrations of products, maps of locations, latest prices. The civilian and military possibilities are by turns fabulous and chilling.

Although multimedia is currently beset by a number of technical limitations, these stumbling blocks are likely to fall away quickly. The main problem facing the future of multimedia is identifying the needs it promises to fulfil. Despite the hysterical claims of the admen heralding the dawn of a communication revolution round the next corner, 'technology in search of an application' remains the most frequently cited criticism in response to the 'state of the art' developments. Certainly, home video and desktop publishing systems were developed for an established market need and their use has already proved their worth. Multimedia by contrast is not truly an application in its own right, but a collection of tools which permit applications to be designed, assembled and delivered. The distinction is critical, for multimedia is a means and not an end. While major market research companies predict multi-billion dollar global markets for multimedia within the first five years, the fundamental questions remain: how will these systems be used, and what benefits do they offer?

As multimedia develops FMV capabilities, feature films on compact discs will gradually, but not immediately, challenge the VHS market. CD programmes are likely to offer the same visual quality obtained on VHS but the near ubiquity of households with VCRs means that video will be hard to unseat. At present CDs have a capacity of 72 minutes which means that most feature films would have to be 'broken' over two discs, interrupting the viewing experience. Sony is currently working on developing a blue laser which will quadruple CD capacity but this is not expected to be commercially viable until the turn of the century.

Random access, the ability to jump directly to any point in the film, might attract prospective CD buyers but compared with video, the read only facility will remain a distinct disadvantage. Being able to record off air and to record one film over another seems preferable to improved image quality, compact size and random accessibility, as Laservision's death in the market-place showed. However, the first recordable CD audio machines are now making their way into the domestic market and real-time motion compression chips will feature as an integral part of home digital recording systems by the end of the 1990s. At that point tape-based systems will begin their speedy and irreversible decline and give way to digital optical technologies.

While the artistic community may be quick to see the creative potential of multimedia, its impact on other areas of human endeavour is less certain. Perhaps the answer lies ultimately in a reappraisal of how we as a society use – or fail to use – the information technology with which we surround ourselves. The arrival of each item of new technology in the home or workplace is heralded as an event which will assist, simplify, or otherwise lend support to existing ways of working. In every case, be it the arrival of the washing machine, the television or the word processor, our patterns of life have not only been supported but for ever changed. New technologies do not simply accommodate our needs, they change patterns of behaviour and cognition. They change as they penetrate cultures, economies and societies. In sleek grey boxes, digital multimedia will do more than simply restyle our furniture.

NOTES

1. Grahame Weinbren, article in *Catalogue* for Experimental Film Congress, Toronto, 1989.
2. Ibid.

REFIGURING CULTURE

Timothy Binkley

The Light at the Back of the Cave

Plato would probably disparage the ubiquitous TV den as a modernised version of his gloomy Cave portending dire consequences for the future of culture. Shackled by nothing more sinister than potato chips and beer in an easy chair, passive spectators watch flickering shadows cast by a reality that passes them by in some remote elsewhere. The progenitor of Western philosophy would most likely agree with his contemporary progeny who deride television as a retrograde cultural force that numbs the intellect while it panders to the appetites.

The Platonic critique of television is based on two related beliefs. Firstly, ideas and images exist in drastically different realms mediated but separated by objects and secondly, their relationship is indirect and unreflexive since images assume the inferior position of representing objects that are in turn subordinate to the concepts those objects instantiate. For example, the Idea, or Form of 'bed' is an abstraction that is imitated (or instanced) by an object made of wood and cotton. This object is in turn imitated by a painting. In this one-way hierarchy, pictures capture only reflected illumination from concepts and hence are twice removed from the pure Forms of Truth and Beauty. Within this framework television stupefies because it traffics in faint imitations of imitations that obscure uplifting ideas with base passions.

When he dichotomised rational forms and perceptual appearances, Plato struck a tonic chord which still resonates. But these well-worn assumptions about the breaches and bridges between spiritual and physical worlds are giving way to new kinds of cultural events. TV images are drawing splendour directly from mathematical abstractions unmediated by any physical events they might represent. The realm of concepts has begun to play its own distinctive apparitions across the cathode ray tube (CRT) as digital media supersede analogue ones and computers take an active role in managing the spectacle. A new intercourse of ideas and images arises as computers perform feats heretofore restricted to people and a pervious screen beckons us to join in the dance.

The intriguing phenomena of **virtuality** and **interactivity** loom over the horizons of the old metaphysical order and challenge it on two major fronts. These two hallmarks of computed experience originate in abstraction. Numbers are the original 'virtual reality'. Despite their intangible nature, they have a concrete impact on our lives, from measuring financial status to gauging the structural integrity of buildings. Our world economy has abandoned gold as the basis of wealth, and a new order is rapidly emerging which traffics in nothing but numbers. A paycheque is simply an addition to the balance in one's bank account, and a purchase is a subtraction. A number identifies who you are and what privileges you enjoy. All this activity is mediated by computers which connect us to numbers in perplexing but vivid ways. They do this by being able to execute formal procedures called 'algorithms'. These procedures permit computers to have a dialogue with us through numerical mediators which are both representatives of events in the world and the subjects of calculations. The mechanised ratiocination that takes place among hidden circuitry is linked to our quotidian world through responsive interfaces which accomplish rapid conversions between numbers and physical events. The virtual reality of numerical descriptions in coordinate space and the interactivity of intelligent machines which algorithmically manage them coalesce to open enigmatic portals into cultural productions more vivid but less domineering than the mimetic ones prevalent since shadows danced in Plato's Cave.

What is a Digital Medium?

Prehistoric artisans wrestled their entreaties to immortality into recalcitrant physical substances long before Plato spurned images in favour of ideas as the best route to eternal verities. Ever since, supplicants striving for an audience with future generations have struggled to chip stone into beautiful shapes or plaster walls of dark rooms with arduously prepared pigment. The earliest creative labours left legacies enshrined in material objects with more staying power than mortal flesh. They have since evolved through a long history of increasing

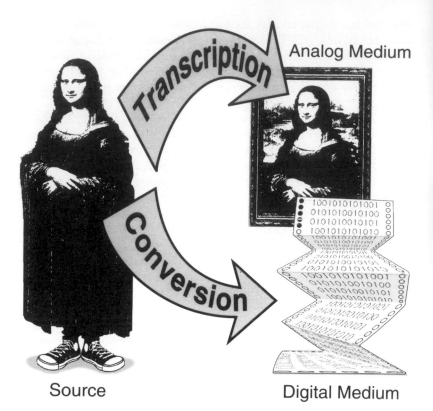

Transcription

Analog Medium

Conversion

Source

Digital Medium

Fig. 1 by William Nelson

automation so that now anyone can capture an image for posterity with pushbutton immediacy.

The protracted course of civilisation has carved a rich heritage of communication channels. From painting to periodicals, from recitals to radio, from LPs to CDs, they have come to be known as the **media** by which messages are spirited across space and time.[1] Until recently, media have conformed to what is called an **analogue** paradigm characterised by an imprinting process. Analogue media store information through some kind of **transcription** which transfers the configuration of one physical material into an analogous arrangement in another (Fig. 1).[2] The Mona Lisa mimics in paint the appearance of a person in the flesh. Even if the Gioconda is not a real person or is an idealisation of an historical figure, the work's representational status is derived from a portrait paradigm: someone could look like that even if no one

94

Source

Analog Medium

101

Mona Lisa
by Leonardo di Vinci

Transcription

Transcription

Fig. 2 by William Nelson

does.[3] When a painting has no representational subject, the medium still registers at least the artist's gestures transcriptively as they impart analogous forms to paint: a straight movement of the hand creates a straight line, while a curved movement produces an arc.

Analogue media imbue objects with resilient marks perceivable either directly through the senses, or indirectly through a display process that carries out an additional transcription. Photography is of the former type, video the latter. By transferring reflected light onto reflective pigment, a camera generates visible film whose recorded images are simply looked at. But when light patterns are embedded in an electrical signal by a video camera, the analogous forms imparted to the current are not visible until they are transcribed back into light as glowing phosphor on a monitor. When a video signal is recorded on tape, yet another transcription imprints electrical impulses onto analogous magnetic ones, and the playback process involves two transcriptions that first conform electric current to the recorded magnetic fields and then match the flicker of light on the screen to the varying flow of electrons. Transcriptions can be joined together in a cascading sequence of media that vastly extend the potential impact of a work of art or a noteworthy event (Fig. 2). Such iterated transcription is intrinsic to the popular 'mass media' of television, newspapers, magazines, books and movies of contemporary culture. These ubiquitous transmitters are all thoroughly immersed in the repeated imprinting that is essential for the promulgation of analogue information. The face of Madonna on the cover of a magazine is transcribed first to film, then to a printing plate, and then to paper before finally reaching the consumer.

Digital media by contrast **convert**, rather than transcribe, the information they preserve. Whereas analogue media store cultural information in the material disposition of concrete objects, digital ones store it as formal relationships in abstract structures. A phonograph record and a compact disc both archive music, but the methods they use are fundamentally dissimilar. Analogue media maintain a concrete homogeneity with what they represent, while their digital counterparts transform originating impulses into heterogeneous quantifications of their sources. An analogue-to-digital conversion process transfigures physical quantities into numbers (Fig. 1). A digitisation of the subject of Leonardo's masterpiece transforms her features into a sequence of numbers rather than trying to analogise them in paint. These numbers might initially be lodged in the electronic circuits of a computer's memory, but they can readily be shuttled back and forth among many other types of media that have been suitably prepared to receive them, from magnetic disc to marks on paper, to optical discs, or magnetic tape.

A digital medium is not virgin territory, but needs to be formatted first before it can receive messages from a communicator. No imprint is pressed; rather a lattice is filled. A digital medium is prepared to receive information not by smoothing it into an undifferentiated continuum, but rather by imposing on it an essential grid that delineates receptacles for data. Although a digital medium may use the same physical material as an analogue medium (e.g. magnetic tape), it functions quite differently since its import lies in stored digits, not in any particular aesthetic qualities of the substrate. Digital media are discontinuous pre-structured arenas where vast multitudes of regimented discrete quanta are episodically hosted for the purpose of articulating messages.

Photographs and phonograph records directly mimic their sources through medium-specific tangible linkages, each engineered to make relatively permanent marks on a particular type of material. The art is then carried to its audience through direct or transcribed perceptions of the medium.[4] Digital machinations, on the other hand, can place the source, artist and audience at remote locations where contact with the material that holds the information they share is essentially mediated not by characteristic physical processes, but rather by conceptual constructs adaptable to a variety of materials.[5] The digital medium is never a palimpsest: no permanent traces are left since messages pass in and out of the theatre of digits without presuming continued residence. Each cipher gently occupies its assigned seat with quiet assurance but then agreeably leaves when asked to make room for another cast of characters. A database constitutes an elusive though powerful creative resource which is diaphanous compared with paints and brushes. Digital media store information, but not in a form that is directly perceivable or by means of a playback transcription. These salient differences can be summarised by noting that a digital medium stores tokens of numbers rather than recording traces of events, as its analogue predecessors do. But what exactly does this mean?

Numbers are abstractions that have no concrete physical existence. The number two is an intangible idea designated by many different instances of markedly different symbols. The arabic numeral for it is '2,' the Roman form is 'II,' and the binary code made popular with computers is '10'. Every time any symbol for the number is written, the marks constitute what is called a **token** of the number. The abstraction that constitutes the number itself is sometimes called a **type**. Different inscriptions of the same symbol can have rather different appearances, as when the arabic symbol is written in different handwriting scripts or printed in different typefaces. The ability of a token to represent a number does not depend upon the particular aesthetic qualities of its appearance, but rather upon the role it plays in a comprehensive formal system. A token for two does not have to look like anything in particular so long as we can consistently identify it and systematically differentiate it from tokens for other numbers. Marks that designate the numbers permit a much wider range of variability than brushstrokes representing Mona Lisa's enigmatic smile. One small change and a smile becomes a frown, but a token for two can be stretched into wildly diverse shapes without losing its meaning. On the other hand, the same token could mean two or twenty depending simply upon where it is placed relative to other symbols. The aesthetic properties of a token are incidental to its mathematical role. A beautifully designed '2' is just as functional as an ugly if legible scrawl.

When an image is transcribed into an electric signal by an analogue video system, a particular amount of light measured in luxes is matched to a different amount of current measured in volts (Fig. 3).[6] This kind of co-ordinated matching is the hallmark of an analogue medium. Quantities of one kind of substance are transferred into isomorphic quantities of another according to a specified physical process. In video, light patterns become electrical ones. When an analogue video signal is subsequently recorded onto tape, the changing magnitude of an electric current is transcribed into similar changes in the magnitude of a magnetic field.

But when a digital video system converts light into numbers, it strips the structure of a physical event away from its underlying substance and turns the incoming signal into a pure abstraction, a file of numbers untethered to any intrinsic material alliance. A digital medium stores numbers without tying them to a unit of measurement. Digital video turns a quantity of light into nothing but a quantity, a bare token that stands only for a number and not for a certain amount of matter or energy measured according to a conventional unit. The process converts an image into a collection of numbers that can be abstractly manipulated using mathematical techniques, a process completely alien to analogue media. When we subsequently want to look at the image represented by an array of digits, the unit of light must be recomposited with the numbers to convert the information back into visible events comprising an image on a CRT. Digital media are supported by both an abstraction process that extracts numbers from events for input and a materialisation process that injects numbers into events for output. But when numbers take up residence in a computer, they exist independent of any particular scale of measurement. Which material unit gets affixed to a set of numbers is to some extent arbitrary since a given file can be output either as a picture or as music equally well, given suitable conversion hardware. Digital systems are strictly independent from material manifestations and yet can easily be converted to and from them. Each analogue medium by contrast is inextricably linked to a particular substance.

States of electronic circuits, arrangements of magnetic fields, or microscopic pits etched in plastic are not things human beings can manipulate as tokens of numbers the way we manage marks on paper or beads on a string. Computers, however, use such arcane symbols to emulate what we do with our humble tokens. The contents of a digital medium are invisible and intangible, but by virtue of the role they play in a computing system, they conform to recognised criteria of numbers.

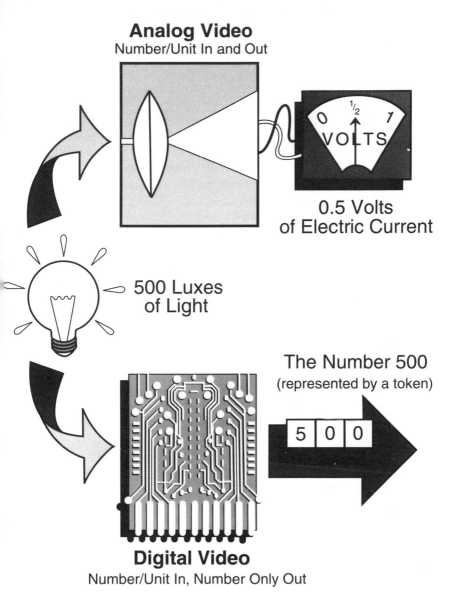

Analog Video
Number/Unit In and Out

0.5 Volts
of Electric Current

500 Luxes
of Light

The Number 500
(represented by a token)

Digital Video
Number/Unit In, Number Only Out

Fig. 3 by William Nelson

For example, they satisfy Peano's postulates that axiomatise the natural number system and are amenable to formal manipulation just like their traditional counterparts.[7] Some of the algorithms used are derived from age-old procedures while others are markedly different: a computer will probably calculate an average in much the way we do it by hand, but it will most likely sort a collection of items or draw a line using unique methods developed especially for machines. Although they may behave somewhat differently, computerised digits still form part of a deductive system which subjects them to familiar activities of inference and calculation. Moreover, it is possible to translate the computer's tokens into ours so that they can readily communicate with us. Indeed, some humanly perceivable manifestations are necessary (whether as tokens or as something else) in order for digital media to have any meaning for us.

That digital media store abstract tokens of numbers instead of concrete traces of events makes them distinctive. One of the most important features of digital media is that they can be manipulated with all the resources of a digital computer to create, filter, augment, refine, or alter the information they contain. This subjects them to a completely different set of rules from those applied to analogue media. Since their creative resources are mathematically instead of materially based, their limits are fixed at logical instead of physical boundaries. Our ability to impart a particular form to an analogue medium depends upon the efficacy of physical tools directed by manual skills. But converting the same form into a numerical format relies upon conceptual skills in formulating algorithmic techniques. A creative imagination roams through digital domains unencumbered by the constraints of corporeal existence that are a way of life for analogue artists. It takes strength and skill to chip a block of stone into a beautiful bust; and once cleaved, elementary laws of physics prevent the stone from becoming whole again. Digital media, on the other hand, are graciously forgiving and will obediently retract any regretted action. But this indulgence carries its own problems and perils. When a steel chisel carves a block of marble, familiar motor skills come into play guided by instinctive hand-eye co-ordination. However, a purely digital chisel will pass right through numerically defined stone without making a mark. It is sometimes difficult to achieve desired results in an intangible medium without carrying out challenging formal procedures that have little intuitive relationship to any visual goal. Moreover, the freedom of unlimited pardon can imprison the artist in a confounding labyrinth of her own making. Having the ability to redo something until it comes out right guarantees perfection on a regular basis, but it can also lead to an endless array of variants that stymie the artist with fecundity. Too many alternatives can cloud the clarity of incisive insight.

One of the important practical differences is that, despite their submissiveness, digital data tend to possess more resilience and hence need less protection than information stored in analogue media. Although a file of numbers can be more tentative than chipped marble, it can also be more lasting. An analogue medium is immaculately primed for imprint, making it sensitive to the slightest nuance. Whether the marks so borne are sacred maculations of art or horrible scars of vandalism depends upon where they stand relative to accepted social practices. Elaborate institutions protect the integrity of certain appearances and prevent the encroachment of others. Museums are built to shelter paintings from the elements and they are staffed by guards to deter mischief. The perceptual qualities of analogue media are paramount, but they are vulnerably stored in fragile physical materials. This is why the various mechanical sentinels of photography carefully guard its sensitive films to discriminate between sanctioned and errant flashes of light. Meticulous rituals are observed to ward off the intrusion of anything that does not come through a camera's shutter. Even a slight change in the material of an analogue medium can significantly alter the message. Digital media, on the other hand, are impervious to a considerable amount of rough treatment. Since they store tokens of numbers, their information content will often remain intact despite significant changes in the material that stores it. The postmark on a stamp will mar the look of its image while not generally affecting the legibility of its denomination. A scratch on the surface of a painting seriously violates its aesthetic integrity, but a similar vandalisation of its digitised counterpart need not affect its contents at all (Fig. 4). The responsiveness of digital media to mathematical formulae gives us the surprising ability to recover lost information or to filter out interfering 'noise' that corrupts an intended message. We can also enhance a digital image or sound to reveal information otherwise unnoticeable. In scientific visualisation, for example, digital images are often processed and coloured to reveal patterns hidden in the raw data.

The vulnerability of analogue media is apparent in their very dissemination where 'generation loss' corrupts the quality of an image as it is repeatedly copied. It is difficult to maintain all the details of an image or sound when it is transcribed over and over again from one material object to another. Even when making multiple copies from

Digital Medium

Analog Medium

Fig. 4 by William Nelson

one source, such as an etched plate, the original tends to deteriorate in the process since direct physical impact is needed for each successive imprint. But there is a sense in which digital media deal only with 'originals' and hence neither propagate generation loss nor corrupt the source through repeated copying. When a token of a number is copied, it is not usually imprinted from one material to another. Rather, a discrimination process is engaged to analyse the token and decide what number it represents. When the copy is written, it is inscribed anew as a token of the same number. In this sense, tokens of numbers are not copies mediated through other tokens, but betoken their abstractions with equal virility. When you transfer a number from a bill to a cheque, your payment is never somehow diminished by being copied. Similarly, when a computer writes a collection of tokens on a disc, they are always equally strong representatives of their numbers, whether they originated on another disc or were computed fresh. A 'glitch' might occur in either case, but such infelicities are easily detected and readily corrected. Tokens are never transcribed, but are always inscribed afresh, which is what gives digital media their resilience.

Both kinds of media store information. Analogue media transcribe it into a material form with aesthetic vitality, but their quest for perceptual analogy limits them to physical repositories which render them relatively passive. Digital media store only cold abstractions that have no inherent perceptual appeal, but since their use of physical material is less intrinsic, they open a gateway to virtual worlds that permit interactive experiences. So computerisation of cultural activities changes the role of media.

Computers make pictures without using the traditional repertoire of image-making tools. In effect they are virtual cameras capable of producing real pictures of imaginary places. It is hardly surprising that our fantasies attribute magical powers to a machine that conjures up photographs of things that don't exist using a camera that doesn't exist either.

The first step in generating much of the computer imagery that appears in film and video today is to **model** an environment mathematically. This is done by fashioning a set of geometrical structures in an abstract coordinate space, called the **object space** (Fig. 5). For example, the spaceships in *The Last Starfighter* (1985) are described mathematically and situated in a three-dimensional Cartesian coordinate system used to reference locations in a virtual universe. A computer manipulates the coordinates of the ship to move it across a starfield and generate sequential files of numbers representing each successive frame

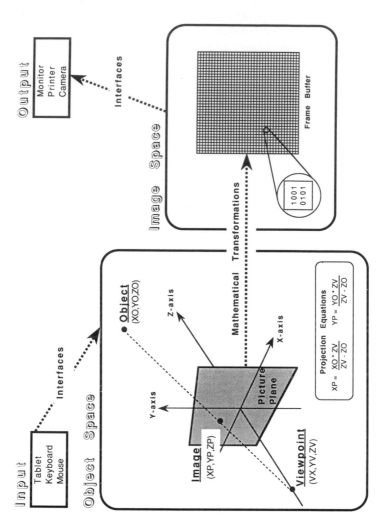

The Virtual Camera

Fig. 5 by William Nelson

104

of the animation. The computed frames contain pictorial information in **image space**, where information about the spaceship and its environment are transferred to a different mathematical structure tailored for output as a real image (recorded on film, video, or paper) that human beings can look at. Popular computer-aided drafting and page layout systems function similarly, except that the object space is usually two dimensional and is populated with the more mundane creations of architecture and graphic design. Object space is stored in the general purpose memory of a computer, while image space typically has its own hardware receptacle called a 'frame buffer'.

In some cases, computed imagery remains entirely in image space. The most common example is the so-called 'paint system', which allows users to make pictures by introducing numbers into the frame buffer with the aid of an electronic stylus or a mouse. Some cinematic applications also confine themselves to image space. A number of noteworthy recent examples show people metamorphosing into animals or into other people, such as the Michael Jackson video, *Black or White* (1991). For these effects, film is shot of the two (or more) subjects and then each frame is digitised into a computer's image space format. By analysing each frame with the guidance of artists, the computer uses special algorithms that seamlessly blend the face of one person into that of the animal or the other person. Once the metamorphosed sequence is finished, the image space is output back onto film.[8] Metamorphoses can also take place in object space, where interpolation algorithms transform the objects rather than the images. Although the results may look similar, the procedures are different for transforming the coordinates of an elephant into the coordinates of a giraffe, as opposed to changing a picture of a car into a picture of a tiger. Technical and aesthetic issues dictate which approach is preferred.

The computer is so deft at such feats because nothing exists for it except as numbers. The data representing objects, the files representing pictures, the equations used for performing mathematical transformations, and the algorithmic procedures used to do the work, are all composited as constellations of ciphers. To create something, a set of numbers is composed; to make it move, a sequence of calculations is performed. Instead of using the constructive tools of Euclidean geometry to capture real objects the way a camera obscura does, the computer's virtual camera uses the computational tools of Cartesian geometry to depict virtual objects that exist for its eye only.[9]

Cultured Ciphers

Although the advent of computerised image making is relatively recent, it is having a widespread if sometimes quiet impact throughout the arts and mass media today. After more than a decade of experimentation with analogue computers, motion-control, and oscilloscopes (most notably by Ben F. Laposky), a number of artists began using computers in their work during the 1960s. The first digital computer-generated film wass produced in 1963 by Edvard E. Zajac at Bell Labs for simulating the motion of a communication satellite in order to help solve the problem of ensuring that the same side always faces Earth. He wrote a programme to compute each frame of the film as a black-and-white line drawing based upon the position of the satellite at a given time. The computer than drew the image on a cathode ray tube being photographed by a movie camera. After each frame was completed, the computer advanced the film to the next frame and then drew the next image on the CRT. This general method of iterated display-and-record is still the standard method for recording computer animation onto film and video, but it is no longer necessary to write a programme for each animation since several software packages are available off the shelf that satisfy most production needs.

Although fine artists have not taken up the computer *en masse*, they were the first to avail themselves of its artistic potential. Soon after Zajac's achievement, film-maker Stanley VanDerBeek collaborated with Kenneth C. Knowlton (also at Bell Labs) on several films including an eight-film series of animated mosaics titled *Poem Fields*. Similar experiments in abstraction were conducted by other fine artists in the early days of computed imagery. One of the foremost pioneers in directing computer technology towards cinematic goals is John Whitney, Sr. He had been making experimental films since the 1940s and constructed his own analogue computer which he used with his brother, James Whitney. When the opportunity arose in the 1960s, he drew on his extensive experience to produce a series of digitally designed films that beautifully choreograph points of dancing coloured light. One of his most renowned is *Arabesque* (1975), whose mesmerising motions were calculated by a digital computer running software written by Larry Cuba. Most of the early computer films were composed of abstract mathematically-based patterns controlled by a computer programme. This tradition in the fine arts has been continued and recently expanded by Larry Cuba and Vibeke Sorensen, among others.

These abstract expressions may have seemed at first to be the only

106

type of art well-suited to computerisation. But rapid advances in programming techniques have since taught computers to fashion images possessed of a surprisingly meticulous realism. The challenging quest for verisimilitude quickly became a guiding light (perhaps even a holy grail) of computer graphics. After dedication and hard work on the part of software specialists, it is now difficult to tell a computer-generated image from a photograph. Picturesque ocean sunsets can be made to order with popular animation systems, and architectural renderings are beginning to look more like photographs of the finished edifice than sketches from a plan. The computer can also augment photography with mathematical image processing techniques that seamlessly manipulate their sources to transform pictorial information without a trace. Computer-altered photographs are often so convincing that our faith in photographic verity is being undermined. No longer will a photograph be able to offer prima facie evidence about truth and reality.[10] Two strangers at opposite ends of the world can be brought together to shake hands in a digitally composited image.

One of the earliest computer films to incorporate representational figures was *Hummingbird* (1967) by Charles Csuri in collaboration with James Shaffer at Ohio State University. They employed an ancient computational tool called 'interpolation' to make a hummingbird automatically disperse into a jumble of meaningless parts and then reassemble. After the key frames were entered into a computer, it was able to calculate in-between frames automatically. These intermediate frames used to be laboriously drawn by hand, but are now often computed. Interpolation is an efficient film-making tool only when computer-assisted, and it has quickly become one of the most pervasive techniques in computer animation. Peter Foldes' *Hunger* employed the same method to transform corpulent figures into skeletons and win the Prix de Jury at Cannes in 1974.

Since computers and video are both currently based on electronic technology, a natural alliance was forged that established the standard conduit for producing computer animation. Even when the final result is film, it is often useful and cost-effective to preview animation in video. And when computed images are filmed, the output device is usually just a camera aimed at a high resolution video monitor inside a fancy box. One of the impressive milestones resulting from this liaison is Ed Emshwiller's well-known classic *Sunstone* (1979).[11] This salient work showed an early use of colour cycle animation, a technique by which the forms in an image remain constant while the colours are cycled through a range of shades. It also demonstrated an important digital process called **texture mapping**, by which a two-dimensional image is stretched over the surface of a three-dimensional object. It relies upon the ability to store a video image in digital format, from which a computer can manipulate the two-dimensional surface into three-dimensional shapes by performing suitable calculations. Since computers are facile with the mathematical formulae that describe geometric shapes, almost any shape imaginable can be wrapped in video with the right programme, from a simple static cube to a contorted whirling vortex. Expensive special purpose machines to perform set repertoires of these tricks on the spur of the moment in a studio (such as ADO, Mirage, and Kaleidoscope) are widely used in broadcast television today, and their sophistication has steadily increased over the past ten years.

Throughout the 1970s, the extent and sophistication of computerised cinema increased substantially so that by the early 1980s it became a readily available resource for mainstream design as well as special effects. A computer imperative descended upon broadcast television to transform the look of logos and title sequences. Today it is difficult to watch any network programming without seeing computer-generated imagery in abundance. Computer artists are also responsible for some of the dazzling new pyrotechnics in feature films that audiences have come to expect, from the astonishing transformation of metal into flesh in *Terminator 2* (1991) to the more subtle but still synthesised scenarios in Akira Kurosawa's *Dreams* (1990) and the phantasmagoric spectacle of Peter Greenaway's *Prospero's Books* (1991). Even relatively traditional-looking animated features, such as Disney's recent *Beauty and the Beast* (1991), are beginning to use substantial amounts of computer animation. Computer imaging is also popular in music videos and advertising. Computers expand cinematic transformation beyond the realm of dissolves and wipes because they function entirely in a digital space where images are carefully analysed, calculated, and composited bit by bit rather than being merged as totalities in an analogue mixer such as an optical film printer or a video switcher. As a result, the computer is not only capable of coming up with entirely new transitions, but also spawns novel generative processes as well.

Professional television production is becoming increasingly enamoured of digital technology's reliability and versatility, and the standard broadcast video systems are moving towards a completely digital configuration. The camera produces a digital signal which is recorded on tape in a digital format that can be edited digitally and played back directly to a monitor. The electron gun of a cathode ray tube is still controlled by an analogue signal, but some of the new flat-screen display technologies may eliminate that analogue element as well. Much television production already uses digital tape systems, which were introduced with the D1 format in 1986. Since then two newer digital formats have emerged (D2 and D3), and analogue recording is preferred only where digital is unaffordable. The analogue medium of film is still superior for many purposes because of its range of colour and depth of field, but it too is on the verge of digital transformation. The roles of film and video as media are changing due to the impact of recent technology. If the recent history of computers is any indication, applications of digital video will expand as costs drop. Some version of high definition video might even supplant film in many venues as this nascent format matures.[12] But as moving pictures become increasingly digital, the differences between film and video could become insignificant or disappear altogether as traditional analogue media evolve into something else.

The impact of miniaturised personal computers (PCs) is being felt throughout our society, and their effect on the arts has not been confined to film and video. PCs next computerised page layout to revolutionise the printing industry. During the second half of the 1980s, graphic design was dramatically changed from a field long based on the manual skills of wielding material tools into a related but very different field requiring conceptual dexterity with abstract methods. Despite a great deal of scepticism and resistance on the part of designers and art directors in the early 80s, page design systems running on microcomputers quickly made themselves indispensable. By 1990 it was simply too expensive to use pencils and T-squares since computerised techniques had achieved greater speed and efficiency while reducing costs. An added bonus was the extension of creative options as previously impractical techniques became not only affordable but easy. Designers can now explore a much wider variety of solutions since the computer has dispensed with a considerable overhead of tedium and made it possible to generate multiple variants quickly. That bane of the designer's existence, a client's change of mind, can now be accommodated with minimal fuss. Knowledge of computer page layout has become essential to the graphic designer.

Photography is the next major visual art standing at the threshold of digital upheaval. With the recent appearance of image processing and photo retouching software for microcomputers, it will not be long before computer skills are a prerequisite in the education of aspiring photographers. The darkroom is being superseded by software that is not only more versatile and faster, but also safer since it dispenses with obnoxious chemicals. Digital cameras are threatening to replace film with discs which store picture information as numbers capable of immediate conversion into a colour print or instantaneous trans-mission around the world via telecommunications.

The history of 'user friendly' software development parallels and complements the domestication of hardware to democratise computer technology. The changes being wrought by widespread access are not wholly the result of reduced cost and size. When Harold Cohen began work on his computerised drawing programme twenty years ago, he had no choice but to write the programme himself.[13] But if writing programmes were still the only way to use computers, few people would be able to take advantage of them. Computers not only open the gateway to virtual worlds, they do so through responsive two-way channels. The management of this interactivity with well-designed human interfaces has been an equally important facet of the PC revolution.

In 1962 Ivan Sutherland developed at MIT his interactive computer graphics system called Sketchpad. The user of this programme could draw directly on a cathode ray tube using a light pen. But the activity is not wholly like what we have come to think of as drawing since the process is managed by an intelligent machine orchestrating the flow of information through a digital medium. When the pen is held up to the screen, the computer calculates its position by taking note of the precise moment when light falls on a photoelectric cell mounted inside the pen's barrel. The computer can then issue appropriate commands to place a line on the screen as the pen is moved in front of it. This is a peculiar sort of drawing since there is no marked surface: the drawing area is not the glass face of the tube, but rather the less tangible space defined by the scanning electron beam. Furthermore, the line itself is not defined by the visible glowing strand as much as by its invisible mathematical coordinates that exist only as naked numbers without any intrinsic material expression. Because of this virtual existence, geometrical objects are eminently changeable and can respond quickly to the operator's whim. Sutherland's Sketchpad is a prototype of cur-rently popular desktop design systems, but prior to the advent of artistic uses, interactivity was fostered by better funded applications.[14]

By the early 1980s complex paint systems offering millions of colours and elaborate special effects were being produced for commer-cial use by such companies as Quantel in England and Aurora in the United States. The cost of these early systems made them feasible only for large industries, most notably broadcast television. Over the course of the past decade, rapid developments have brought professional computer paint systems within reach of individual artists working with desktop machines, and much of the expensive technology for other types of interaction has been downsized at an astonishingly fast pace to bring us video games and information kiosks.

Interfaces and Paradoxes

The meaning of a digital message is not usually explicated by reciting tokens of numbers. We experience (the reality of) what lies hidden in a digital medium through an **interface** which transforms numbers into events (or vice versa) by implementing a systematic and automated connection between them. It either quantifies qualities by detaching an abstract digit from a concrete unit or it qualifies quantities by attaching the two. A video camera, for example, is used to input particular colours and intensities of light that are turned into corresponding numerical values, and a monitor is used to do the reverse by outputting coloured light based on a digital file. This transformation is ordinarily realised in a piece of hardware, called a **converter**, that connects peripherals – such as a keyboard, tablet, mouse, monitor, or camera – to a computer (see Fig. 6). There are two primary types of interface converter: the analogue-to-digital (A/D) converter that digitises events into numbers and the digital-to-analogue (D/A) converter that reverses the process and reifies invisible numbers as perceivable events.

The abstraction and materialisation processes which stand at the input/output portals of a computer system are quite different from making pictures, whether done by hand (drawing and painting) or by machine (photography and video). One important aspect of the difference can be characterised by noticing that picturing is **recursive** while interfacing is not. The pictorial media of photography and its second cousin video have become the paradigmatic mimetic forms for our age, and it is useful to contrast computerised imaging with them. We have seen that analogue transcriptions can be concatenated, and that highly developed recursive chains in certain media function as foundations to our contemporary culture. Although digital media can be disseminated with even greater facility than analogue media, their proliferation is not recursive since they use a process of inscribing tokens rather than transcribing events.

Consider photography as a function which maps one piece of the visible universe onto another:

111

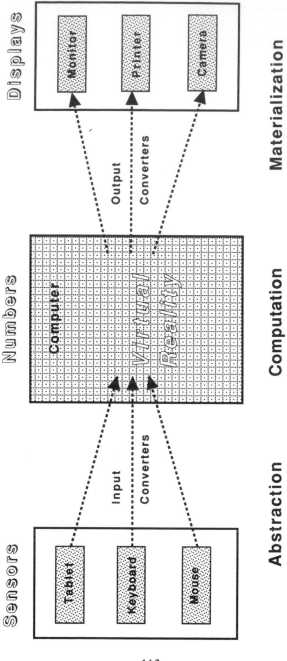

Fig. 6 by William Nelson

112

$$p = T(s),$$

where **p** is the photograph that results from placing a subject, **s**, in front of a camera that performs the transcription, **T**, when the shutter is released. This relationship is called a **mapping** in mathematics because it correlates items in one set (the world photographed, represented by the independent variable **s**) with items in another (the photographs, represented by the dependent variable **p**). It is a particular type of mapping called a **homomorphism** since the **domain** (the results of the picturing function) is a **subset** of the **range** (the collection of all things that can be pictured). In other words, photographs are the kind of thing that can themselves be (re)photographed, just as a painter can depict a previous painting in a new one. The contiguity of homogeneous causes and effects in an analogue medium is essential for establishing the mapping correlation by means of an imprinting process.

The function **T**, like most picturing functions, is recursive. The exposed film can be removed from the camera, developed, and placed in front of the camera to make a picture of a picture in a characteristically postmodern antic by which artists such as Sherry Levine and Mike Bidlo have attained some notoriety. The relevant formula might be

$$p = T(T(s)) \text{ or perhaps } p = T(T(s) + s'),$$

depending upon whether the second photograph includes solely the first, **T(s)**, or incorporates some of its surroundings as well, **s'**. The dominant analogue channels of communication typically mix media as they iterate images. The process of publishing art books or magazines (as in Fig. 2) involves a sequence of transcriptions moving analogue information from a person to a painting to a photograph to an inked metal plate to a printed page.

If a tripod-mounted camera is left in place after taking a picture, and the processed film is subsequently put in front of the lens while another picture is shot, one can make a photograph that appears to incorporate a copy of itself. A similar result is produced in video by aiming the camera at the monitor. Pictures that picture themselves pose something of a dilemma when we try to understand what they do. Strictly speaking, they can never be finished since they lead to an infinite regress of pictures of pictures like the unending reflections you see when situated between two parallel mirrors. In practice, they are truncated at the limits to the resolution of a particular medium: in photography, for example, one eventually gets down to a single grain of the emulsion. We avoid the unending chain by not making pictures that completely picture themselves. This regress underscores the one-way communication of analogue media. A change in the subject or the picture will change the picture of the picture, but a change in the latter will never change the original picture or its subject. The transcription process is not reversible. Playback of tapes or records only iterates transcription into another medium (e.g. from magnetism on tape to electrons in the recorder's circuits to sound emanating from the speakers). Playback proliferates transcription, it does not invert it. You can readily picture a picture to generate a copy, but you cannot generate an original from a picture. Once locked into analogue media, you can only go deeper into them. This is because they store information in concrete objects, where it is inseparable from individual chunks of matter that can only be re-transcribed, rather than in abstract concepts that can repeatedly be inscribed anew.

The recursive process also gives rise to a paradox, which might be called the Russell Picture Paradox since it derives from Bertrand Russell's famous paradox about sets.[15] Some pictures picture themselves and some do not. Now imagine making the picture of all pictures that do *not* picture themselves. This picture would have a prodigious subject matter defying actual execution, but we need not be daunted by this nettlesome detail when contemplating it in a thought experiment. Now let us ask, Does it picture itself? Does the picture of all pictures that do not picture themselves picture itself? If it does, then it pictures itself and should not be included among its subjects, which means that it does not picture itself. On the other hand, if it does not picture itself, then it should be included among its subjects which means it does picture itself. If it does it doesn't, and if it doesn't it does. Either way we get a contradiction.

Interface mappings are immune to Russell's paradox for a simple reason: they cannot recurse. Once you have digitised a sound or a shape by transforming it into numbers, you cannot turn the process on itself due to the *hetero*morphic character of the mapping function. At one end is an analogue aperture receptive to physical events; at the other is a digital format prepared to store numbers. Since the input and output of the conversion process in an interface are heterogeneous, you cannot redirect the output channel into the input channel (see Fig. 6). The domain is not a subset of the range. A quantity of illumination is not a number, and a bare number cannot be measured by a light meter.

Furthermore, when tokens are transcribed, they do not recurse. Pictures of tokens are tokens of the same numbers, undiminished by being pictured. A photograph of a photograph is not the same as the original, but a photograph of a mathematical proof written on a blackboard is just as valid as the original inscription, whose essence consists of abstract symbols rather than concrete marks.

Moreover, in order to complete a digital system, you need the agency of a computer to introduce yet another function which manipulates numbers with calculations. So the process by which a digital image gets made is represented by a function that looks something more like:

$$p = M(C(n)),$$

when n is a number (or perhaps a set of numbers) that is subjected to calculations, C, whose results are subsequently materialised through an interface, M, which turns numbers into perceivable events. If the process accommodates digitised input, which is usually the case, then the formula becomes:

$$p = M(C(A(s))),$$

where the A is an abstracting conversion that turns physical events into numbers. Digital media do not make analogue ones obsolete, since interfaces are needed to make numerical abstractions tangible, and these converters usually connect digital numbers with analogue events. The computer does not supersede its physically grounded predecessors, but rather breathes new life into them.

By moving numbers from one digital format to another, computations can simulate the projective geometry that takes place in a camera. They can even recurse it to simulate Russell's Picture Paradox so long as the range is within the domain. But once the interface conversion is applied to manifest the results of computation, numbers are turned into events which cannot be subjected to calculation without turning them back into numbers again through another interface. One cannot in general recurse the process of computer imaging even when two interface functions are used (an input and an output) because the analogue aperture of each will not necessarily be compatible. For example, A might be realised by a digitising tablet (the input) and M by a video monitor (the output). There is no direct way to make the output of one aperture, which consists of light emanating from the face of a tube, compatible with the input of the other, which responds to movements of a stylus over a surface. Moreover, even when the two can be mated (say, if the input is a video camera), the recursion that could occur is radically different from the picturing recursion of standard video feedback. This is because the intermediate calculation function can transform the video input differently each time through so that the output bears no apparent visual relation to the input. The computation could even ignore the video input entirely. Only if C is some sort of identity function which moves numbers 'directly' from the digital format stationed at the input to the one stationed at the output, can the system be made to simulate recursion.[16]

An image which is paradoxically both an invisible set of numbers and a perceptible collection of colours is realised through interlinked heteromorphisms and calculations. This type of system brings together measurement and perception in a cognitive synthesis which has until now been the exclusive province of sentient beings. Concepts and percepts are integrated and manipulated in ways characteristic of conscious behaviour. What the computer does is more like the artist painting from imagination than the camera recording from reality. The achievements of Renaissance painting have been described using the metaphor of a transparent window overlooking depicted reality; digital media function more like inscrutable portals to another universe – perhaps something more like the *Star Trek* transporter. The Renaissance window stands as an impenetrable barrier while nevertheless providing a direct view into a scene that appears continuous with the coordinate space of the viewer. You can look at a Millet landscape, but not reach into it, since your oustretched hand collides with the canvas. The digital gateway of an interface, on the other hand, is unable to reveal any glimpse of the space that lies behind it; but it can transport the user into another dimension altogether, defined by an alternative coordinate system.

Interacting with Virtual Realities
Monologue is the analogue model for discourse.[17] Once a message is transcribed into an analogue medium, all the audience can do is receive it in a one-way exchange epitomised by broadcast. Digital media, on the other hand, readily accommodate two-way interactions that support one-to-one exchanges within the context of the medium itself, because they are managed by computers configured for input and

output. Although digital media can be used for broadcast, they support a much wider range of activities since the systems in which they are embedded take dialogue as their model for discourse. They are not dedicated to taking something and passing it on, but instead receive, reflect, and respond in a repeated cycle. Apart from making shopping lists or writing diaries, people do not usually send messages to themselves through analogue media, but they can sit alone for hours communicating with themselves through a computer. This is because the computer has become more than a medium, it is an agent.[18] Not designed to sustain impacts and brandish their marks, its purpose is rather to analyse events and initiate actions. So interactions with computers are less like the soliloquies that take place before a typewriter or a blank canvas and more like dialogues with a partner.

Digital media are meaningless without the machines that enliven them by moving numbers in and out of storage and performing myriad calculations upon them with potentially multiple meanings. A digital medium is not a blank slate, but a replete system of communication. The ability of its laconic ciphers to respond implies the presence of something like a communicator able to manipulate and display symbols in ways which respond specifically to each individual approach. Digital media cannot be passive repositories of cultural information, but introduce perforce active partners into the creative process which add an entirely new dimension to it. The computer is neither a medium nor a tool, but a new kind of cultural agent – a digital deputy charged with refiguring the network of social interaction. Computed imagery plays a major role in the new digital forum.

Analogue media are adept at recording events by storing concrete representations of them deposited in physical materials. Digital media enlivened by computers are able to do something completely different. They can simulate situations by manipulating their conceptual representations couched in abstract symbols. Digital media do not mimic what they represent in analogues, but model it in formal structures. A numerical model does not transcribe, but rather transfigures what it represents. It is able to simulate the workings of its subject rather than merely record its states since computers can continuously and responsively update an abstraction in much the way events play themselves out in the reality it represents. Digital media invite interactions with the lively microcosm of events they have captured, rather than simply record and playback.

When digital interfaces connect a user to a computer they accomplish something which is more like perceiving than picturing. Unlike the comparatively rigid recitations of media in the museum or the theatre, computation can be spontaneous like experiencing and thinking. Simulations offer you experiences of a virtual reality which are more like experiences of reality pictured than experiences of pictures. Even though these exploits are often constructed with the aid of pictures, they transcend the simple display of imagery because of their interactivity. As a result, digital media give rise to what might be called 'digital domains', sometimes referred to as 'hypermedia'.[19] These domains are composed entirely of numbers betokened in digital media functioning as operational components of a computing system (which could be a person).[20] Although numbers must be couched in media as tokens, they transcend the scope of media by virtue of their abstractness. Some things can only be represented by numbers, and those things that can be represented in other ways can be accessed differently when digitised. Anything quantifiable is picturable and interfaceable, hence we are able to see and touch types of phenomena never before accessible except through tables of numbers. A digitally defined object must be interfaced to be experienced, but no particular interface has any priority in manifesting such virtual entities. So we are able to concoct new 'multimedia' presentations that immerse us in abstract worlds.

A person can manoeuvre in the space-times of these digital domains. Not only the images, but also what they represent can be instantiated as numbers so that you can manually grapple with what the media depict, unlike painting or sculpture. Using a computer you can do something unavailable to you with a real camera: create virtual objects and then picture them. A painting cannot make a person out of paint and then picture her. A novel cannot make a character out of letters or words and then describe her. But a computer can permit you to fashion denizens of a digital domain out of numbers and then take pictures of them which are equally numerical. An interface is needed to hypostatise these abstractions and in the process it allows you, in a fashion, to step through the canvas. Simulation shares qualities with both art and life. Like art, it uses imagery to represent, but like life, it permits you to interact with what it represents. One might say it bridges the interstices between art and life to make imagination veridical.

Our dealings with reality itself are becoming increasingly mediated by interfaces to computation.[21] Digital media continue a tradition of surrogate reality inaugurated with the camera. The computer adds two novel twists: the reality behind the picture may be virtual, and it can interact. While Russell's picture paradox has practical import primarily

118

for artists working in media where feedback risk is imminent, it can be relegated to the closet of philosophical curiosities for much artistic creation. But paradoxes about virtuality intrude upon the conceptual frameworks by which we live our daily lives. Exactly what this all means is in the process of being discovered. The need to describe virtual reality paradoxically simply demonstrates how inadequate our traditional categories are for understanding this novel phenomenon and serves to challenge us to rethink them. Exploring simulations will teach us a great deal about what reality is while dramatically changing the reality in which we live.

Virtual reality may be an imaginary reality, but it is some kind of reality and not merely a mimetic ghost. It may require a change in our ontology as well as our epistemology. In the ongoing debate about artificial intelligence, John Searle points out that simulating something is not always enough to make it the real thing.[22] He then uses this point to argue that we cannot give machines consciousness merely by making them follow algorithmic procedures. The problem is, how do you ultimately decide whether something is a simulation? How complete does a simulation have to be before it is real? And are there phenomena (possibly consciousness itself) whose simulations are no less real than what they simulate? Whether something is real might be a question of whether it is hypostatised at the other end – whether the simulator is actually connected to a real picture or a real plane via an interface. In one sense, the computational system is indifferent to whether the subject is virtual or real. Is ontology a function of which interface you have plugged in? The ontological problem easily metamorphoses into a strange epistemological one.

The channels through which culture flows are crystallising into intricate lattices fleetingly populated by effervescent informational atoms. The inveteracy of cultural repositories is weakening and their identity dissipating as serious challenges to accepted notions of intellectual property and copyright undermine hallowed customs of attribution and reward. Our tidy methods and concepts for conducting artistic enterprises are thrown into disarray, and rarefied reticular domains invite activities which challenge some of the most basic distinctions we have come to accept.

People who use computer imaging systems experience something of the wonder and (over)excitement that must have possessed those ancient artists who discovered that they could (paradoxically) materialise bison on the walls of caves. But computer simulations objectify imagination in a new way. Not only are the visages of beasts materialised with the wave of the hand, but their reciprocating vitality as well. The cultural transformations subsequent to the invention of mimetic reality must have been profound. Synthetic virtual reality poses a similarly dramatic challenge to our media-based culture as we try to comprehend the paradoxes of interacting with virtual entities through their computed visages. Interfaces to the noetic constitution of numbers enable us to visualise things and events heretofore invisible or unimaginable.

Divisions between sense and intellect are persistent themes in Western civilisation, surviving a host of cogent philosophical and scientific challenges. Vernacular expressions in many languages echo Plato's metaphysics, dichotomising appearance/reality, body/mind, emotion/thought, percept/concept and other binary antipodes which organise our understanding of the universe. As we marshal computer resources to serve our needs, oxymoronic discord interrupts these harmonious categories of thought. The very idea of a 'thinking machine' is anathema to Plato's idealism and the concept of a 'digital image' assembles two traditional opposites in a contradictory amalgamation of the invisible and the visible. Some of the philosophical unease about entrenched dualism is discovering a kind of avatar in computers, which are beginning to support growing doubts about disparities between mind and matter.

NOTES

1. Joseph Margolis defines a medium as 'a cultural instrumentality manifested in a physical material', in 'Film as a Fine Art'. *Millennium Film Journal*, Fall/Winter 1984–85, p. 95.
2. Figures 1–6 have been created by William Nelson.
3. I do not mean to gloss over the complexities of the concept of representation here. See Kendall L. Walton, *Mimesis as Make-Believe* (Cambridge, Mass.: Harvard University Press, 1990) and Nelson Goodman, *Languages of Art* (Indianapolis: Bobbs-Merrill, 1968). My concern is with the specific methods of recording information, not with its general cultural interpretation. As a curious aside, Lillian Schwartz manipulated a Leonardo self-portrait with a computer to adduce evidence from which she concludes that Leonardo himself was the sitter for the Mona Lisa. See Lillian Schwartz, 'The Mona Lisa ID: Evidence from a Computer Analysis', *Visual Computer* (No. 4, 1988), pp. 40–8.
4. Some aspects of musical notation and literary inscription bear similarities to digital media, but there are important differences as well. A word has a characteristic sound and look which its ASCII counterpart coded for processing lacks. Without being converted to numbers, written musical

notes and letters of the alphabet cannot be subjected to computation as part of an axiomatic system. Literature is based in culturally-defined languages where the type-token relationship obtains between letters or words and their inscriptions. But no numbers are represented. Numbers have a universality that linguistic concepts don't. 'XX' betokens the same number as '20', but 'kennen' does not designate quite the same concept as 'to know'.

5. The Belgian artist Jan Fabre dislikes computer drawing because he cannot 'hurt' the surface by gouging it with his pen, as he does in many of his works. This inability to make a mark comes from the fact that a computer image has no physical surface.

6. If colour information is to be preserved, the wavelengths of incoming light must be transcribed as well.

7. In 1889, Giuseppe Peano proved that all properties of the natural numbers can be derived from five axioms:
   (a) 1 is a number.
   (b) Every number, n, has precisely one successor, n + 1.
   (c) 1 is not the successor of any number.
   (d) Distinct numbers have distinct successors.
   (e) If a set of natural numbers contains the number 1 and contains, together with any number, also its successor, then it is the set of all natural numbers.
   The natural numbers are the counting numbers: 1, 2, 3, 4, 5, etc. By supplementing Peano's postulates, it is possible to axiomatise the integer, rational, and real number systems, which are the ones used by computers.

8. See Peter Sørensen, 'Morphing Magic', *Computer Graphics World*, January 1992, pp. 36–42. Sometimes these computerised special effects are augmented by traditional methods, as in *Willow* (1991), where a tiger is turned into a sorceress with the help of actual props for some of the key positions.

9. I discuss the virtual camera more extensively in 'Camera Fantasia', *Millennium Film Journal*, Fall/Winter 1988–89.

10. See Fred Ritchin, *In Our Own Image* (New York: Aperture, 1990). See also Binkley, 'Camera Fantasia'.

11. I have concentrated here on some of the early developments in applications of computers to cinema, but equally important strides were made in still imagery. No comprehensive history of computer art exists, but parts of it are covered in Cynthia Goodman, *Digital Visions: Computers and Art* (New York: Harry N. Abrams, 1987), Robert Rivlin, *The Algorithmic Image* (Redmond, WA: Microsoft Press, 1986), and Herbert W. Franke, *Computer Graphics – Computer Art* (Berlin: Springer-Verlag, 1971).

12. For further discussion of HDTV, see the chapter by Jean-Luc Renaud in this volume.

13. See Pamela McCorduck, *Aaron's Code: Meta-Art, Artificial Intelligence, and the Work of Harold Cohen* (New York: W. H. Freeman, 1991). Cohen's work is revolutionary for the way he has introduced artificial intelligence into the creative process.

14. See Rebecca Coyle's chapter in this volume for further discussion.

15. Bertrand Russell, *The Principles of Mathematics* (Cambridge: Cambridge University Press, 1903).
16. Mathematics is replete with recursive functions, and the function represented by C could certainly contain some recursion. Fractal images, for example, are generated this way. However, the **formal** recursion involved in such computation is very different from the **physical** recursion inherent in analogue media. Computational recursion maps numbers into numbers, while pictorial recursion maps objects and events into objects and events. The latter can be representational, the former is not. When we compare analogue and digital media, it is important to contrast the material representation of events, which can be recursive, with numerical representation, which cannot.
17. A telephone system might consist of paired, inverted analogue electrical signals to make person-to-person conversations possible. But at some level, the system is digital to permit individual addressing: each telephone has a number. Of course, now phone companies are using digital data transmission as well to maintain signal integrity.
18. I discuss this idea at greater length in 'The Computer is Not a Medium', *Philosophic Exchange* (nos. 19 & 20, 1988–89), pp. 152–73, and 'Medium or Tool?', *Computer Graphics World* (February 1989).
19. Or even 'hyperreality' by those bold enough to dare. See Jean Baudrillard, *Simulations* (New York: Semiotext(e), 1983).
20. Before the advent of electronic digital computers, a 'computer' was a person whose job was to perform numerical calculations. Only in the late 1940s did the word come to refer to machines.
21. See David Gelerntner, *Mirror Worlds* (New York: Oxford University Press, 1992).
22. See John R. Searle, Paul M. Churchland and Patricia Smith Churchland. 'Artificial Intelligence: A Debate', *Scientific American*, January 1990, vol. 262, no. 1.

INTERACTIVE GAMES

Leslie Haddon

Since electronic and computer games were certainly the earliest form of interactive software to find a mass market they provide the most common introduction to the principles of interactivity and as such may have a profound bearing on any interactive media in the future. This chapter examines three related histories.[1] First, the development of games hardware, to show that interactive games descended from a number of technological vehicles, of which the home computer is only one manifestation.

The earliest games originated in research computing departments in the early 1960s. Given that the large computers of the 50s were used mainly for serious purposes, their unlikely origins need some explanation. So too does their subsequent diffusion throughout the computer establishment as they were taken up by microcomputer hobbyists from the mid-70s. Video games machines, the coin-operated machines in amusement arcades and home video games products (especially programmable consoles) were the interactive games' other lineage. Both these routes eventually saw the emergence of an independent games software sector with some of the characteristics of other media industries, but it was the coin-ops and consoles which laid a basis for the popularity of the microcomputer games of the 80s, which in turn led home computers to become predominantly games machines.

The second section focuses on the evolution of software industries and on specific game texts. A number of genres, such as adventure games, originated on larger computers, but the most significant type of game was the fast 'action' genre, initially associated with shooting games. Both the nature of the game-play and of these narratives can be

123

understood in terms of the researchers' contemporary interest in interactive computing generally and the particular tastes of early male game designers – action games later fitted conveniently in the arcades. Coin-op and home video games attracted interest from other media industries whose licensing deals affected games content. These ties with other media were later re-established when microcomputer games appeared, but only after the early cottage industry of small software producers had been replaced by larger games publishers. Interactive games are currently an established but still fringe media industry with their publishers constantly seeking a far wider audience.

The final section examines the nature of games-playing itself, and the frequently negative reception which this activity generated among pressure groups and academics. Moral panics about games, including fears of addiction, the 'effects' of desensitisation and of escapism have spanned a range of political campaigns, media attention and academic, mainly psychological, analysis. The origins of such concerns are complex topics in themselves, deriving partly from more traditional criticisms of television and partly from more recent anxieties about the experience of computing. Relevant to this inquiry is why games were initially so interesting to the first computer hobbyists. This group was significant as both early consumers and producers of this software, and their whole approach to games as a means of learning about programming shaped the experience of others outside their own community. Computer games were fundamentally different from the previous video games in that users could combine programming with games. Looking into, altering, or breaking the copyright protection on programmes, as well as creating their own games and special effects meant that for many, playing the game was only part of a package of experiences.

To date, many of the commentaries on games-playing have focused on either the nature of games as masculine texts or the masculine appeal of mastering interactive technology. The emphatic interest of young males in games-playing needs to be addressed, but too narrow a focus neglects the history of games-playing as an *activity*. The crucial stage in the evolution of games was their appearance in arcades where playing became a collective form of leisure amongst young males. Later, with the advent of the micro, programming expanded the activity of 'games-playing' beyond the moment of sitting at the screen with a joystick, and closer inspection of what constitutes this more varied consumption highlights the particularity of young male interest. It will be argued that the content of games themselves is more liable to reflect this interest than to determine it.

Hardware: the First Computer Games

During the late 1950s and early 1960s, computer science was in the process of being constructed as an academic discipline.[2] MIT introduced the first courses on computing for undergraduates in 1959 and set up an 'Artificial Intelligence' research department. The military had been funding computer development since the early days of the space programme. When this programme was transferred to the civil body NASA, the military decided to increase its support for computing and basic research projects in particular. The new AI department was able to deploy these funds with a considerable degree of discretion and employed the first enthusiastic students emerging from MIT's new courses. Meanwhile, the university department was developing a close relationship with the young company DEC, then at the forefront of the newly emerging minicomputer industry. DEC provided MIT with a free minicomputer and any assistance that was requested. In return, the minicomputer company benefited from MIT research and advice, received a range of free programmes from the AI department, and eventually recruited a number of staff from this source.

Within these institutional arrangements, the AI department was in the process of developing new forms of computing. At that time, the only model of computing was the batch-processing system dominated by IBM. Anyone wanting access to mainframes had to submit programmes to operators and pick up the results later. Using a small research computer and a DEC minicomputer, the MIT unit explored a more direct style of computing with these machines, whereby users could receive immediate feedback. MIT researchers developed a range of facilities to support this new type of 'real time' computing, formulating some of the principles by which microcomputers were later to operate.

Even prior to the new MIT courses, a male community had evolved in the university's model railway club, where members used their technical expertise to construct and investigate systems – telephone and railway ones in particular. These students continually tried to perfect new 'features' for their systems. The set of values operating in this culture led them to develop their own terminology, in which a key concept was the 'hack': a stylish technical innovation undertaken for the intrinsic pleasure of experimenting – not necessarily fulfilling any more constructive goal. Defining themselves as 'hackers', the students were soon attracted to the new computer systems in the AI department. In the course of displaying their programming skills, these hackers explored and enhanced the capabilities of these new machines.

125

As 'hacks', projects which tested and demonstrated the computer's abilities were often of little use in themselves. For example, these enthusiasts worked on programmes to play chess and to solve puzzles generated by solitaire. This approach to computing was very different from the traditional, 'serious use' of the machine. Rather than treating computers as mundane tools, the hackers played with the machines as if they were toys. While heretical to many of their contemporaries, the AI managers regarded these projects as vehicles for learning about interactive computing. There were also tangible spin-offs. Hackers wrote the operating systems for their first machine, the *TX-O* and then improved it for DEC's minicomputer, the *PDP-1*, as well as supplying other programmes which would have been very costly to design commercially. More particularly, the hackers produced innovatory software to handle real time computer graphics and later made considerable contributions to the development of time-sharing.

The first games were just such exploratory projects. Demonstration programmes which created visual effects already existed. For example, one such programme controlled a row of flashing lights which simulated the motion of a ball in table tennis. Another project entailed the construction of a maze on a VDU in which a mouse would search for cheese. But the start of interactive gaming as we now know it developed with the space battle programme *Spacewar*.

In the years between the first *Spacewar* and the advent of the micro, games became an established feature on larger computers because of programmers' interest in games-playing and because games were useful to computer manufacturers. In 1962, MIT exhibited *Spacewar* to the general public. DEC requested a copy, and *Spacewar* was soon supplied to all their clients. Apart from their diagnostic utility in checking if machines were in order, games were also used by the DEC salesforce as demonstration pieces. *Spacewar* showed the accessible and friendly face of computers. Later, when graphics capability became an important consideration, games were often used to demonstrate the sophistication of these machines. By the 70s, games had become established as 'traditional' and legitimate programmes.

Hardware: Arcade Games

Nolan Bushnall was mainly responsible for the transfer of games to the arcades.[3] An engineer who had played the original computer games as a student, Bushnall had also worked in amusement parks. Once the price of chip technology fell sufficiently he attempted a coin-op version of *Spacewar*. Designed in 1971, the game was not an immediate commercial success. But his subsequent effort – the electronic table-tennis game *Pong*, made with the help of a colleague – proved very popular. With this product, Bushnall and his colleagues founded the company Atari, a company which was to become the major force in the new games industry.

Other companies entered this new market very quickly. Within a few years there were thirty manufacturers of coin-op video games, reducing Atari's market share to 10 per cent by the end of 1973. But by the late 70s, Atari, now supported by Warner Communication funds, came to dominate the industry again, producing for both the coin-op and home video games markets. Following the introduction of *Space Invaders* in 1979, the arcade game reached new heights of popularity. This can be measured by sales of game machines which rose from approximately $40 million to $500 million between 1979 and 1981, by which time coin-op games had become an international phenomenon. Their proliferation and profitability attracted growing media attention as well as provoking considerable critical comment.[4]

Coin-op machines were located in American bars and shops as well as the actual arcades from which they took their name. Amusement park owners were particularly motivated to adopt these machines. The new games were part of a widespread attempt to discard the sleazy image of the arcade. These managers felt that the new product would help to introduce respectability to the amusement park, making it a place for family entertainment. The homely table-tennis game may have been particularly attractive from this perspective but the clean electronic high-tech form of the new games generally helped signal the arcade's more modern look. These electronic games specifically appropriated the role pinball had occupied: within a few years of the introduction of video games, pinball sales had declined by two-thirds. Meanwhile, the major pinball manufacturers were among those companies moving into the production of the new coin-op machines.

Hardware: Home Video Games Machines

Sanders Electronics, an American defence-orientated company, was responsible for developing the first home video game technology as an alternative use for TV sets.[5] The first commercial product, released in 1972, was licensed to the TV distributor Magnavox. The *Odyssey* machine was capable of playing twelve games, including simple hockey, tennis and maze games, many of which were similar to each other. Users had to place plastic overlays on the television screen to provide the background setting for the video games. To reprogramme the machine for different games, players had to plug in circuit cards. These 'TV games' initially had a much lower profile than the coin-ops, although they were reasonably successful in the market as a consumer electronic.

In 1975, Atari released *Pong* for the home market. The home version of *Pong* added new features such as sound effects and ricochets and introduced integrated circuit technology. These components, otherwise known as silicon chips or semiconductors, were to be the basis of general microelectronics development up to the present day. From 1974, other companies also started to enter the market, with leisure specialists and semiconductor firms competing with pinball manufacturers. Over thirty new companies started producing for this home market in 1976 alone. The particular appeal to the semiconductor companies, such as Fairchild and National Semiconductor, was that video games machines arrived when they were diversifying from capital goods and in the process of building up a consumer products division. These firms had seen the profitability of utilising chips in digital watches and calculators and once video games started to use chips, they perceived them as ideal for their new divisions.

After *Pong*, TV games technology had consisted of one chip or a combination of chips on which there were fixed programmes. By 1976 several companies were working to replace these chips with a microprocessor. This technology had already been introduced into the coin-ops, where the sale price of each unit justified its cost. In 1976, Fairchild Camera and Instruments introduced the *Channel F* or *Video Entertainment System*, which would accept programmable cartridges. As far as the semiconductors were concerned video games provided just the type of dedicated application for the new microprocessor technology which they had been seeking. Soon other programmable consoles were available from RCA, Bally, Magnavox, Coleco, and Atari.

This move to microprocessors affected the nature of the video games product. Programmable machines, or consoles, created a flexible division between hardware and software. Thus, a distinct software industry could emerge once video games cartridge manufacturers could sell games separately from the hardware they were played on: games machines were now potentially 'software players' like hi-fis and other home-based 'delivery systems'. Games software could be bought, collected and compared in the same way as records.

The console market started to boom in the late 1970s, with sales of hardware and software peaking in 1982. Although many of the early manufacturers had already left the field, leaving only Magnavox, Mattel and Atari,[6] as the boom accelerated various companies from the toy industry diversified into this area, Coleco being the most successful newcomer. Atari remained dominant with 80 per cent of the home market by 1980. In that year, 3.5 per cent of American homes had consoles, and by 1981 this had risen to 8 per cent.

There were always dissenting voices which discussed games as a fad, although the general view aired in the trade press in the early 80s was optimistic. The one cloud on the horizon was the growing home computer industry. Microcomputer products were initially much more expensive, and were thought to cater for a different market, but as home computer prices fell, the new product started to appropriate the role of consoles and distract sales from the video games market. The consensus in the trade press by the end of 1983, a year after video games actually reached peak sales, deemed the video games 'boom' to be over. In fact, sales did not simply disappear. The consoles had now been relegated to toy departments at reduced prices, where they continued to sell steadily but in smaller quantities.[7]

Hardware: Microcomputer Games

Microcomputers had first emerged in the USA as a hobbyist product during the mid-70s.[8] However, some of the leading hardware manufacturers and industry observers foresaw a more lucrative future for this machine as a mass market consumer electronic. The most ambitious long-term scenarios, such as those cultivated by the semiconductor giant Texas Instruments, envisaged micros which would not only run a variety of software, but which could eventually be connected to telecommunications systems and even have home control facilities. The home computer could become a central part of the household, routinely used by all the family. In the shorter term, difficulties implementing telecoms and control functions meant that American producers pitched the micro as a more restricted, albeit still versatile, 'software player'.

In fact, the first British home computers, launched in 1980 and 1981 by Sinclair, were a different type of machine, extensively sold as products able to explore the world of computing. This 'computer literacy' theme was to remain stronger in Britain than many had originally expected and it also had a significant bearing on the very experience of games-playing.

As the boom in home computers expanded, producers for the British market, including the leaders Sinclair, Acorn and Commodore, hoped along with their American counterparts that their micro would find more wide-ranging applications. Consequently, these hardware manufacturers maintained an ambivalent attitude towards games. In their favour, games provided a familiar application for the micro requiring no expensive additional equipment such as printers. Some microcomputer firms even recognised the possibility of taking business away from the profitable video games market. On the other hand, too strong a games identity threatened the status of the micro as a more general purpose machine, and indeed pushed the micro towards being a child's toy. Hence, early advertisements for micros never overtly emphasised games as their central function; if anything, the key stress was on the educational potential of the machine. While games were always mentioned in advertisements and fostered by the software support that manufacturers offered, games-playing was depicted as being only one option within a range of applications.

The Microcomputer as Games Machine

By 1983, the sudden entry of a range of new companies culminated in considerable competition and price cutting, straining the profitability of many firms. As a result, a number of manufacturers left the industry or went bankrupt. In 1984 a slight decline in demand occurred just as retailers overstocked for the Christmas sales; price cutting in the New Year to clear this stock and the consequent fall in retailer orders precipitated several company collapses. Acorn had to be rescued, and later even Sinclair ran into difficulties. The national news media which covered these developments suggested that the 'bubble had burst', giving rise to a widely held public perception that the home computer had somehow faded away.

However, assumptions that the home micro had disappeared were incorrect. Hardware and software sales remained at high enough levels to support the fewer companies still operating in the market. The temporary financial problems experienced by many firms were eventually resolved, as most companies gradually moved into profit. Although slightly fewer magazines were to be found, the computer press still occupied a firmly established section of newsagent shelf space. Home computers may have had a lower media profile and commanded less prominence in the multiple retail departments, but the industry was far from dead.

Even by the time of the crisis, the home micro had already become established as the new vehicle for electronic games. The computer had been appropriated by users as a games machine, despite the wishes of manufacturers. All the quantitative data on usage, and contemporary interview-based research indicate that this is still the case. The peak of interest in games had passed, but games were still routinely played by many boys and girls.[9]

Nevertheless, the original reservations that games narrowed the micro's potential and devalued it persisted, together with a disappointment that early ambitions for a more all-purpose machine had not been realised: the technological 'revolution' had gone astray. In order to broaden the identity of the existing computer product, hardware manufacturers and software publishers (e.g. Atari, The Digital Muse) have promoted other, non-game entertainment software, such as art and music packages (e.g. Degas Elite, Virtuoso), and applications derived originally from the business market (chiefly through database, word-processing and spreadsheet software). Other industry commentators have seen the route to a more general purpose computer in more powerful machines, exemplified by the Atari ST and Commodore Amiga series. However, such micros have tended to build upon the appeal of games rather than challenge their predominance.

Hardware: Recent Developments – Consoles and Micros

Recent moves to reintroduce dedicated video games machines may be taken as a measure of optimism about the permanency of this form of entertainment. In the light of a clear and established demand for games, it was argued that machines which have design features geared to games might once again be viable.

Despite quips such as 'Home Computer Wars II: The Console Strikes Back', the micro has not yet been displaced by the console. The huge success of the Nintendo games machines in Japan and the US, followed by rival Sega with NEC machines waiting in the wings, prompted an array of stories in the late 1980s computer press heralding the transformation of the games market. In practice, by the 1990s there had been only a limited sales push, matching a lack of demand. At that point it certainly appeared that the home micro had become too established as the games machine in this country. Nevertheless, console hard- and software sales have started to rise and a range of other companies, including Commodore, Amstrad and the toy maker Hornby, have added their own brands to this market.[10] By Christmas 1991, it was clear that consoles had established a huge presence in retail stores.

An opposite tendency has been for games to expand from the early machine formats onto those very micros which are trying to break

131

away from the games machine identity. The Amstrad PCW series and PC series of micros have attracted games support, and 1990 saw the release of *PC Leisure*, a magazine for Personal Computer (i.e. IBM compatible) games. Some software producers have even seen these machines as constituting a major new sales base for games software, again keeping an eye on their success in the US. However, despite some growth in other European countries, the PC still has a relatively limited installed base in Britain's homes.[11]

Various industry pundits had been even more optimistic about the extent to which games would eventually migrate to the more technologically sophisticated 16-bit micros. This view has proved more justified given the rise in software sales for Commodore's Amiga and Atari's ST machines, which overtook the Spectrum and Commodore 64 in 1990. Yet, these prognoses concerning the PC and 16-bit micros reveal conflicting views. While computer firms and enthusiasts may hope that the growing popularity of 16-bit micros in particular will give the micro a more sophisticated image than the 'games computer', others in the software industry see the best prospects for games in this new hardware.

Software: Computer Games
In *Spacewar*, two spaceships engage in battle, using torpedoes to shoot at each other. The programme operated in real time, in that the graphics reacted instantly to the players' control, either when turning the spaceship or firing. Action was continuous, leaving little pause to stop and plan. It called on physical reflexes as much as on strategy.

Why did the first interactive game take this form? In its narrative content, the space battle reflected the interests of its designer, Steve Russell, who was an avid science fiction reader and a fan of 'space opera', where heroes engage villains in galactic battles. Whereas descriptions of spaceship encounters and space fleet manoeuvres inspired the game's scenarios, the game-play itself – the action – came from a different source. Russell had wanted to create a more visually stunning 'hack', demonstrating the potential of interactive computing in general, and so translated the fast pace of a written narrative into rapid physical action of a game. In so doing, he also acknowledged the influence of an existing product which was so important in shaping the later development of games: *Spacewar* reflected the game-play of pinball.

Once *Spacewar* was presented to the hacker community, others added new features such as gravity effects and details of solar systems and developed the first computer game joysticks to control the motion. There were soon to be other variations on battle and shooting themes, with *Star Trek* becoming the best-known game on mainframe computers. When alternative types of game were developed, the tastes of game programmers in the male-dominated computing field continued to be reflected in these texts. (For example, simulations had been one of the earliest uses for computers – especially simulations of battles for military purposes. The popular mainframe game *Lunar Landing* was once again located within a space setting, simulating control of a spacecraft approaching the moon.)

Mathematically-based programmes were also popular. One such programme, *The Game of Life*, simulated ever-changing communities of 'cells' as they formed patterns over 'generations'. The other best-known genre started with the game *Adventure*. Appearing much later, in 1976, this computer game drew on the structure of fantasy wargaming and, in particular, on the *Dungeons and Dragons* interests of some programmers. The player directed an explorer through an underground world where the protagonist fought off enemies and overcame obstacles through clever tricks in order to find some treasure. This latter genre became, like *Spacewar*, a cult game in Computer Centres. On the home computer, this adventure format was later to provide the main alternative to the fast-action games predominating on video games machines.[12]

Software: Arcade Games

The mix of strategy, speed and physical co-ordination involved in action games well suited the logic of the arcades – hardly surprising given that this action style of interactive games had been modelled on pinball. The excitement of fast action provided the type of thrill which initially attracted players to the coin-op while the brevity of games (until skill had been acquired) maximised earnings. Yet the new video games were different from their arcade precursor in one respect: they had at least some narrative content. Albeit 'thin', the storyline of the games allowed commentators to see the new games as being comparable to other media texts. Indeed, it was this feature which so easily enabled concerns about violence on TV and film to be transferred to the new entertainment machines.

This narrative quality, along with a variety of different possible manoeuvres on screen, allowed the rate and form of innovation to be very different from the pinball predecessor. Whereas pinball had evolved very slowly and differences between machines at any one time were often cosmetic,[13] a continuous stream of new arcade video games started to appear by the late 70s. New releases contained not only different scenarios, but whole new configurations of action: for example, *PacMan*, where players control a blob fleeing from danger through a maze. As this pattern of innovation emerged, video games became part of a 'cultural industry', in much the same way as film and music were.

Software: Video Games
Most of the early home video games were variations on the bat and ball idea found in the *Odyssey* machine and in *Pong*. *Pong* itself was an example of a game making the transition from arcade to the home machine. Driving games also made this transition, but the early chip technology caused a considerable time-lag in any such transfer. The dedicated integrated circuit chip needed for the home games machine could take a year to develop.

The companies which introduced microprocessor-based technology widened the options by adding cartridges containing other game forms besides those found in arcades: noughts and crosses, blackjack and chess. A countervailing tendency arose once software programming enabled a more speedy transfer of games from the coin-ops. Home versions could be released while a game was still in vogue in the arcades. The coin-ops became even more extensive testing grounds for products which might then be cross-licensed to the home market.

This relationship bore fruit when one particular arcade game first boosted sales of the domestic machine. *Space Invaders* enjoyed unprecedented success as a coin-op, increasing overall sales in that sector after its introduction in 1978. After Atari had bought the home licence and was able to offer a version for their consoles, programmable sales also increased considerably. Atari was by now the training ground for many games designers, a number of whom later set up companies to supply the software cartridges for the Atari console and for competing machines.

Besides cross-overs from arcade favourites, a number of film companies, such as 20th Century–Fox, set up software arms and arranged licensing deals. For example, Atari and Lucasfilm arranged joint projects. Games were seen by the film industry both as competition for the same 'entertainment dollar' and as a new outlet for cross-licensing. However, although scenarios and plots of home games became more varied, the action game-play remained a stable product in the industry.

While it lasted, this growth of the video games industry led to innovations in publicity and distribution. The increased rate of new releases was now covered by video games magazines, carrying news and reviews of the latest games available. Meanwhile, existing games producers experimented with novel means of delivering games to players, whereby telephone companies downloaded the games to homes by phone. Both these moves were repeated when games appeared on home computers.

Software: Microcomputer Games

Initial interest in microcomputer games came from the hobbyists who both produced and consumed this software. The hobbyist magazines had always devoted some space to games, providing this software genre with respectability. Within a few years of the first home micros being released, a wave of books introducing programming to a more general public relied on games to explain the structure of computer languages. Eventually, even the manuals which were packaged with the hardware adopted this approach.

Microcomputer games soon proved popular outside original hobbyist circles, especially among male youth. Since the previous video games consoles had made less impact in the UK than in the US, micros provided many people with their first chance to play home-based games. This demand encouraged more hobbyists to establish their own part-time mail order ventures, selling software for the new home computers. Aided by the cheap cassette technology, these initiatives developed into a small cottage industry. Within a few years, teenagers who had received the early micros as gifts provided a further source of games programmers. Although this software industry was relatively small, the national press carried stories of successful entrepreneurial schoolboys and this fuelled further interest. Consequently, software which aided game design proved to be very popular.

By 1983, several substantial publishing, record and video companies (e.g. Mirror Group, Virgin) had entered the computer games field and transformed software production for this increasingly lucrative market into an industry organised on the same model as their other interests. In this restructuring process, a majority of the small start-up firms, as well as others who had tried to cash in on the games boom, went bankrupt, amalgamated, or left the market.

The 'burst bubble' coverage micros received in 1983–84 made some wonder if games, like the hardware, had also been a fad. But this was certainly not the case. Like hardware, computer games had a lower media profile by the mid-80s and games were commanding less shelf

135

space, but following the reduction in the number of software houses, the games industry achieved an overall degree of stability which has continued to the present day. Meanwhile, since the early 80s international sales have become increasingly important to British software houses, the UK becoming a major exporter of games once micros became popular in other European countries.

Under the new industry regime, games writing became routinised and continuous instead of haphazard and occasional. Active marketing of the latest product guaranteed sufficient chart hits for profitability while cheaper 'budget' software gave old products a new life in compilations. There have also been innovations in distribution: software is now sold through a wide range of outlets including garages and corner shops.

Finally, the industry operated in conjunction with a new type of computer magazine, geared mainly to leisure and entertainment. These journals gave far more coverage to game developments than their hobby-orientated predecessors. These new publicity outlets had the effect of systematically promoting games, often relegating other software to the fringes. Yet the newly emerging magazines also went beyond reviewing games, carrying regular features on how to break into games programmes in order to see their inner workings and how to make changes so that the games operated differently. The hobbyist project had infiltrated games-playing, adding a new dimension to the activity for some users.

Software: Innovation in Games

Despite all these signs of the durability of games, publishers felt that they nevertheless remained a 'fringe' entertainment, rather than a 'mainstream' one like music. One problem which the games industry has identified is its low profile in the mass media, so there have been occasional attempts to gain prominence for programmers as media personalities and to obtain newspaper and TV coverage through promotions. Several trade associations have been created over the years to promote the industry as a whole.

Equally important has been an ongoing concern in the industry about the perceived lack of creativity in actual games content. Admittedly, part of the worry about lack of 'real' innovation relates to the mechanism whereby successful new games are immediately followed by a spate of near copies. This process is not very different from the record and film industries, where producers follow successful formulae.[14] In general, there have been incremental improvements in such matters as enhanced graphics detail. Some of the late 80s games, such as *Tetris* and *Little Computer People*, have not fitted easily into existing genres and there are always new arcade hits to convert and new items to license from the other cultural industries. Occasionally, totally new sub-genres have appeared, such as the Kung-Fu, quiz, and horror games. Even soap operas such as *EastEnders* have found their way onto the games format. But some ask whether this level of innovation is enough. Do changes in scenario and slight changes in the playing skills required provide enough novelty? While the games industry has been kept ticking over so far, competition for disposable income from the other cultural industries is always a threat. Industry commentators point out the new lower-priced videos and compact discs taking shelf space from micros in many of the multiple retailers' stores.

One approach to changing the content and nature of games has been to separate the role of programmer from games designer. This involves drawing on the expertise of staff from other entertainment media, such as music, television and film, to complement the technological skills of existing games writers. Other analysts have placed their longer-term hopes in the software innovations made possible by more advanced hardware which include both the faster processing power of 16-bit chip machines and the greater memory capacity offered, especially by CD-ROM peripherals. Both these options are now being realised in software development for multimedia CD.

Dangerous Games-playing

Despite hopes that interactive games would give arcades a new image, the new coin-ops were starting to arouse opposition by the end of the 1970s.[15] The criticisms emanating from the anti-games lobby were diverse.

In the US, moral panics resulted in some much publicised by-laws to regulate arcades. At a national level, the Surgeon General issued a warning that video games might be dangerous and that children might find them addictive, while the National Coalition on Television Violence extended its area of interest to include the new games. The US was not alone. Perhaps the most vigorous attack on video games came from the Philippines where President Marcos ordered 300 machines to be dismantled, smashed or surrendered to military police within fifteen days because of their detrimental effect on morals and on youth discipline. Even in the UK, the Labour MP George Foulkes led a campaign in 1981 to curb the 'menace' of video games, mainly because of their addictive properties. His 'Control of Space Invaders (and other Electronic Games) Bill' was only narrowly defeated in the Commons.[16]

One set of worries focused on the effect of the technology underlying these games. Critics feared what they saw as the 'compulsive' behaviour engendered by electronic games – an issue previously raised in relation to the 'narcotic' effect of television.[17] This fear of addiction was reinforced by discussions of the 'holding power' attributed to computer environments *per se*, as manifest in earlier concern about the 'unhealthy' attraction of hackers to computer technology.[18] Those opposed to games argued that players were becoming adjuncts to the machine, and thus antisocially disposed. Anxiety intensified because the majority of users were adolescent, that time in their life thought necessary for developing interpersonal skills rather than for being isolated with 'things'. A number of American psychology studies followed from these commentaries, trying to evaluate whether the use of these electronic devices was addictive, or led to lack of social skills. Some studies tackled slightly different concerns about the violent nature of games. Although seemingly about games content and their scenarios, these debates also referred to the underlying technology of the media which was supposed to desensitise users to aggression.

Other critics painted a very different picture, focusing instead on the collective nature of a video games culture. Many parents and local community spokespeople recognised that arcade machines were a gathering point for youth.[19] The games were felt to be encouraging young people to 'hang around', a view which tapped into traditional fears about arcades being 'corrupt and corrupting places'.[20] Arcade video games were seen as the new locus of a separate youth culture, distracting young people from more constructive activities. Consequently, a number of studies framed their analyses of arcade life in terms of delinquency.

The location of video games within arcades meant that the new machines were incorporated into the existing social activities of these milieux and thus reactivated old anxieties. Amusement parks and many of the other public sites where coin-op machines were found, were part of street culture. They were mainly male, particularly young male, preserves. Some girls were present in these contexts and there were some girl players; after all, the arcade and other public locations were meeting places. Yet observational studies found that the proportion of boys varied between 70 and 90 per cent.[21] So, while the new technology may have been brought in to mark changes, it was soon slotted into a nexus of relations. Very traditional fears about 'deviancy' and working-class, male youth underlay some of the apparently new alarm about video games-playing.[22]

The values, rules, and rituals which these young males had built up in the pinball arcades were transferred to the video game. They shaped the experience of interactive games-playing. For instance, many would-be players served apprenticeships as spectators. The public display of skill was important. There were times for discussing tactics and giving tips. Rules governed waiting for a new game. In sum, while the games were played individually, the activity remained grounded within the social life of the peer group.

Games-playing: Gender and Games

Just as many of the fears about microcomputer games persisted from the arcade days so analyses of gender and games have not changed significantly from when they were first formulated in relation to the coin-ops.

The most frequent argument has been that the aggressive/destructive/violent/mastery nature of many games is a masculine quality.[23] Early critics also argued that scenarios such as science-fiction settings were male-orientated.[24] Stereotypical male and female characters appeared in the plot, or were offered as roles which players could adopt.[25] The nature of the colour in graphics was also discussed in gender terms (e.g. more colourful graphics being more attractive to women).[26] The case against sexist content seems more plausible when some of the more pornographic 'adult' games are considered. For example, the controversial arcade game *Custer's Revenge* had rape as its goal.[27] The next step taken by some of these commentators was to explain the content by reference to the conditions of production – that the vast majority of game designers were male.[28] Clearly, a number of the early male designers of arcade games had come from a background of playing *Spacewar* – which seemed to have severely restricted their creative horizons.

However, the picture was rendered a little more complicated when, in the late 70s, the game *PacMan* was found to be nearly as popular with women as with men, challenging assumptions about the masculinity of arcade games. Analysts sought explanations in the particular content of *PacMan*. One commentator argued that 'directing the faceless featureless *PacMan* through its model-home maze is less threatening and more closely related to hide-and-seek games than to nuclear holocaust'.[29]

The few female games designers in the industry suggested a very

139

different mode of analysis, emphasising the changing context of games-playing.[30] *PacMan* appeared when coin-op games were becoming more pervasive than pinball and video games had achieved some respectability outside the arcade in places such as lounges and restaurants. These designers argued that whereas the arcade atmosphere had been less comfortable, the new sites were more socially acceptable places for women. A similar point, in fact, had been argued in relation to pinball itself. It was only when American suburban shopping centres decided that it was profitable to allow arcades into the plazas earlier in the 1970s that some of the plusher chains first managed to attract a few women pinball players. The history of pinball thus supports the argument that an important factor in the success of *PacMan* with women was that video games were becoming generally more accessible.

Yet, even this analysis fails to address the nature of the 'interest' which is involved. As in the case of a record, a particular game may be enjoyable to a wide range of people. Alternatively, games-playing may be an activity in which many people would happily engage on an occasional basis. *PacMan* benefited from this less 'committed' form of interest. But the situation where games have a public currency within particular groups of young males is another matter. This involves a continuous interest in games in general, and entails a more regular participation in a collective activity. It was to this core of enthusiasts that the constant flow of new game releases appeared to be principally addressed and it was this level of interest associated with the arcades and other male-dominated locales which formed the basis for a greater enthusiasm among young males for both home video games and the later computer games. The arcade not only provided a familiarity with games-playing skills, but communal practices were carried into the use of domestic machines – despite the image of the isolated games-player in the home.

Games-playing: Games and Hobby Micros
Although video games players were very significant, they were not the only key actors shaping the experience of games: we also need to account for the interest of computer hobbyists. As with the hackers who designed the earlier games, the enthusiasts who built and bought the first microcomputers in the mid-70s sought ways to show this black box in operation. The first demonstrations involved controlling sound, and these were soon followed by programmes which produced a display of flashing lights. Games played the same role, demonstrating

the micro in action and illustrating the computer's capabilities. In fact, games became one of the first forms of software to be sold as a product, with some hobbyists converting the classic mainframe and minicomputer games to the smaller machines, as well as copying the arcade favourites.

Games also constituted a new type of programming challenge: squeezing the complex structures designed for minis and mainframes onto the small memory of a micro. More generally, games were still vehicles for learning about the machines. Programmes such as *Spacewar* could be justified as an exercise in controlling animated computer graphics, while adventure games involved planning and familiarity with the structure of databases. Moreover, it was possible to programme and run games even with very limited equipment.

Finally, these male hobbyists also saw games-playing as being of interest for its own sake for reasons that went beyond the particular narrative content of these products. Games were puzzles within a computerised environment. As such, they were somewhat like programming itself. Thus, early computer magazines presented games-playing as acceptable activity – as a source of relaxation in the midst of programming. This community never rejected playing as a misuse of machines: games were one of their many applications. These hobbyists were not only to provide a market for the new computer game products, they were also a legitimising force, pointing to the potentially constructive side of this software genre in contrast to the commentators who later cast games in a dimmer light.

Games-playing: Male Youth and Computer Games

Microcomputers reached a far wider audience during the 1980s, especially amongst male youth.[31] Part of the appeal lay in computing *per se*, part in the fact that micros provided a new vehicle for interactive games. But there was always more to games-playing than the moment in front of the screen.[32]

Talking about computers and games, both in and out of school, became an important dimension of boys' discussions. As with music, there was always scope for evaluating the latest releases and, as in the arcades, passing on game-play tips. Moreover, because the micro was programmable, homebrew games and special effects could also be shown to or even developed with peers. Then there was the exchange of software within school, either for copying purposes, or simply to borrow. Nor was school, including computing clubs, the only location for such interaction. Enthusiastic games-players sometimes transformed existing computer clubs and microcomputer shops into alternative arcades. Shop managers shared mixed feelings about such development with exhibitors at computer shows: hordes of players monopolising machines might be deterring other, less game-orientated, custom.

All these public settings provided opportunities to try out products, to play in collective settings and to make contact with those who shared an interest – which could mean a chance to exchange games and other software. Moreover, by appropriating these public spaces boys, albeit perhaps relatively few boys, became very visible to the producers of hardware, software and magazines. Little wonder that these staff and other commentators so easily assumed that micros and games-playing were a totally male domain, and showed surprise that girls demonstrated any interest at all. The actual situation was far more complex.

One reason for detailing the nature of boys' collective interest is to underline the fact that this social dimension simply did not exist for girls. In contrast to the beliefs of some commentators, available statistics show that girls did actually use computers – mainly for playing games. But behind the figures we need to see the difference in the experience of games. Like boys, girls were not simply isolated users, they played with other family members and with friends who visited their homes. But unlike boys, that was usually the limit of their interest; for girls the currency which computer talk and games play had among some young male peers did not exist. Girls would usually rely on brothers to inform them about the latest game and there was simply not the same amount of talk about games, nor the practice of exchanging them. Few girls visited or played games in the various public sites which were geared to microcomputers and when they did, attendance was not so much with male peers as with family. At home, girls tended to have less say than boys as to which games should be purchased, often playing whatever games were available. Hence, despite all the analysis of masculine games texts, the majority of games played by girls were also of the fast, arcade-style action, reflecting the general predominance of this genre.

The Future of Games
This chapter has indicated the complex history of interactive games which have been made available through a range of different hardware, and all of them have had some bearing on game development and their meaning in everyday life. In the case of the micro what has also

emerged is the tension between whether games merely migrate to a new hardware product or take it over so that it becomes merely the latest incarnation of a games machine. This dilemma may well face future vehicles for games, such as multimedia CD.

At about the same time as videodiscs emerged, CD-ROM, another variant of laser disc technology, found a function as a storage medium for computer data and since it promised a further lease of life to the home computer, CD-technology generated interest in the computer press.

In practice, the implications for home computers are far from clear. One line of development has involved using CD-ROM as a peripheral for the micro; CD-ROM games and other software (e.g. *The Guinness Book of Records*) became available in the early 1990s. The other line of development was to combine the same CD technology and microprocessor in a new product which was not conceptualised as a micro. Philips has for years been the driving force behind the development of such a machine – CD-I – and was joined by Commodore which announced its own multimedia product, CDTV (based on its Amiga system) at the end of 1990. While these products can achieve the functionality of a micro mainly by adding keyboards, marketing policy has deliberately distanced multimedia from computer products.[33]

This makes little difference to games software publishers, for whom multimedia is just another hardware vehicle like the video games console: in fact, it has the additional advantage that software on laser disc cannot so easily be pirated. On the other hand, games are far more problematic for hardware manufacturers. Although Philips and Commodore have signed up a range of publishers to support their machines, having learnt a lesson from the micro industry, they are still wary of games. Ultimately both manufacturers want their products to become home entertainment centres, occupying a permanent place in the living room and used by all the family – echoes of the general purpose micro – and not just the latest games machines.

Virtual reality games are a little further away – at least as home-based products. The software trade press is only just starting to get to grips with this new medium, although a number of those in the VR industry have seen games as a probable application. It is early days yet, but they might be expected to face the same dilemma as multimedia: games will threaten to dominate and give the new media narrower connotations than their hardware producers would prefer.

This chapter has shown how the software industry's shaping and reshaping has had ramifications for games texts. The concerns of software houses to establish games as more mainstream entertainment apply equally to multimedia games. Since their proponents hope that products such as CD-I will eventually compete for free time with broadcast TV, work on multimedia games now involves bringing in specialists from other media to achieve higher production values.[34] The capacity of the new hardware promises to open possibilities for radically new game products, but to date there has been little more than the enhancement of existing ones. Incremental but significant improvements include providing more detailed and smoother graphics and lifelike sounds in CD-I games than in traditional home computer versions, and adding video clips and digital audio quality music to animation sequences. While these developments introduce a greater sense of realism, efforts to give games a higher profile continue. Children's television will include *Cyberzone*, where contestants compete within a computer-generated environment.[35] Since participants have to make physical movements to attain virtual movement (e.g. by walking on a pad containing sensors), this will also be the first showing of a programme with elements of virtual reality. Even before its release, a number of countries have bought rights to show the series, which could broaden interest in this new type of interactive game considerably.

The central argument of this chapter has been that games-playing must be situated within a wider range of games-related activities. The history of the arcade and micro have made games-playing into the particular preserve of young males and it is not at all obvious why this should change with the advent of multimedia. The first commercial virtual reality product to be released for a consumer market was, in fact, a 3-D simulation for use in arcades.[36] Concerns about games never really disappeared, as the 1990 *Q.E.D.* television programme on the dangers of computer addiction made clear.[37] Reinvigorated anxieties about escapism and antisocial behaviour can be confidently expected once Little Johnny is equipped with virtual reality headset, data gloves and body suit and goes beyond the screen.

NOTES

1. This chapter is based on the author's doctoral thesis on the history of home computers and interactive games, which entailed interviews with a variety of producers. An earlier version appeared as Leslie Haddon, 'Electronic and Computer Games', *Screen* vol. 29 no. 2, Spring 1988, pp. 52–73.

2. This section is mainly based on: Steven Levy, *Hackers: Heroes of the Revolution* (Garden City: Doubleday, 1984); Stewart Brand, 'Spacewar: Fanatic Life and Symbolic Death Among the Computer Bums', *Rolling Stone*, 7 December 1972; and Paul Freiberger and Michael Swaine, *Fire in the Valley: the Making of the Personal Computer* (Berkley: Osborne/ McGraw-Hill, 1984).

3. For the history of arcade developments see Tekla Perry et al., 'Video Games: the Electronic Big Bang', *IEEE Spectrum*, vol. 19 no. 12, December 1982, pp. 20–33; Craig Kubey, *The Winners Book of Video Games* (London: W.H. Allen, 1982); John Price, 'Social Science Research on Video Games', *Journal of Popular Culture* vol. 18 no. 4, Spring 1985, pp. 111–25; Peter Bernstein, 'Atari and the Video Games Explosion', *Fortune* vol. 104 no. 2, July 1981, pp. 40–6; Judith Larsen and Everett Rogers, *Silicon Valley Fever: Growth of High Technology Culture* (London: Unwin, 1984); Sidney Kaplan, 'The Image of Amusement Arcades and the Differences in Male and Female Video Game Playing', *Journal of Popular Culture*, 1983, pp. 93–8; Sue Smith, ' "Coin Detected in Pocket": Videogames as Icons', in C. Geist and S. Nachbar (eds.), *The Popular Culture Reader* (Bowling Green: Bowling Green University Popular Press, 1983), pp. 145–51; Aaron Latham, 'Videogames Star Wars', *New York Times Magazine*, 25 October 1981, pp. 100–12.

4. Eric Egli and Lawrence Meyers, 'The Role of Video Game Playing in Adolescent Life: Is there Reason to be Concerned?', *Bulletin of the Psychonomic Society* vol. 22 no. 4, 1984, p. 309.

5. For the history of home video games developments, see Ralph Baer, 'Television Games: Their Past, Present, and Future', *IEEE Transactions on Consumer Electronics* vol. CE-23 no. 4, November 1979, pp. 496–504; M. Jones, 'Video Games as Psychological Tests', *Simulations and Games* vol. 15 no. 2, June 1984, pp. 133–4; Thomas Murrey, 'The Boom in Video Games', *Dun's Review* vol. 108 no. 3, September 1976, pp. 54–5; *Screen Digest*, 'Video games', July 1977, pp. 127–9; Stephan Bristow, 'The History of Video Games', *IEEE Transactions on Consumer Electronics*, February 1977, pp. 58–68; Perry et al., 'Design Case History: The Atari Video Computer System', *IEEE Spectrum*, March 1983, pp. 45–51; Peter Nulty, 'Why the Craze Won't Quit', *Fortune*, 15 November 1982, pp. 114–24.

6. A number of the firms which first entered the market saw a potential in programmable consoles which went beyond games, as a more general entertainment software player. Part of the reason for leaving was that this usage never materialised.

7. Author interview with Atari management in Britain (8 July 1986).

8. See Leslie Haddon, 'Home Computers: the Making of a Consumer Electronic', *Science as Culture* no. 2, 1987.

9. This is clear from surveys, my own samples and other qualitative research including a longitudinal study at the Centre for Mass Communications Research in Leicester University, and David Skinner's current PhD research at Brunel University. The Leicester work is discussed in Graham Murdock, Paul Hartmann and Perry Gray, 'Contextualising Home Computing: Resources and Practices', in Roger Silverstone and Erich Hirsch

145

(eds.), *Consuming Technologies: Media and Information in Private Spaces* (London: Routledge, 1992).

10. Many of the details and viewpoints in the following pages are derived from issues of the home computer industry trade press *Computer Trade Weekly*.

11. The UK installed base of PCs in the home is estimated at 350,000, while PC game sales account for about 5 per cent of the UK total (compared with 15 per cent of Europe as a whole). Estimate in J. Minson, 'The Quiet Revolution', *Computer Trade Weekly*, 2 July 1990, pp. 8–9 and p. 19.

12. Gillian Skirrow provides a history of the adventure genre which traces its features back to previous texts. This piece contains by far the most sophisticated analysis available of games as texts. Gillian Skirrow, 'Hellivision: An Analysis of Video Games', in Colin MacCabe (ed.), *High Theory/Low Culture: Analysing Popular Television and Film* (Manchester: Manchester University Press, 1986), pp. 115–42.

13. Edward Trapanski, *Special when Lit: A Visual History of the Pinball* (New York: Dolphin Books, 1979).

14. M. Litwark, *Reel Power: The Struggle for Influence in the New Hollywood* (London: Sidgwick and Jackson, 1987), p. 100.

15. See Terri Toles, 'Video Games and American Military Ideology', in Vincent Mosco and Janet Wasko (eds.) *The Critical Communications Review, vol. III: Popular Culture and Media Events* (Norwood: Ablex, 1985), pp. 207–23; Nancy Needham, 'Thirty Billion Quarters Can't Be Wrong: Or Can They? A Look at the Impact of Video Games on American Youth', *Today's Education, 1982–3 Annual*, 1983, pp. 52–5; John Price, 'Social Science Research on Video Games', pp. 111–25; Eric Egli and Lawrence Meyers, 'The Role of Video Game Playing in Adolescent Life', pp. 309–12; *EL News*, 'Anti-Video Game Movement Gathering Momentum', *Electronic Learning* vol. 1 no. 3, 1982, pp. 12–13.

16. Neil Frude, *The Intimate Machine: Close Encounters with New Computers* (London: Century, 1983), p. 68.

17. This same concern has been carried into writing from an overtly socialist perspective, as in Tony Solomonides and Les Levidow, *Compulsive Technology: Computers as Culture* (London: Free Association Books, 1985), p. 6.

18. Discussed in Sherry Turkle, *The Second Self: Computers and the Human Spirit* (London: Granada, 1984).

19. Tom Panelas, 'Adolescents and Video Games: Consumption of Leisure and the Social Construction of the Peer Group', *Youth and Society* vol. 15 no. 1, September 1983, pp. 51–65.

20. Desmond Ellis, 'Video Arcades, Youth and Trouble', *Youth and Society* vol. 16 no. 1, September 1984, pp. 47–8.

21. There seems to be little public market research available on arcades. These figures are derived from a compilation of small-scale observational studies.

22. This concern about antisocial behaviour and isolation also partly reflects a general reservation about male over-involvement with 'things', and especially with technology.

23. An example of this type of analysis would be Nancy Kreinberg and Elizabeth Stage, 'EQUALS in Computer Technology', in Jan Zimmerman

(ed.), *The Technological Woman: Interfacing with Tomorrow* (New York: Praeger, 1983), p. 255.

24. Nancy Needham, 'Thirty Billion Quarters Can't Be Wrong: Or Can They?', p. 54.

25. Terri Toles, 'Video Games and American Military Ideology', p. 214.

26. Tekla Perry et al., 'Video Games: the Electronic Big Bang', p. 26; John Price, 'Social Science Research on Video Games', p. 122.

27. D. Talbot, 'Pac-Man Kills Kids: Video Horrors', *Mother Jones*, April, 1983. The game was withdrawn after a campaign by Women Against Pornography.

28. Perry and others estimated that there were about 100 video game designers in the US when they were writing – about 4 or 5 of these were women, mostly designing home video games. Tekla Perry et al., 'Video Games: the Electronic Big Bang', pp. 28–9.

29. Sue Smith, ' "Coin Detected in Pocket": Videogames as Icons', p. 150.

30. Tekla Perry et al., 'Video Games: the Electronic Big Bang', p. 31.

31. As a rough guide, surveys suggest that boys' use of, knowledge of and desire for computers is at least twice as great as that of girls. Boys are by far the biggest users of micros, followed by girls and then adult males. Details are outlined in Leslie Haddon, *The Roots and Early History of the British Home Computer Market*, unpublished doctoral thesis, University of London, London, 1988.

32. Based on the author's research which involved interviews with boys and girls and observations in a boys' computer club.

33. Many of the details concerning multimedia are derived from recent research by the author and colleagues at Sussex University to be published as Alan Cawson et al. *The Shape of Things to Consume* (London: Sage, forthcoming).

34. Discussed by various speakers at 'CD-ROM Europe '91' conference, Novotel Hotel, London, 21–23 May. See also, Frank Rickett's chapter in this volume.

35. Previewed at the 'Virtual Reality' conference, Sedgwick Centre, London, 5–6 June, 1991 produced by Broadsword Productions, and broadcast on BBC2, in Britain.

36. W. Industries released a virtual reality games unit for the arcades in August 1991. 'Virtual Reality' conference, 1991.

37. 'My Best Friend's a Computer', *Q.E.D.*, 24 January 1990.

THE GENESIS OF VIRTUAL
REALITY

Rebecca Coyle

Terminology, Principles and Technology
Cyberspace and **virtual reality** are two of the terms used to refer to
the electronic environments produced by a new generation of interactive computer technologies. Although the terms are often used inter-
changeably in popular journalism, they are distinct in emphasis.
Cyberspace refers to the cybernetic data 'space' of the computer
apparently 'entered into' by the systems user, whereas **virtual reality**
is the apparent world (or 'reality') the user experiences while using the
system.[1] Drawing on these definitions, this, and following chapters,
use the term **cyberspace technology** to refer to the mechanical-elec-
tronic apparatus which facilitates interaction with computer **cyberspace** and thus the **virtual reality** experienced by the system user.

Traditional computer systems allow the user to interact with data –
usually represented on a computer monitor screen – by means of a
keyboard, joystick, mouse or data-pen. Cyberspace technologies,
though still cumbersome, permit a far greater degree of interaction
through the use of three main elements:[2]

- Sophisticated three-dimensional (3-D) graphics systems presented
  to fill the user's field of vision;
- Interactive software programmes designed to enable the user apparently to interact with the representation of physical objects and
  locations;
- Sensor devices which
    (a) allow the user apparently to move within and scrutinise the
    presented visual environment and

148

(b) allow the user to manipulate apparent objects within the presented environment by making physical movements in 'real' space which conform to those apparently required by the presented visual environment.

Current hardware allows users to perceive the computer's synthetic world via a helmet in which two tiny colour liquid crystal display (LCD) monitors are mounted directly in front of the user's eyes. These produce a 3-D effect by screening a slightly different computer-generated view before each eye. The monitors are fitted to a tracking mechanism connected to a computer. As the viewer's head moves, the image correspondingly moves in the virtual space. An increasing number of programmes also allow multi-directional or binaural audio information to be fed to the user by headphones fitted into the helmet.

Users can currently interact with the virtual environments they encounter – or rather those features in cyberspace programmes designed to be interactive – by means of four principal, hand-operated interfaces. These are the 'data glove' (discussed in detail on pages 157–8), an updated version of the joystick, a pistol grip apparatus or a small spherical control. These enable users to 'move about' in the synthetic world and to manipulate the apparent objects they encounter there by moving their hand. The hand-operated interfaces are embedded with fibre-optic cables that detect how the hand moves and what spatial position it occupies, and send this information to the computer. 'Real' hand gestures are thus translated into movement in the virtual world.

Conventions have developed whereby certain gestures are linked with particular movements in the virtual world. In systems using dataglove interfaces, the action of forming a fist around the image of an object usually allows the user to 'hold' and 'move' that object in the programme. Similarly, in many systems, pointing up with the glove enables the user to 'fly'. Programmes provided with force feedback enhance the reality experience for the user by offering apparent resistance, so that the user can seem to sense a weight in the objects they move or come up against. To interact further with the cyberspace system, it is also possible to wear a 'data suit' – a sensor system embedded into a body suit. Sensors in this suit project an image of the wearer's body into the computer-generated space before the wearer's eyes. The user can thereby see him/herself *within* the computer system.

To date, the medium has attracted significant research and development investment from three key agencies: companies wanting to use cyberspace as the medium for a new generation of computer-video games; military organisations wishing to use such systems for surveillance and combat; and space agencies (particularly NASA) developing systems for remote sensing and exploration. As the following history of the medium details, the character of these agencies is not only likely to determine the future development of the form but has also determined much of its development to date.

The Antecedence of Cyberspace
Cyberspace systems have a complex history. They derive not only from a technological tradition but also from a range of other strategic, commercial and cultural initiatives. As is widely acknowledged, the term 'cyberspace' was first used by Canadian science-fiction author William Gibson who used the term in 1984 in *Neuromancer* – the first of his trilogy of 'Cyberpunk' novels – to describe the imaginary world experienced by those engaging with a globally networked 'data space'. In his terms it was 'a consensual hallucination experienced daily by billions of legitimate [computer] operators. ... A graphic representation of data abstracted from the banks of every computer in the human system.'[3]

Alternative realities have, of course, long been a staple of fantasy and science fiction writers.[4] Various modes of entry into these systems have been posited. Lewis Carroll's memorable fantasies, for example, created other worlds, either physically located (as in the subterranean fantasy world of *Alice in Wonderland*) or else conceived as a 'parallel' reality (as in *Alice Through the Looking Glass*). More contemporarily, Marge Piercy's *Woman On The Edge Of Time* features a main character who moves in and out of an imaginary world. Her 'alternative reality' is one in which solutions to social problems and new models of social behaviour can be found.[5] Nevertheless, Dr Brenda Laurel, Managing Director of Telepresence Research in California, argues that the search for alternative realities has been an abiding theme throughout history:

> The notion of Virtual Reality is actually on a continuum that's older than science fiction by a lot. Enactments around pre-historic campfires, Greek theatre, performance rituals of aboriginal peoples the world over have all been aimed at a similar goal, and that is heightened experience through immersive, multi-sensory representations.[6]

Thus, Gibson's work clearly derives from an existing tradition but what has made it so influential is how he conceptualised the manner of entry into this other plane. The global computer matrix he envisages is an 'alternative reality' which computer users enter, explore and engage with through interactive systems. Instead of mystical, fortuitous or simply unexplained ports of entry to 'other worlds', Gibson imagined access by means of a commonly available technology whose actual production was only just beyond the range of science fact at the time of his writing. In short, he set an imaginative agenda bringing together some of the formative pieces of cyberspace technology. Although Gibson was unaware of it, the components of the interactive 'entry' interface he imagined in his novels were in development at the very moment he was describing them in print – as Philip Hayward describes in Chapter 9. Indeed, they preceded his work. Although Gibson may be the 'father' of the imagination of cyberspace, it is the pioneers of technology who ultimately created the conditions for the final leap into cyberspace accomplished in the late 1980s.

The most significant aspect of cyberspace to users is that it gives them the impression of actually being in a synthetic world rather than simply observing images and events. Such an experience has long been the aim of media practitioners. Indeed there are a number of notable precedents where earlier technologies have been deployed to produce such an effect. Edwardian stereoscopes, holographic stereograms and 3-D film all form part of the pre-history of the medium. The endeavour still continues in non-computer media: IMAX and OMNIMAX wide-screen motion picture systems, for instance, can be seen as an attempt to immerse viewers more effectively in the world presented to them. However, possibly the earliest experiments which most closely approached contemporary cyberspace systems were the 'Stereoscopic-Television Apparatus for Individual Use' (STAIU) and the 'Sensorama Simulator' patented by Morton Heilig in 1957 and 1961 respectively.

The headgear designed by Heilig for the STAIU included wide-angle optics and individual lightweight display screens for each eye of the viewer. The Sensorama extended this idea further to incorporate 'color, visual movement, complete peripheral vision, 3-D, binaural sound, breezes, odor and tactile sensations'.[7] These effects were accomplished through the use of film loops, odour canisters triggered electromagnetically from information on the film track, vibrating knobs and a seat. Unlike the single-user systems most commonly available at present, Heilig's prototype could accommodate four people simultaneously.[8]

Despite the considerable accomplishment of Heilig's prototypes, they were still based on a passive model of user perception and it is only advanced computer systems which have enabled users to create substantial aspects of their own experiences (within the limits of the software) rather than experience precisely pre-determined ones. Computer scientist and graphics expert Ivan Sutherland, initially based at the Massachusetts Institute of Technology (MIT) and later at the University of Utah, was a key contributor to the earliest phases of cyberspace system development. As early as 1963, his doctoral thesis described the design of a system known as *Sketchpad*, arguably the first real-time interactive computer graphics system.[9] *Sketchpad* allowed the user to 'draw' onto a screen with a 'light-pen' and to modify the images via a keyboard. Further computer graphics research led Sutherland to create 3-D simulations of, for example, aircraft landing on a carrier.

Sutherland's work represented the first (scientific) step towards creating a virtual reality beyond the flat screen of the monitor interface. The key breakthrough, however, was the helmet device he built in 1968, nicknamed the 'Sword of Damocles'.[10] Too heavy to wear, the helmet was suspended from the ceiling and hung over the user's head. It featured two video displays, and sensors connected to the helmet recorded the user's head position and movement. Sutherland's experience with this system led him towards further developments of the technology, extending its graphics and display potential.[11] His aim was to produce a helmet display which featured a 'room' within which the objects would be computer-generated and able to be manipulated.

Thomas Furness's work in flight simulation took crucial steps in the halting realisation of cyberspace technology. He began working in visual display systems for the US Air Force in 1966. In 1981, while based at the Wright-Patterson Air Force Base in Dayton, Ohio, his team launched their Visually Coupled Airborne Systems Simulator, known as the 'Super Cockpit'. This was designed to assist training pilots to fly high-speed aircraft like the F-16 fighter jet. A specially constructed helmet allowed the pilot to see a computer-synthesised simulated environment on the inside of a face shield. The pilot's 'flight' through this world was mainly controlled by voice commands and eye movements. The pilot's glove was lined with position sensors so that by pointing to virtual buttons various functions, such as missile launches, could be controlled. Furness's work in this area has been widely adapted by various aviation agencies.

Airline companies and defence services now use adapted forms of these early flight simulators and the equipment is generally manufactured alongside the aircraft for use in training and skills upgrading. However, flight simulators for passenger and civilian freight planes do not include helmets as part of their systems, since helmets are not used for real flights and would therefore detract from the veracity of the simulation. Prior to the introduction of computer-generated imagery (CGI) systems in the late 70s, flight simulation systems achieved real-time visual scene representations by using flat-screen projection systems. The scenes generated for these systems were produced from large-scale model landscapes on moving belts or else flat terrain models whose images were relayed to system users by closed-circuit video cameras. In the late 70s, however, CGI systems allowed users to experience a larger field of view with better image definition (although the images were very basic representations and lacked scene content). More recent developments have allowed landscapes and urban areas to be rendered with 'photo texturing' to give a more realistic appearance. The images are screened either on 'window' screens fitted into cockpits or on projection optics in domes.

Flight simulation programmes now have sophisticated computer graphics and offer more specified virtual experiences designed for the particular purposes of the training agency. After basic instrument training in generic models, pilots are given advanced training in specifically designed copies of actual aircraft cockpits. The simulator cockpit is suspended on hydraulics so that the pilot experiences most of the physical sensations of being in the air, landing, taking off, taxi-ing, and so on.[12] Sophisticated computer programmes comprise computer-generated images, video excerpts or a combination of these and allow instructors to test pilots' responses to a variety of weather conditions and emergency situations, to different times of day, and to different airport and aerodrome layouts. The value of these simulations is that they are effective enough to induce symptoms of anxiety in pilots similar to those experienced in real aircraft flying. Brenda Laurel of Telepresence Research observes that, 'Even at very low frame rates and very low resolution, something quite extraordinary happens to you when your visual sense and your auditory sense and your kinaesthetic senses are all working in tight linkage with one another. And that's the essential trick of the medium.'[13] The Australian airline Qantas, with one of the best safety records of any airline, has been using flight simulators since the 60s. A measure of the sophistication and efficiency of current systems is evident in their considerable reduction in real aircraft flying for training and skills advancement.

The development of flight simulators is associated with initiatives in cyberspace technology in three main areas: 'real time' animation, display hardware and sensor electronics. The American National Aeronautics and Space Agency (NASA) has been a key organisation in developing all three of these and extending them into the field of **telepresence** – the use of virtual reality to 'place' humans in inaccessible and/or hostile environments. Recognising the limitations of the human astronaut in space or on hostile planetary surfaces, NASA's Virtual Environment Research Lab has been involved in developing remote sensing and manipulation systems which do not require the human astronaut's physical presence or intervention at sites of exploration. These programmes can also be applied in underwater exploration, nuclear power plants and at other inaccessible sites.

The use of robots for the completion of dangerous, boring, repetitive and specialised tasks is not new. The difference between the robots being developed for routine tasks in industry and those in research laboratories like MIT, Stanford and NASA is in the creation of robots that can move on their own in the real world and can thus be used for (relatively) complex exploratory tasks. This robotic technology includes aspects of artificial intelligence, sophisticated sensors that allow the robot to react to changes in the environment, and different forms of locomotion. NASA's research into telepresence links into the work on 'teleoperation' and 'tele-existence' by, for example, the Japanese government's Mechanical Engineering Laboratory. Tele-existence involves a hybrid of human and machine in that the autonomous robot performs specialised tasks operated by a human who makes judgements and manipulations via computer at a separate location. The operator 'sees' the environment via cameras located in the robot's eyes.[14]

In the mid-80s, NASA researchers at the Ames Research Center, Michael McGreevy, James Humphries and Scott Fisher, constructed a helmet which would enable an astronaut working inside a space station to visualise what a robot operating outside could 'see' through its optical sensors. This system used advanced LCD video screen technology first launched by the Japanese Citizen Watch Company in 1985. When the astronaut's head turned, the robot's camera eyes swung in the same direction. This was accomplished by an electronic sensor registering the user's head position and orientation and sending electromagnetic pulses from three transmitter antennae to three receiver antennae on the robot. In both the transmitter and the receiver units, the antennae coils were positioned at right angles to one another forming a Cartesian-coordinate system. As this system mathematically locates a point in terms of its perpendicular distance from a set of mutually perpendicular axes, it ensures a high accuracy response. (See Chapter 8 for Sally Pryor's and Jill Scott's discussion of Cartesian philosophy and virtual reality.) The sensor or tracking device in this system is often referred to as a 'polhemus' since it was devised by the Polhemus Navigation Sciences Division of the McDonnell Douglas Corporation. It is now a standard device in a range of cyberspace systems. In addition to the position sensors, the helmet technology also incorporates eye-tracking sensors that bounce a beam of light off the cornea of the eye to record its micro-movements. Later versions of this system also allowed the helmet to be used in conjunction with a data glove designed to pass signals of hand and finger movements on to the robot.

The particular developmental path followed by trainer-simulator designers and robotics experts has led to a number of spin-offs which have demonstrated other potential uses. As early as 1985, for instance, Australia's Channel 7 TV coverage of the Australian Masters Golf Competition included an ambitious computer graphic sequence created by Qantas's Chief Engineer in Simulator Development, Vern Cottee. This sequence gave the viewer action at the third hole from the *perspective of a golf ball* – a perceptual simulation effect similar to that used six years later by the US military for bomb guidance in the Gulf War. The involvement of the military in this form of advanced technology is hardly surprising. Whereas the golfball simulation project was something of a curiosity, a one-off, there is a more enduring strategic motivation for military research and, of crucial importance, a massive potential source of funding in the military–industrial combine.[15]

Toys and War Games – the Strategic Interface

The research into cyberspace technologies conducted by American military organisations and associated industrial companies has paralleled research pursued by the commercial aviation and space industries and developed the technologies in specific ways. Indeed, it is estimated that around two-thirds of the global simulation and training market is dominated by the US military. Simulation technologies are now used for battlefield modelling and combat management for both individual combatants and strategic planning purposes.

The advantages of many systems being developed for combatants take them beyond simple training simulation. Civil aviation companies

155

have established that advanced simulators allow pilots to 'virtually experience' and test their reactions and responses to difficult and unusual circumstances of a kind they could not be expected to experience in training. To give one example, a British Airways' pilot who successfully flew through the dense smoke and particle cloud caused by a volcanic eruption in the early 80s claimed that his experience in simulators enabled him to negotiate successfully a hazard otherwise unfamiliar to him. New systems being developed for the US military take this one step further and maintain the graphic representations and data-scheme of display simulations in actual flight and combat situations – the real is constantly rendered 'virtual' in order to be more manageable.

US military researchers, in collaboration with CAE Electronics in Germany, are developing the fibre-optic helmet-mounted display or FOHMD. This system's helmet includes a pair of 7.5 cm by 5 cm display panels which create a seamless cyclorama around the pilot's head, sealing him away from the external environment. The FOHMD seems likely to replace the current 'Head-Up Display' visual superimposition system in designs for the American Advanced Tactical Fighter project and the US Army scout attack helicopters. Software that will use this technology to display a computer-enhanced real-time landscape on the pilot's visor is being developed. In addition to software that responds to voice commands like 'select', 'zoom', 'god's eye', 'fire', Stewart Brand has described a sophisticated optical sensor which allows the pilot to point 'fire' with his eyes, 'the definitive piercing glance'.[16] The US Air Force helmet that reportedly projects cartoon-like images of the battlefield with flashing symbols for enemy planes and 'a yellow-brick road leading right to the target'[17] emphasises the links between military applications and the research and development being conducted by computer games manufacturers. As Kevin Robins has pointed out in his report *Into The Image: Visual Technologies and Vision Cultures*, it is as if 'the commander and fighter were engaged in mastering a game logic, rather than involved in impassioned, bloody and destructive combat'.[18]

There are a number of convergences and reciprocal influences between the military and the games sector. As many observers have noted, trainee pilots are often avid arcade game players.[19] This emphasises the extent to which both systems require manual dexterity, hand-eye co-ordination, quick reactions and the ability to predict likely developments. They also stimulate and excite their users in similar ways. This parallel provided the scenario for the 1984 film *The Last*

Starfighter. In this, aliens plant advanced *Space Invaders*-style games on Earth which they then monitor to select the best player. When this individual, a young boy, is found, the aliens contact him and inform him that the games machines have in fact been assessment and training simulators for space fighter pilots required to save the galaxy from attack. Despite initial reservations, the boy becomes a pilot and leads the successful battle with the hostile aliens. Of course, *The Last Starfighter* is fiction, yet the film underscores the extent to which many arcade and home video games are based on battlefield scenarios.

Furthermore, recent events have seen the production of games based on entirely realistic scenarios. Arcade and home video games manufacturers are constantly searching for new machines and programmes that can capture the imagination and maintain popular appeal among the (mainly young male) consumers, and the Gulf War in particular generated a profusion of games. One such game is the *MicroProse F-15 Strike Eagle II*. This simulates the combatant experience by allowing the player/pilot to have full control of the simulated fighter bomber and to make strikes with 'high-tech smart weapons like infrared-homing Maverick missiles, Paveway glide bombs and HARM anti-radar missiles'.[20] In this manner the (actual) war functioned as a great free prime-time promo for the games products which flowed on after the event.

Besides capitalising on defence technologies and 'combat events', games manufacturers have made significant contributions to interactive systems by developing screen graphics. Many current interactive devices are limited to two dimensions.[21] Even manipulations of 3-D simulations are usually specified through 2-D devices such as the mouse. The breakthrough was the creation of an interactive device that had all the precision, control and agility of the human hand: the electronic glove or data glove. The DataGlove was initially developed in the mid-80s by Thomas Zimmerman and L. Young Harvill for VPL Research Inc., a small California-based company. Their invention was then developed further for the games market by brothers Anthony, John and Chris Gentile of Abrams/Gentile Entertainment Inc. (AGE).

As Philip Hayward discusses in chapter 9, the original idea was to make an 'air guitar' – a virtual instrument that could actually be played rather than being a notional shape around which rock fans mimed the motions of actual rock guitar playing. Under the direction of musician-cum-computer entrepreneur Jaron Lanier, Zimmerman and Harvill created a 'hand' to strum the virtual guitar strings.[22] The glove comprises fibre-optic cables along each finger and thumb, sandwiched

157

between two layers of lycra fabric. Both ends of the cable connect to an interface board near the wrist. Movement in the fingers sends signals via the interface to the computer and broad hand gestures are recorded by the Polhemus sensor mounted on the back of the hand. The hardware was complemented by software devised by Jaron Lanier and Chuck Blanchard and called 'Body Electric'. This software maps the actual movements of the DataGlove and EyePhone head-mounted display onto the virtual (computer graphic) landscape and allows the user to interact with all aspects of the 'world'.

Though the DataGlove was ready for manufacture in 1985, a slump in the games market meant that it was not taken up until later. The AGE concept for the electronic glove was co-licensed (with VPL) to Mattel Toys and marketed as the Power Glove in October 1989.[23] Within six weeks the Power Glove made $50 million in sales. Consumers can now programme the glove to interact with any Nintendo home video game software, such as the *Mike Tyson's Punch Out* and the *Super Glove Ball*. AGE plans to make a child-orientated version of a VR system available by 1993 and intends it to retail for US$200. The perception of market demand has therefore driven the development of low-cost manufacture of lightweight technology in ways which directly contradict the cost-intensive slow product development for the military–industrial market, where margins are enhanced by delay, obfuscation and general overpricing.

One important development of glove technology now under way offers the user force and tactile feedback, that is, the ability to 'feel' the weight, texture and pull of various materials, substances and objects. Force feedback systems have been attempted before. A significant predecessor of current systems being developed for glove use was devised by a group headed by Frederick P. Brooks Jr. at the University of North Carolina at Chapel Hill in 1968. The team adapted for force feedback a remote manipulator device of the kind used today to handle radioactive materials. In the 80s, the 'joystring' (named after its predecessor, the joystick control) was developed by Richard J. Feldman of the National Institute of Health. It requires the user to grip and manipulate a T-shaped joystring control which is held suspended in space by nine wires. The computer reads the user's movements through shaft encoders and generates appropriate force and torque feedback via the servomotors. Despite being somewhat awkward, the joystring remains one of the more effective force-feedback devices.

Other methods of interacting with the computer currently being developed include integrated voice and gesture recognition. Since the mid-70s, Nicholas Negroponte and Richard Bolt of the MIT have been developing these forms of technology for tasks requiring the use of both hands (such as the testing of electronic assemblies). In the late 80s, Kenneth Davies of the IBM Corporation's Thomas J Watson Research Center developed a system with a vocabulary of over 20,000 words. Meanwhile, at the same centre, James R. Rhyne developed a system that recognised hand gestures made in two dimensions with a penlike positioning device. IBM envisages integrating these technologies in spreadsheet display programmes, for instance, where a total for a group of figures could be requested by a circle and summation sign made by the user's hand.

NASA's Ames Research Center (Aerospace Human Factors Research Division) is currently undertaking work on all of the principal technologies described in this section. The centre has established an interactive Virtual Interface Environment Workstation (VIEW) which former research leader Scott Fisher recently claimed offers 'a new kind of media-based display and control environment that is closely matched to human sensory and cognitive capabilities'. It provides 'a virtual auditory and stereoscopic image surrounding that is responsive to inputs from the operator's position, voice and gestures' and consists of 'a wide-angle stereoscopic display unit, glove-like devices for multiple degree-of-freedom tactile input, connected speech recognition technology, gesture tracking devices, 3-D auditory display and speech synthesis technology, and computer graphic and video image generation equipment'.[24] It is a measure of the pace of development in this field that such a system would have been beyond the immediate expectations of the computer industry as recently as five years ago. VIEW represents the elements of virtual reality systems that require further research, but also demonstrates how these goals are known and achievable. Questions around why, who and how the systems will be used in which the research goals are less clearly defined.

Although the military–industrial combine has played a major role in the development of the medium, virtual reality has also excited the interest of groups and individuals wishing to use it for broader and more peaceful learning and experiential purposes. Indeed, as Philip Hayward discusses in chapter 9, its technologies have even been seen as innately 'counter-cultural'. These counter-cultural associations predate the canonisation of William Gibson as the 'father of cyberspace' and were largely initiated by Myron Krueger, who claims to have coined the phrase 'artificial reality' in a book first published in 1983.[25]

Krueger, an artist and former computer science teacher, began working on Technology-Art pieces in the late 60s. Many of these comprised interactive environments that encouraged full-body sensory participation by users. His installation for the 1985 SIGGRAPH (Association for Computer Machinery, Special Interest Group on Computer Graphics and Interactive Technologies) show, for instance, allowed individuals and groups to 'interact with images of themselves that were projected onto a facing wall'.[26] His *Video Place* installation at the State Museum of Natural History in Storrs, Connecticut has expanded on this and allows participants in separate rooms to perform physical feats, tickle each other, fingerpaint together and interact in other ways. Video cameras record the behaviour and send images to a computer. This information is then rescreened on the walls of other rooms for participants' responses. Participants are unencumbered by the currently available virtual reality paraphernalia of goggles, gloves and suit, although the images they interact with are only 2-D at present.

Krueger's pieces, and the work of other interactive artists like Australia's Jill Scott and Simon Veitch,[27] are important for the manner in which they stress the interactive potential of existing systems (however limited) and the active role system users can play in the creative – rather than purely consumptive – process. This concern also informs the work of Brenda Laurel, whose theatre training, doctorate on interactive fantasy (completed in 1986) and over ten years' experience with the games industry have led her to research a version of virtual reality that attends to the 'emotional, cognitive and aesthetic dimensions of human experience in virtual worlds'.[28] While enthusiasm for interactivity pre-dates the arrival of virtual reality systems, cyberspace technologies offer artists opportunities to extend the potential of interactivity. Krueger has gone on to argue that

> most importantly, artificial realities are a medium of expression and experience, as well as a new way for people to interact with each other. ... Increasingly, people are products of artificial experience. Vicarious experience through theater, novels, movies and television represents a significant fraction of our lives. The addition of a radically new form of physically involving, interactive experience is a major cultural event which may shape our consciousness as much as what has come before.[29]

This rhetoric also informs the sales pitches and self-promotion of the small group of advanced computer companies, such as Autodesk and

VPL, who have located themselves on America's West Coast and have become leading publicists for the idea of cyberspace technology as an innately 'alternative', and even 'consciousness raising', medium. This has not, however, prevented them from becoming embroiled in the commercial competition that has characterised the early development of the medium. The struggle for pre-eminence and credit for each other's prototypes is a long story in itself. There is, for example, the curious affair of Autodesk's Eric Gullichsen's registration of Gibson's term 'cyberspace' as an Autodesk trademark – an action which Gibson responded to by applying for trademark registration of the term 'Eric Gullichsen'. ... On a more serious level, VPL has been engaged in legal battles with Stanford University and with AGE toy developers to protect their rights to the DataGlove.

Companies such as VPL and Autodesk have none the less been at the cutting edge of a series of exciting – and often wildly imaginative – developments of the medium. Of late, VPL has turned its hand to developing 'VR tourism' (virtual travel), sophisticated sensory control programmes and a new high-fidelity auditory technology called *AudioSphere*. In addition, along with other companies, they are prioritising the development of new hard and software systems to be manufactured and retailed at substantially less than the current asking price of around US$250,000. A wide range of marketplace applications is already expected, virtual reality systems are already in operation, for example, in architectural visualisation. Frederick Brooks and his team at the University of North Carolina recently created a programme to conduct tours through a new addition to the local Orange United Methodist Church before it was built. The system used virtual reality-like hardware and the sensation of walking was provided by a treadmill and handlebars on a device to permit directional control. Japan's Matsushita Electric Works corporation has pioneered an extension of this application, incorporating imported American virtual reality technology in a 'virtual kitchen' showroom launched in Tokyo in April 1991 (now also in North American showrooms). In this facility, customers can experience what a custom-built kitchen would look and feel like before it is built. They can, according to Gene Bylinsky, 'not only lay out their dream kitchens but also turn on faucets, pick up dishes – and even break them, if they happen to drop them while setting the table'.[30]

Academic and medical research institutions are also becoming increasingly involved with product applications. The University of North Carolina (UNC) at Chapel Hill has, for instance, attracted significant attention through developing programmes for architectural 'walkthroughs', scientific visualisations and medical analyses. Significant medical research projects are also under way at MIT, Stanford, Northwestern and UNC in conjunction with Apple Computers. These projects are perfecting systems that will allow surgeons to rehearse complex operations in virtual reality prior to surgery. Drug designers are another group of interested specialists, hoping to research the behaviour of pharmaceuticals on the molecular structure of diseases through new virtual reality simulations. While virtual reality offers exciting possibilities for education in general, it seems unlikely that the technology will be affordable to most schools and colleges in the immediate future. The museum and display gallery sector, however, is already exploring the use of virtual reality systems, with the San Francisco Observatory and the Smithsonian both investing in research and development.

As major studies such as Howard Rheingold's *Virtual Reality* have detailed, there are myriad possible applications of virtual reality technology to existing cultural, communicative and scientific practices.[31] It is, however, the integration of a whole series of computer-dependent media into a new 'meta-media' which makes virtual reality a truly distinct and innovative phenomenon. The nature of that phenomenon has yet to be realised. Gibson has offered us one vision in his novels, the military–industrial combine presumably imagines another, and cyber-gurus like Lanier and researchers like Laurel and Fisher posit others. As a meta-media, virtual reality is likely to be so all-encompassing that its 'reality' will need to be grasped philosophically rather than identified as a discrete area of communications practice. The 'ethical' component of this philosophy may well be crucial to the future of human society, and the inscription of human values into this new cyberspace is likely to be a long and complex process.

Thanks to Jill Scott and Sally Pryor for their assistance on this chapter.

NOTES

1. In a talk given at the University of Technology, Sydney, on October 9, 1991, Brenda Laurel explained the terminology thus: 'We use the word **telepresence** because the term virtual reality is an oxymoron. ... Most of us in the business dislike it a lot. The word 'virtual' is okay because in fact we're creating environments or realities that don't necessarily have concrete physical components to them. But the use of the word 'reality' in the

162

singular belies a certain cultural bias that most of us are not very comfortable with. And so perhaps a better word is the word that we use to define our company which is Telepresence. And the definition of telepresence is, a medium that allows you to take your body with you into some other environment. That's kind of metaphorical. What it really means is that you get to take some subset of your senses with you into another environment. And that environment may be a computer-generated environment, it may be a camera-originated environment, or it may be some combination of the two.'

2. Expanding on this, Randal Walser has identified a 'complete' cyberspace system as comprising:
   (a) a **cyberspace engine** to generate a simulated world and mediate the player's interaction with it;
   (b) a **control space** (a box of physical space) in which the player's movements are tracked;
   (c) **sensors** to monitor the player's actions and body functions;
   (d) **effectors** to produce certain physical effects and stimulate the player's senses;
   (e) **props** to give the player solid analogs of virtual objects and vehicles;
   (f) a **network interface** to admit other players to the simulated world, and
   (g) an **enclosure** (or some sort of physical framework) to hold all the components
   in his chapter 'Elements of a Cyberspace Playhouse', in Sandra K. Helsel and Judith Paris Roth (eds.), *Virtual Reality, Theory, Practice, and Promise* (Westport, CT: Meckler, 1991), pp. 57–8.
3. William Gibson, *Neuromancer* (London: Grafton Books, 1986), p. 67.
4. See, for example, the cyberpunk novels of Bruce Sterling.
5. Connie, the central character in Marge Piercy, *Woman On The Edge Of Time* (London: The Women's Press, 1976) escapes the horror of her personal circumstances and global problems by flipping into the panacea of her imaginary world.
6. Laurel, talk, University of Technology, Sydney.
7. Morton L. Heilig, US Patent 3,050,870 filed in 1961.
8. VPL have recently released their *Reality Built For Two* system that enables two users to interact in the virtual world. Flight simulator technology is also being used for applications such as *Star Tours* in Disneyland and *Tour of the Universe* in Toronto. These allow up to forty people on a motion platform whose movement is synchronised with a simulated display of a ride through the universe. The video display combines model-based and computer-generated images.
9. Ivan Sutherland, 'Sketchpad, a man-made graphical communication system' (PhD thesis, Massachusetts Institute of Technology, 1963).
10. This Sutherland helmet was significant in that it was designed for use with advanced graphics. Devised at MIT in the late 60s, Sutherland's helmet allowed the viewer to see computer-generated graphics superimposed on 'the real environment'. Other helmets, however, had been devised before the 'Sword of Damocles'. In 1958, the Philco Corporation developed a remote stereo-camera pair of goggles and head-mounted display that en-

abled 360-degree graphics. In alternative uses of the medium, some current head-mounted devices show a 2-D display to one eye while the other sees the real world (see notes on the Private Eye device in 'Living In A Virtual World' in *Byte*, July 1990, pp. 215–19. An offshoot of this is the development of helmets that can present computerised flight data in the form of holograms while also allowing see-through visibility and eliminating the need to look down at instrumentation. Such helmets are described in H.J. Caulfield et al., *Holography Works, Applications of Holography in Industry and Commerce* (New York: Museum of Holography, 1984).

11. See descriptions of Sutherland's and other work in Andy Darley, 'From Abstraction to Simulation: Notes on the History of Computer Imaging' in Philip Hayward (ed.), *Culture, Technology and Creativity in the Late Twentieth Century* (London: John Libbey/Arts Council of Great Britain, 1990), pp. 39–64.

12. The creation of more effective air pressure chambers, wider visibility and greater depth of field on the vertical spread requires further work.

13. Laurel, talk, University of Technology, Sydney.

14. For more detail about the Japanese robot industry, see Frederik L. Schodt, *Inside The Robot Kingdom: Japan, Mechatronics and the Coming Robotopia* (Tokyo: Kodansha International, 1988). Also, the huge but related area of artificial intelligence and the work of Marvin Minsky (an early founder of AI principles, commonly associated with MIT) is worth some examination.

15. However, Alan Kay (founder of the Vivarium project at MIT's Media Lab) with animator Glen Keene has been using the highly advanced flight simulator at Evans and Sutherland, Utah (the computer corporation founded by Ivan Sutherland), to create 'Infinite Reef', an underwater world with animated sharks that can be piloted by the user.

16. Stewart Brand, *The Media Lab: Inventing The Future At M.I.T.* (New York: Penguin, 1988), p. 139.

17. Evan Thomas and John Barry, 'War's new science' in *Newsweek*, 18 February 1991, p. 21.

18. Kevin Robins, *Into the Image: Visual Technologies and Vision Cultures* (mimeo, Centre for Urban and Regional Development Studies, Newcastle University, Newcastle upon Tyne, April 1991), p. 22.

19. Captain George Lindeman, formerly Manager of Flight Simulators for Flight Operations Training at Qantas (now retired), observes that, 'Trainee pilots enjoy playing [arcade] games because, in some ways, they're practising what they're doing here. They'd enjoy the simulators too, except for the instructors sitting at their backs!' Tom Wolfe's novel of the early American space race, *The Right Stuff* (New York: Bantam Books, 1979) also explores the connection between test flight pilots and games-playing.

20. Phil Campbell, 'Grab a slice of the Gulf War action, it's on again' in *Sydney Morning Herald*, 1 July 1991, p. 17.

21. 3-D images in the form of holographic displays are being developed, although experts predict that it will be some time before these are sufficiently advanced to be used in VR systems.

22. Lanier also collaborated with NASA researchers to develop a virtual drum kit.

23. An AGE precursor to the Power Glove was prototyped in 1986 and later abandoned. Called 3-E, to suggest a step beyond 3-D, it mixed live-action with computer-generated videos. The Gentile brothers claim their inspiration for the Power Glove to be a favourite episode of the 1960s television series *The Outer Limits*, entitled 'Demon With the Glass Hand'. Research into sensors and tracking devices has continued for more than fifteen years. At Ohio State University, there's been work on mounting light-emitting diodes on dancers' bodies to gain information on where the body is in a prescribed space. Brenda Laurel has been involved with 'non-encrusting interfaces' for body-tracking such as 'smart' floors that know where users are stepping and predict trunk movement by the shape of a foot, and bodies breaking infra-red beams or curtains of light and this movement being recorded, and so on. See detailed technical information on data gloves, sensors, and force feedback systems, in a seminal article published in October 1987 in *Scientific American* by James D. Foley, 'Interfaces for Advanced Computing', pp. 82–90.

24. Scott S. Fisher, 'Virtual Environments: Personal Simulations & Telepresence' in Sandra K. Helsel and Judith Paris Roth (eds.), *Virtual Reality*, p. 105.

25. Myron W. Krueger, *Artificial Intelligence* (Reading, USA: Addison-Wesley, 1983). The book derives from a dissertation manuscript prepared between 1972 and 1974 and has since been updated and reprinted.

26. Paul Brown, 'Metamedia and Cyberspace' in Philip Hayward (ed.), *Culture, Technology and Creativity*, p. 235.

27. See Rebecca Coyle, 'Treading Terra Technic: Advanced Technology Artworks by Paula Dawson and Jill Scott' in *Artlink*, vol. 10 no. 4, Summer 1990, pp. 46–8. See also the work at MIT including that of the Architecture Machine Group which, in the late seventies, created the Aspen Movie Map, a virtual representation of the town of Aspen, Colorado. Users could move around the representation of the town via a touch-sensitive screen.

28. Brenda Laurel, 'Virtual Reality Design: A Personal View' in Sandra K. Helsel and Judith Paris Roth (eds.), *Virtual Reality*, p. 99.

29. Myron Krueger, 'Artificial Reality: Past and Future' in Sandra K. Helsel and Judith Paris Roth (eds.), *Virtual Reality*, p. 25.

30. Gene Bylinsky, 'The Marvels of "Virtual Reality"' in *Fortune International*, vol. 123 no. 12, 3 June 1991, p. 96. Bylinsky goes on to relate that the first customer in the virtual kitchen spent an hour in the virtual room and then 'had to pay with real money when she wound up buying $30,000 worth of appliances'.

31. Howard Rheingold, *Virtual Reality* (London: Secker and Warburg, 1991).

VIRTUAL REALITY
Beyond Cartesian Space

Sally Pryor and Jill Scott

Indented text is from a diary kept by Jill Scott while visiting Virtual Reality (VR) research centres in the United States in 1990; non-indented text is by Sally Pryor.

Seeing Reality

> At the University of North Carolina at Chapel Hill (UNC) they encourage me to 'hop in'. I am given a yellow ball whose magnetic field tells the computer its position and orientation in space. I put on the heavy VPL EyePhones and the room suddenly disappears. It is replaced by the interior of a geometric, plastic-looking, green and pale blue room. If I point the ball, my body seems to move forward in the room. The EyePhones sit heavily on my cheeks, forcing my eyes open even wider to gaze closely at the rather bad resolution.
>
> Floating ahead of me is a cluster of protein molecules. My first response is to move around and become orientated. The magnetic tracker on my head tells the computer how my head is positioned, so I can look up and down and around the room. There is a slight lag as the frames try to keep up with my movement, but I am really tricked into thinking I am inside the room.
>
> I turn around to look at another floating cluster which represents a drug called mucotracyne. I can grasp this with my tracker ball by placing an arrow over the image; when I press the cursor button the drug follows the movement of my hands. I then try to complete the required task – that is to dock the drug into

the protein cluster so that it fits tightly. I do this successfully and with surprising ease. The task's completion gives me new confidence. I 'hop out'. It is nice to see everyone again but it is surprising to have to re-orientate myself to the natural light of my surroundings.

I ask to see more . . .

Since the word 'reality' is used extensively in discussions of Virtual Reality (for example in VPL's product, 'Reality Built for Two'), it would be appropriate to look at the way reality is represented and manipulated in a virtual world. When the user 'hops in' to Virtual Reality (VR), she enters a computer-generated world which usually consists of objects in a three-dimensional space. The user enters this space through viewing a series of images (on the EyePhones for example) and perceiving sound and other sensory information (such as force feedback) that give the impression that she is interacting and moving within it. The visual images are calculated by computers, based on the view of this space that would be seen by a camera attached to the current position of the viewer's head. Each object in the space has been defined as a three-dimensional (3-D) shape located within a 3-D Cartesian space, that is, a grid calibrated with X, Y and Z axes (Fig. 1). Objects have also been numerically described in terms of position, orientation, movement, shape, colour, surface qualities, behavioural

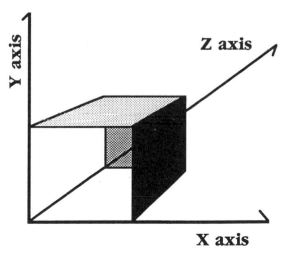

Fig. 1 The Cartesian Coordinate System

167

characteristics and so on. These parameters can change with time, interactions and context.

This space has certain limitations. Artificial shapes are easier to digitise (that is, to convert to a digital description) than natural ones. Whereas a cube could be described by the location in 3-D space of eight points and six faces, a rock or a human face is much more complicated. It is much easier to work with manufactured, regular objects than those of the natural world, which is possibly what Laurie Anderson meant when she said. 'There's no dirt in here' after experiencing VR.[1] In order to give the user the impression of moving and interacting within a space, VR systems must calculate and display a new image up to sixty times per second. As a virtual world becomes more complex, the time required to compute and deliver a response becomes longer: one frame of a contemporary, state-of-the-art, 3-D computer-generated animation can take as much as thirty minutes' computer time to calculate. It is clear that compromises and simplifications must be made in order to approximate a 'real-time' response. Various strategies are being used to make this computation fast enough to simulate 'real time', but for a while we must accept rather simplistic imagery and sluggish responsiveness in VR.

For these reasons alone, current state-of-the-art VR worlds are not convincing enough to be seriously confused with the 'real thing'. More importantly, the representation of 'reality' in VR is actually a highly specific view of the world, a view which unthinkingly assumes a Western tradition and ideology. VR rests on an unstated foundation of conventions such as Cartesian space, objective realism and linear perspective. It is easy to assume these conventions to be neutral and transparent, to be part of the way everybody sees reality, but in fact they are deeply rooted in an historical philosophy that privileges perspective, with its implications of detachment, objectivity and observation. This positions the Self behind a 'camera' looking at a window on the world, separate and distinct from his/her environment. VR adds something unique to this familiar approach in that the detached viewer is mapped back into the space and is able to interact with it to some extent, but this sense of separation between viewer and the represented world still lingers.

Interacting with the World

> ... I hop in again. I spontaneously walk toward the door in the artificial room and simultaneously walk toward the real door in

the actual room. My intuitive response causes strange things to happen. Voices tell me I have ventured outside the range of the magnetic polhemus sensor near the computer. I trip over some cables and it reminds me that I am connected. Restricted by being connected. Soon, I become used to the fact that my head and my hands are moving me in this artificial space, not my feet. It takes a while to register. It also takes time to sort out exactly how to place my body, but the system is hampered by magnetic interference outside my control. Now it is flashing, I obviously tilted my head too far. Interesting to be so concerned about the body's exact position in space!

... They tell me the addition of sound and force feedback will make the worlds much more convincing. Later at VPL I am given the chance to test this for myself as samples from a sound library are triggered with the completion of certain visual tasks. It is true, the sound really helps me to feel transported into the particular worlds.

I wonder what it would be like to add the sensations of smell, touch and taste?

How does the user relate to the world in VR? Not so long ago, input and output were terms that described the information that went into and out of a computer. Today these terms are also used when referring to the information going into and out of the person who is in VR.[2] This information is classified into categories such as visual (what the user sees), auditory (sounds and the user's voice), haptic (touch, temperature, pressure), proprioceptive (current body configuration), vestibular (orientation, movement, acceleration), olfactory (smell) and taste. Thus in a virtual world, a person sees, hears and feels things that encourage her to believe that she is within this world and that it is responding to her.

At the current state of VR development, the primary inputs to the user are visual, auditory and, to a lesser extent, haptic (such as force feedback devices which give the impression of weight or pressure). The primary outputs come from magnetic tracking devices which measure the user's movements and from haptic devices (such as buttons or joysticks) which record touch and the exertion of force. In the experiences Jill relates above, for example, she communicates with the virtual world through the tracker ball. She moves through its space via head and hand movements, not her legs. She sees herself represented in this world in a rather disembodied way – as an arrow cursor – the most minimal representation of oneself in VR.

Devices such as the data glove and data suit enable not only a wider range of inputs from the user's body but also the construction of more complex images, increasing the amount of computation required. Although these images can approximate to the way the body appears in 'real' life, they do not do so necessarily. Moving a data-suit-clad arm could lead to the sight in VR of one's arm moving, someone else's leg kicking, an octopus tentacle waving, a wave breaking – there are endless possibilities. The Challenger astronaut Judy Resnick operated a mechanical arm which was controlled from within a space shuttle but was capable of lifting solar panels and performing other tasks outside the ship. Her job involved looking at a monitor and manipulating sensitive electronic controls to manipulate this arm, her training involved learning to experience this gigantic arm as an extension of her body. In a similar way, VR represents a kind of extension and re-mapping of the body, a de-naturing of its organic, holistic nature and a reconstruction of it in 3-D space as digital cyborg (part machine, part human). This represents a kind of uncoupling of oneself, an interception and substantial manipulation of a presumed space between thinking and doing, mind and body. VR gets under your skin.

Metaphysics, the Body and Technology

Now I am poised on the top of a roller coaster path which winds in a hilly way before me. This world responds only to my head movements. The visuals simulate the sensation of riding in the first car of a roller coaster whose tracks meander dangerously, gliding toward me. Up and down I go, I cannot help bending at the knees as I slide down. 'Do I look ridiculous from out there?' 'Yes,' they all say. Would children mind if their body moved in such a silly way responding to the motion of the graphics?

I imagine how strange it would be to look in through the door of a Virtual Reality game parlour with the cable-connected bodies and terminals. Perhaps Virtual Reality could make them feel sick? This roller coaster is certainly a stomach test.

The technicians change programmes to another game. I'm in a maze of rooms with an elevator. I immediately bang into the wall, disoriented. I use the arrow to fly around. 'Turn around,' they yell. As I turn, a simple diagram of a flying bird comes towards me, its mouth opening and closing aggressively. It's trying to eat

170

me. 'Point backwards at yourself', they yell. I immediately zoom
away from the bird.

What are the metaphysics of this body in virtual space? Answering this
question means considering its origins. Despite recent philosophical
and scientific theories,[3] a dualist tradition permeates the metaphysics
of science and technology which is especially apparent when the mind
and body are conceptualised. The influence of René Descartes lingers
on. For Descartes, the mind/body split was a reality. The body was
defined by its capacity to occupy space whereas the mind was conceptual, based on Reason. Thus the body was spatial and not conceptual;
mind was conceptual but not spatial. Subjectivity, that is, the sense of
being 'I', was identified with the conceptual side of this opposition, the
mind, thus relegating the body to the status of an object, outside of and
distinct from consciousness. This binary opposition is commonly associated with a number of other binary pairs: self and other, subject
and object, culture and nature, reason and emotion, male and female,
public and private. The mind is associated with culture, rationality, the
self, even the masculine; body is correlated with nature, the emotions,
the object and, of course, the feminine. Elizabeth Grosz adds that
'Within this structure the opposed terms are not equally valued: one
term occupies the structurally dominant position and takes on the
power of defining its opposite or other ... by negation.'[4] These dualistic values emerge from a logocentric presupposition that being, language and knowledge are self-evident, neutral and transparent terms
rather than social and cultural constructions. They are a powerful,
almost unstated, subsconscious framework for so many Western
philosophical, scientific and technological traditions.

There has always been an intimate relationship between the latest
technology and how human beings are conceptualised. Descartes, for
example, thought a sick man was like a badly-made clock. This mechanical metaphor is now shifting to one based on computers or robots,
spreading from its birth in scientific and technical circles as the use of
computers proliferates – the input/output model for the user in VR is
one such example.[5] What does it mean to be like a computer? The
computer is made of software (programmes) and hardware (the physical components), categories which align themselves all too easily along
the dualistic mind and body model. Linking software to mind and
hence to the Self, we derive a concept of the Self as software, as a
disembodied set of rules, processing, instructions and knowledges.
Hans Moravec, director of the Mobile Robot Laboratory at Carnegie

Mellon University, postulates a post-biological world, in which a human mind is freed from its brain and loaded into self-improving, thinking machines that he calls 'mind children'.[6] He talks of our 'uneasy truce between mind and body' and recommends that 'human thought [be] released from bondage to a mortal body'. Moravec considers the essence of himself to rest in 'the pattern and process going on in his head and body, not the machinery supporting that process ... the rest is mere jelly'.

Leaving aside the assumption of the mind residing in the brain and the question of whether a mind/body separation is actually possible – it seems highly unlikely – this idea of a disembodied, cerebral self exerts a seductive appeal. Western socialisation involves experience of sexism, racism, power and control and produces an ambivalent and highly-gendered combination of feelings – such as fear, loathing, pleasure and desire – around the notion of the body. It is not surprising that the body, subject to vulnerability, pain and mortality, can become something from which it seems desirable to escape. Could you feel pain if you had no body? Could you experience racism or sexism? A somewhat disembodied self, mediated via telepresence (see Rebecca Coyle, pp. 148–65), might be appropriate in environments such as hazardous radioactive situations, modern warfare or in space, where the body is truly obsolete. But it would not be much fun when holding your baby, to cite just one activity. My experience of the computing and high technology world is that it is populated by men like Moravec who are strongly identified and involved with their thoughts and ideas, and not so much with their bodies. Without being particularly aware of it, they reproduce the mind/body split in the technologies they produce.

Remapping Oneself, Interaction, Symbiosis

The introductory segment of the Body Electric software at VPL offers a pre-selection room where simply designed computers sit on a table. I can fly through the monitor screens into the world of my choice. Even though the ease of getting in through these screens is restricted by magnetic tracking, they still show the potential for a greater element of choice. This awkwardness of movement really needs solving. The technicians tell me about the use of an optical tracker instead of a magnetic one and how this, in combination with better response (refresh rate) and better resolution and sound makes the interaction more convincing.

172

... I enter a space where a mirror is hanging. As I move my head an x moves with me in the mirror. 'That is you', one technician yells. I play with my x clone in delight. The technicians tell me not to go through the mirror because I will shrink. Shrink in what way? I have to try it as the comment doesn't compute. I find myself in a replica of the same room I left. The response to everything is suddenly very slow so I fly backwards, out again. The contact points vary again. Suddenly I feel like the computer may have control over me. Resistance starts to build up inside my real body. I tear off the EyePhones and hop out quickly. I have a splitting headache ...

The development of VR seems to reflect this fantasy of a disembodied self and a dualistic world view. It is as if the user is assumed to be separate from her (Cartesian) world. Her view of it is mediated through the detached eye of a camera, delivering objective realism and linear perspective. The only place she cannot see is inside her head. Her body is mapped back into this world, but in a semi-abstract sense that uncouples her from her real body even while the dominant impression is of her body acting within and around the virtual space. In VR the user becomes a source and a consumer of a variety of information. She becomes a kind of computer, or more accurately, a cyborg. Naturally there are both positive and negative aspects to this. Working with a computer is a somewhat disembodied process – eyes, mind and hands are the only things directly involved. Sore shoulders, headaches and Repetitive Strain Injury (RSI) soon alert you to the folly of ignoring bodily sensations for too long, although it is extremely easy to do. Personally, I long to transcend the limitations of keyboard and mouse and express myself with the computer by involving my body more. I have a fantasy of wearing a data suit and doing dance movements not only to tell the computer what I want it to do (find a file, start another programme and so on) but also to create an image, an animation or music. I want the computer to read body language. Since VR implies this might be possible it might allow communication with the computer to become much more intimate, more personally involved.

There are potential applications of VR which are very interesting and would be socially useful. An example is implied by Jaron Lanier's story of teaching himself juggling in VR by slowing down time – this has fascinating implications for people with physically challenged bodies.[7] As a scientist, I find the possibilities for visualisation and manipulation of complex processes thrilling. As an artist, I can imagine

VR enabling an art-form involving the audience in a truly unique way. As a teacher, I can see immense benefits for students, particularly as they can learn at their own pace. But as a human being, am I willing to work in strong magnetic fields, to be so intimately connected to the machine? Has anyone investigated the effects of VR technology on our not yet obsolete bodies?

Broadly speaking, communication between people and computers will be the most fruitful application of VR but, as with the telephone and more recently, electronic mail, it will be disembodied information that is exchanged. Certain frustrations will remain, for example trying to communicate with one's intimate partner over a long-distance phone call, you can talk all you can afford but there are some things you cannot communicate through speech. VR could alleviate this by enabling communication through a kind of body language which will extend the possibilities considerably. Interacting with people in VR will certainly be fruitful and exciting, but it will still be disembodied numbers that will be exchanged. This cannot be the same as communicating in person.

Virtual Bodies/Virtual Sex

In a new world, I can grab a silly character and throw it around the room. This slippery little yellow toy creature squeals with delight but as I pick it up it stops yelling, like a baby. When I drop it, it makes a loud thud. It seems to scream with delight especially when it is thrown against the wall, and I am reminded once again of the violence VR is capable of procuring under the guise of entertainment. ...

They tell me that sound in combination with force feedback will really change things especially in relation to interacting with others in VR. They demonstrate a world they are currently making. I watch transfixed as the technician manipulates a ball on the monitor. A sexual sigh happens as repeatedly it is sloshed slowly into another object and extracted again. With simultaneous sound the ramifications for sexual interface are considerable.

The concept of Virtual Sex (VS) sneaks around the periphery of many discussions about VR, although developers are uncomfortable with the fascination this topic arouses. It is mentioned at least once in many general articles about VR and whole features are being written about it, accompanied sometimes by a picture of a current sex symbol, who

174

would presumably be 'invited' to the VS session.[8] This writing is mostly overexcited speculation, as the technology has not advanced much past simple interaction with a virtual body, such as the enormous so-called sex goddess conjured up by VPL for a visiting, nameless Hollywood director.[9] According to the story, as related in chapter 9, he enjoyed flying around her enormous nipples and then moved on to something else. ... The terminology of VS is puzzling. When a man has intercourse with a blow-up doll, it would be more likely to be called masturbation than sex. However, sexual activity in VR is being called Virtual Sex or Teledildonics rather than masturbation, which is what it actually resembles. The user enacts sexual activity with (say) Julia Roberts in VR, but the images he sees are not directly connected to the device(s) that are providing sexual stimulation, although they may seem to be.

The excitement about VS makes uneasy reading. It seems to perpetuate the well-documented objectification of bodies, particularly women's bodies, in pornography. Many assumptions are made in these effusive articles – the equivalence of a 'sensitive' interactive system with a living partner, the importance of the penis in sexual pleasure, the notion that women would find VS as desirable as men would, that VS represents a sensible solution to loneliness and isolation, the threat of AIDS and so on. A look at contemporary computer-based pornography is not reassuring. *Macplaymate*, a widely circulating, Macintosh-based programme, offers the user a selection of implements (hand, dildo, surrogate partner) with which to disrobe and stimulate a 'woman'. 'She' is there as a graphics image, displayed in a Playboy-type pose, to have things done to 'her' and to make the user feel powerful and excited – click with the mouse button to remove 'her' shirt and bra ... and so on. To be thrilled by the idea of VS, I would need to be sure that *Macplaymate* is not its 'father', but if involvement of the lucrative pornography industry can be assumed, VS is more likely to encourage notions of power over, detachment from and objectivity towards other bodies (mostly female) than to help resolve our complicated ambivalence about real bodies and intimacy. Al Goldstein, publisher of amongst other things *Screw* Magazine, has described his desire for a robot lover: 'My fantasy is to ... phase the wife out of the picture, to come home and hear a robot greet me ... My wife knows she's on the way out. She's like a buffalo. She knows she's here temporarily until technology catches up.'[10] While being Al's wife does not seem like a bad job to lose, his comment articulates a movement that, together with developments in Reproductive Technology, has

175

profound implications. If, through the development of these technologies, women's bodies were ever to be made redundant for sexual intercourse and for creating new life, discrimination against women (mediated as it is through presumed ties to the body) would have no basis. Alternatively, there might be no socially perceived role for real women at all.

Virtual Conclusions

... I find myself inside a kitchen with all the appliances and cons intact. I can open the refrigerator (clunk) take out the rather unappetizing pizza (swaab) from the shelf and put it on the table. I can carry the plates to the kitchen sink where taps can be turned on and off (sound of water), and generally busy myself with a tidy up or a mess. We find out that this VR world is the only one we have seen designed by a woman. A fair amount of detail has been given to the structure and the mobility of objects within the kitchen but I still manage to slip up and collide with the pizza. I make a joke about wishing to change the velocity, to clean up in fast mode and the technicians say they are working on it.

... I fly above the artificial world of Vancouver Harbor where 'vehicles' are ferries slowly leaving from one dock and travelling to another. The water is in simulated motion and there is a simulated Revolving Restaurant Tower on one of the Headlands. As I move toward the Restaurant I can hear voices of the clients inside. If I go down onto the dock I hear seagulls and the horns of the ferries. I ask whether I can dive into the water. 'Sure can,' the technician replies. I go through the surface with my own squeal accompanied by a pre-recorded splash. I don't exactly have the feeling of floating but a couple of simple-looking fish swim by. I like this world a lot. It seems easier for me to interact in my own time and space. I fly out, WOOSH, and try to fly as high as possible into the sky. The landscape shrinks below me to the size of a tabletop miniature set.

... We talk about the fact that VR may replace TV, but I am concerned about VR becoming the cause of a new type of couch potato. Unless it remains very interactive and allows the spectator to participate in the creation of new worlds, VR will remain a novelty. At VPL, Jody Gillerman and I talk about the hyperbole which promotes VR as invention, the ultimate VR computer able to control the existence of matter. Unless it can help us solve the shocking conditions of the planet, why would we want it to take so much control?

The popular and the computer press are leaping on the VR bandwagon with an understandable but rather disturbing euphoria. VR can be seen to represent a retreat from direct experience of the senses, the body, each other and our (polluted) environment. Is this really a solution to the problem of modern life – to turn a blind eye to what is happening and to what we are doing to this world by re-mapping ourselves into digitally-mediated, synthetic fantasy worlds?

It is hard to comprehend fully the development and implications of VR: aside from its technical complexities, it engages with potent philosophical constructs. Supposedly dualist alternatives, such as mind and body, culture and nature, self and other, inside and outside, presence and absence, reality and fantasy, sex and love are open for re-inspection. VR has the potential to change definitions of reality, of presence, of point of view and of identity – the question is, how will those definitions be changed?

When Francis Bacon wrote in the sixteenth century, 'We will place nature on the rack and torture her secrets out of her', he articulated an approach to the world that defines Women, Nature and the Body as mysterious Others, in opposition to and separated from the Self. Although contemporary philosophy has moved far beyond this dualist model, its conceptual framework lingers, particularly in the world of technological development. As we have seen, VR may be used to reassert rather than question or dismantle it. In this light it is impossible to ignore the involvement of military and space applications in the development of VR and for this reason it is very important to extend debates about VR and about its development. We all, not a select few, have to decide what relationships we want to have with computers, what we want them to do with, to and for us. Donna Harraway points out that information technologies are bringing far-reaching changes in the way that boundaries are conceived and constituted. 'There are ... great riches for feminists in explicitly embracing the possibilities inherent in a breakdown of clean distinctions between organism and machine and similar distinctions structuring the Western self. ... Any objects or persons can [now] be reasonably thought of in terms of disassembly and reassembly.'[11] This violation of boundaries can be seen as a liberating opportunity to discard oppressive constructs and/or as a chance for new but equally restrictive definitions.

Virtual Reality is located at a major point of intersection between

Humans and Computers: it makes disturbingly intimate symbioses possible. This is an important historical moment. Can we use this opportunity to dismantle oppressive dualistic divisions or will the limited variety of people involved with technological development unwittingly reinvent or re-erect them, becoming 'ghosts lost in the cosmos of their own abstractions'?[12] This re-encoding of dualisms is, as we have seen, intrinsic to VR technology. We are not compelled to perpetuate this model of the world in VR, but it could happen very easily.

> ... I can hear the sounds of the technicians talking 'outside' who try to orientate me 'inside'. My brain is having some trouble differentiating between the real and the artificial. Could this be dangerous?
>
> ... Later another artist, Sally, and I discuss other societies' different attitudes toward time. We in the West have been trained to exist in linear time, a stressful habit we have adopted for convenience and progress, while some other societies exist in polychronic time with flexible schedules and simultaneous constructs, or in circular time where all history is fiction because all things return to a former state. I think we tend to exaggerate this in the form of narrative film, where the plot unfolds in a linear construction. By comparison, in VR, I am able to move in this type of simultaneous time as I can move in simulated real time, backwards and forwards, up and down, by choice. I ask Sally if she thinks interactive experiences of simultaneous time may influence our approach to time in real life. She agrees the very term 'real-time' sounds like a paradox. Perhaps there will be no effect as we disconnect from the fiction of electronic space and time and lock back into the 'rush hour' of reality. I would like to try to experiment with the notion of circular time. We talk about savouring the moment or just the fact of being in VR without having any tasks to do. Perhaps it could become a great device for meditation after all.

Thanks to Rebecca Coyle for her assistance on this chapter.

NOTES

1. Laurie Anderson quoted in 'Brave New World' by Stephen Levy, in *Rolling Stone*, vol. 448, October 1990.
2. Richard Holloway, University of North Carolina at Chapel Hill, 'Virtual Reality and Art', a paper given at the Second International Symposium on Electronic Art, Gronigen, Holland, 1990.
3. Poststructuralist theories (for example the work of Jacques Derrida) and chaos theory.
4. Elizabeth Grosz, *Sexual Subversions* (Sydney: Allen and Unwin, 1989), p. 27.
5. Sally Pryor, 'Thinking of Oneself as a Computer', *Leonardo*, vol. 24 no. 5 (1991).
6. Hans Moravec, *Mind Children* (Cambridge: Harvard University Press, 1988), p. 4.
7. Stephen Levy, 'Brave New World', in *Rolling Stone*, vol. 448, October 1990.
8. See for instance Howard Rheingold's 'Teledildonics: Reach Out and Touch Someone' in *Mondo 2000* no. 2, Summer 1990.
9. Stephen Levy, 'Brave New World'.
10. Quoted by Geoff Simons in *Silicon Shock* (Oxford: Blackwell, 1985), p. 130.
11. Donna Harraway, 'A Manifesto for Cyborgs: Science, Technology and Socialist Feminism in the 1980s', in *Australian Feminist Studies*, Autumn 1987, p. 29.
12. Robert Romanyshyn, *Technology as Symptom and Dream* (London: Routledge, 1989), p. 101.

SITUATING CYBERSPACE
The Popularisation of Virtual Reality

Philip Hayward

Diffusion and Resonance

Cyberspace is currently a 'hot' topic. The mainstream press, TV News and current affairs programming have all approached it as a news-worthy phenomenon. Recent innovations in interactive computer technologies have therefore seemed to burst onto the scene, to have moved from prototype to primetime in one easy leap. The spread of news about the phenomenon has, however, been less explosive than this model suggests. Analysis reveals a more gradual pattern of diffusion through a range of (sub)cultural channels whose character and concerns have moulded the public image and perception of the phenomenon itself.

The first publication to break the news of the developments in computer interfacing which precipitated virtual reality was the monthly popular science magazine *Scientific American*. The cover of their October 1987 issue carried the following proclamation:

> The next revolution in computers, the subject of this issue, will see power increase tenfold in 10 years while networks and advanced interfaces transform computing into a universal intellectual utility.

The image chosen to accompany this bold prophecy was seemingly modest – a picture of a data glove and its computer graphic double – but as James Foley's article 'Interfaces for Advanced Computing' emphasised, the technology offered a profound breakthrough in interacting with the 'artificial reality' of computer graphic programmes.[1]

180

The implications of this 'next revolution' stimulated interest in a variety of circles.

Detailed technical description and information soon began to appear in specialist computer magazines and speculation about the technology's potential also began to feature in more general publications. This, in turn, led to the establishment of magazines such as the American *Mondo 2000* and the Australian *Index*, which combined coverage of the new computer media with rock and other 'counter-cultural' topics. By 1990 this diffusion had reached the mainstream media with publications such as the *Wall Street Journal* (US) and the *Guardian* (UK) running major features on cyberspace and virtual reality. Mainstream radio and television subsequently followed suit. In Winter 1990 ABC TV News (US) ran their first item on it and the Virgin/MTV youth magazine programme *Buzz* produced a report which included an interview with virtual reality pioneer Jaron Lanier. By 1991, coverage of the phenomenon had become widespread as information and speculation diffused further and as cyberspace systems and their advocates became more readily available to journalists.

Enthusiasm for the phenomenon has, in part, arisen from the substantial technological innovations in computer technology that have been achieved over the past five years. However, this steady rise in interest more accurately reflects the manner in which the medium's developers and advocates have successfully publicised their radical claims for it. The credence and enthusiasm accorded to Lanier and his fellow pioneers by their adjacent subculture have, in publicity terms, created a major 'buzz' about their activities. Cyberspace – as a promised phenomenon – has caught the imagination first of a subculture and now of a wider public. The medium's heightened rise in profile can be seen to have resulted from a mutually supportive convergence of interests and affinities between practitioners, aficionados and writers.

Unsurprisingly perhaps, given the continuing male dominance of high-tech research and development, the key players in the promotion of cyberspace have principally been white middle-class American males in their thirties and forties. Its main advocates belong to a specific social group comprising individuals who have clung to residual 'counter-cultural' notions, most often articulated within terms of a loose Green–Libertarian rhetoric, while being assimilated into certain sectors of the American professional classes. This group is most notably represented by the computer industries, the culture of Silicon Valley itself and key generational figures such as Apple founder Steve Job. Lanier's interests, rhetoric and background appeal strongly to this group. His impeccably 'counter-cultural' appearance distinguishes him, and other key figures of the 'new wave', from the preceding generation of cyberspace pioneers whose interests and profile were representative of their positions within the American military-industrial combine.

By 1991, cyberspace and 'virtual reality' existed as much as figments of a (sub)cultural imagination as they did as 'real' phenomena. A group of (often overlapping) popular cultural discourses has preceded the medium's introduction by framing, contextualising and predicting the development of cyberspace systems and their virtual experiences. These have served to fix cyberspace in the popular imagination in particular configurations. As this chapter will go on to argue, along with the Techno-Futurist aesthetic discussed in this book's introduction, the most influential of these have been science fiction, rock culture, psychedelia and 'New Age' mysticism.

These discourses are significant because they have shaped both consumer desire and the perceptions and agenda of the medium's developers. In a particularly ironic twist of what must now perhaps be considered 'Late Postmodernism' they have created a simulacrum of the medium *in advance* (against which its products will be compared). As Kevin Robins has emphasised:

> As the idea of virtual reality entertainment comes to public awareness, what is clear is that the imaginative mould has already been set: there is already a wholehearted agreement about its 'revolutionary' significance and a deafening consensus about its 'challenging' potential.[2]

Derived from a set of existing cultural discourses, the 'imaginative mould' of cyberspace substantially replicates a number of their characteristics and ideologies. Analysis of these provides us with a base from which to assess the nature of those radical claims made for the new medium. In particular, an understanding of contexts enables us to analyse the central role played by figures such as Lanier and William Gibson, who, repeatedly interviewed about similar issues, have produced a sizeable, if repetitive, body of argument, characterisation and prophecy. As Robins has also pointed out, frequent reference to Lanier and Gibson is almost *de rigueur* for any study of cyberspace; as is a checklist of other references for discussion.[3] In this manner, this analysis of paradigms of critical and descriptive discourse mirrors its object of analysis but, in doing so, aims to establish the highly tendentious nature of the discourse's key themes and motifs.

Gibson – Science Fiction and Prophecy

> At the time he wrote *Neuromancer*, Gibson had no idea that NASA was working on real artificial reality, or that artificial intelligence researchers were trying to make thinking machines, or even that some physicists were theorising that the universe could be a computer and God a hacker. ... But these themes were all 'adrift' in the zeitgeist' of science fiction which was Gibson's guilty literary pleasure.[4]

Discussions of cyberspace have principally addressed its potential in terms of a set of applications which appear to be just beyond the technological horizon. In this sense, even when most sober and technically informed, discussions of likely social and cultural developments premised on the delivery of new technologies have followed the classic mode of (predictive) science *fiction*. And just as science fiction in general has tended to inform – or even determine – the nature, character and perceptions of subsequent science fact; so writing on cyberspace has created the conditions for a form which still principally exists in prototype. Writing ahead of actual technologies and accomplishment, virtual reality practitioners have fired the imagination of writers and the public about cyberspace much as early science fiction magazines stimulated interest in the potential of space travel (that voyage into *outer* space whose representation in many ways prefigured today's voyages into the virtual space of the computer programme).

Whereas the well-established tradition of science fiction can be seen to have produced a group of predictive 'fathers' for such science *fact* developments as space travel (Jules Verne, Arthur C. Clarke etc.), the emergent cyberspace scene has one principal literary progenitor, William Gibson. Almost all sustained pieces of journalism on the topic have acknowledged his influence. Gibson and subsequent writers are seen to have modernised and reinflected the technological aspect of science fiction. The 'Cyberpunk' genre initiated by Gibson has been credited with shifting the advanced hardware preoccupation of the mainstream science fiction genre towards the world of computer software and its interaction with human 'wetware' (the brain).

Although Gibson's work has provided a significant reinflection of the genre, such themes were present in earlier science fiction. As Robin

183

Baker emphasises in Chapter 2 of this anthology, mainstream cinema, for instance, produced some of the earliest prefigurations of cyberspace in films such as *Tron* (1982) and *The Last Starfighter* (1985). These, and other films, attempted to take the interactive computer games that were coming into vogue in the early 80s and posit alternative 'realities' constituted by (and *within*) these. *Tron* is particularly significant in this regard for its attempt to show the human literally inserted into the 3-D computer world – a harsh electronic reality every bit as complex as the first generation of virtual 'worlds' currently being designed. Although its population of sentient games-players is unlikely to be matched by any cyberspace programme until both memory capacity and super-intelligent (SI) computer systems are considerably more developed, its computer game antecedence renders it a convincing model of what the first fully interactive cyberspace games may be like.

The science fiction connection is not just a convenient basis for comparative discussion but has been a major influence on the development of the medium. Key cyberspace pioneer, publicist and director of leading company VPL, Jaron Lanier, for instance, comes from a background infused with such ideas. His father was a science fiction author and acquaintance of fellow writer L. Ron Hubbard (who went on to found the science-fiction-inspired Church of Scientology). Prominent critics such as Paul Brown have declared themselves 'avid fans' of the genre.[5] More significantly, though, rather than a computer hacker, Silicon Valley whizz-kid or games company executive, it is Gibson who is almost universally cited as 'father' of the concepts and imagination which have shaped the cultural perceptions and directions of new computer media.

Gibson's novel *Neuromancer*, tapped out on a manual typewriter and published in the auspicious year of 1984, was the first of his now famous 'Cyberpunk' trilogy. Its successors *Count Zero* and *Mona Lisa Overdrive* appeared in 1986 and 1988 respectively. Gibson's significance and predictive acuity have been acclaimed by a range of critics and practitioners. Timothy Leary, the Sixties drug guru, now a passionate advocate of 'revolutionary' electronic technologies, has described Gibson's novels as presenting 'an epic-encyclopedic guide book to the cybernetic world that is already emerging'.[6] Critic Paul Brown has also described Gibson's work as 'canonical texts' which have been a 'main source of inspiration'.[7] Fredric Jameson has singled out Gibson, and the Cyberpunk genre, as 'the supreme literary expression ... of late capitalism'.[8] And, at its most inflated, Gibson has even been characterised by Leary as the 'writer who was to define the politics, culture and philosophy of the Information Age of the Nineties'[9] and provider of 'the underlying myth of the next stage of human evolution'.[10]

Yet, as some observers have noted, the promotion of Gibson as herald of a new age of computer media is a somewhat curious enterprise. Firstly, it requires the relegation of the development of cyberspace technology to a secondary role. Gibson, after all, neither initiated the development of the technologies which combined to produce cyberspace systems, nor exerted any influence on their early application. Its origins can instead be traced back to Ivan Sutherland's and Myron Krueger's initial experiments and to NASA's early experimental programme – all initiatives of which Gibson was unaware when writing the early novels.[11] Secondly, the adoption of Gibson as prophet to a generation of hackers, scientists etc. requires a highly selective reading of the fictional trilogy; one which extricates the conceptual system of cyberspace (and its applications) from the overall context his books establish.

The perception of the trilogy as a blueprint for a technologically utopian society involves a particular process of reinterpretation or, perhaps more accurately, 'skewing'. Despite the bleak, violent, polluted and amoral world Gibson sketched in his novels, many readers – and, significantly, many computer aficionados – have interpreted the domain of cyberspace as an imminent technological utopia. Much to his surprise, the dystopian elements of his best-known novels have been largely ignored. As he has repeatedly emphasised:

> I was delighted when scientists and corporate technicians started to read me, but I soon realised that all the critical pessimistic left-wing stuff just goes over their heads. The social and political naivete of modern corporate boffins is frightening, they read me and just take bits, all the cute technology, and miss about fifteen levels of irony.[12]

Although overstated, Gibson's characterisation is broadly correct. There have been few engagements with the more cautionary or critical aspects of his work in the public fora of the emerging cyber-culture. In one sense, responses to his novels can be seen to reinforce perceptions of the general apoliticism of science, scientists and the technology industries. More broadly, they could be seen as further evidence of the much-vaunted 'retreat from politics' in Western culture. But there is also another reading of this position, one which addresses Gibson's assumptions about the nature (and efficacy) of the science fiction genre itself. Science fiction has been seen to operate as a *cautionary* genre. By situating social problems (current or imagined) in an imminent future, it functions, in a manner akin to Victor Hugo's fiction, as a 'laboratory experiment' where the consequence of circumstances can be examined through the development of a fictional world. Gibson's concern is that the cautionary aspects of his work have been overlooked. Yet there is little evidence to prove that science fiction has *ever* been significantly effective as a cautionary genre – least of all where technology has been concerned. Perhaps only the series of nuclear horror films such as *The War Game* (1965), *The Day After* (1983) and *Threads* (1984) can, in association with major anti-nuclear campaigns, be seen to have had any profound cautionary effect on public and professional perceptions. Their 'target' issue, however, is notably starker and less equivocal than the subtler predictions of Gibson's fiction.

Gibson's work, and the Cyberpunk genre in general, have principally served to excite interest in newly developing interactive computer systems. In a social order whose economic and technological rationale still seems centred on a Marinettian notion of progress – where 'progress is right, even when it's wrong' – the lack of address to the cautionary aspects of the genre is perhaps understandable. It is not surprising that a society preoccupied with technology and consumerism can more readily grasp the potential pleasures of new media rather than predictions of the social decay they might cause. Whatever Gibson's (best) intentions, his work has created a desire for cyberspace technologies in advance of their production. Their current unavailability thereby renders them objects of desire *par excellence* for a high-tech consumer culture untroubled by vague speculations as to their dystopian potential.

In one sense, Brett Leonard's 1992 film *The Lawnmower Man* proves an exception to this tendency. Its plot involves a scientist who uses virtual reality programmes to boost the intelligence of Jobe, an intellectually disadvantaged male, to genius levels. In the process, however, Jobe develops pronounced telekinetic and psychic abilities and a messiah complex. After a confrontation in cyberspace between the subject and his scientific mentor Dr Angelo, Jobe evades a fatal data-trap and escapes, as 'pure intelligence', into the global data-grid. The film ends with the outcome Jobe prophesies, his birth as a new super-intelligence is proclaimed in the sound of every telephone in the world ringing simultaneously.

As this brief synopsis might suggest, the film combines a number of classic horror and science fiction themes and gives these contemporary colour through its representation of VR environments and the quasi-Gibsonian twist of its conclusion. The representation of sophisticated virtual reality systems within such a scenario, let alone the story of their development by sinister militaristic agencies, makes it distinctly darker in tone than even the bleakest aspects of Gibson's fiction. In Leonard's film, even the possibilities of virtual sex are represented in the bleakest of imaginable scenarios – a (literally) monstrous virtual rape which leaves its female victim permanently deranged. In this manner, the film is a classic exploitation picture which uses its virtual reality theme as a science–horror motif in a similar way to 1950s and 60s B-Movies such as *The Fly* (1958), *The Crack in the World* (1964) or *Attack of the Fifty Foot Woman* (1958).

As director Brett Leonard has emphasised, he became interested in virtual reality while living in 'northern California where a lot of the virtual reality technology was spawned'.[13] Together with co-writer Gimel Everett, he 'had been wanting to do a cyber film for quite a while' before embarking upon the *Lawnmower Man* project.[14] Like Stanley Jordan's *What's Goin' On* video (discussed further in the next section) one of the functions *The Lawnmower Man* fulfils is the simple *representation* of 3-D VR systems in a 2-D medium. The sequences which show the principal protagonists' transformed, computer-graphic bodies interacting in cyberspace are significantly successful in this regard. Indeed, these sequences, designed and animated by Angel Studios, who have also worked for agencies involved in actual 3-D VR development (such as NASA, the American Federal Aeronautics Administration and Nintendo), are perhaps the most impressive aspects of the film.

The director's stated intent in *The Lawnmower Man* was, however, not just to represent VR but to consciously produce 'a cautionary tale'[15] about it. Using Stephen King's eponymous short story as starting point, the director saw himself as developing a scenario which showed 'a man being transformed by this new technology in a kind of classic way like Mary Shelley's *Frankenstein* or *The Fly*'.[16] Leonard has gone on to emphasise how he drew upon this tradition to allow his film to address the 'big questions' raised by virtual reality, namely, what's going to happen to the human–machine interface and what does that mean for culture and communications in the 21st century.[17] Yet these questions are barely touched on by the film. The blend of generic themes and traditions, and the influence of horror writers such as King

187

himself and author-director Clive Barker produce a thematic momentum for the narrative which mediates and transforms any conscious representative intentions the director might have had. Indeed, perhaps the aspect most singularly lacking in interviews with the writers and director and in promotional material surrounding the film is the extent to which the film's scenario and narrative rely on the administration of mood and consciousness-altering drugs to its protagonists. Jobe's eventual psychosis is, after all, drug-induced and caused by an intentional overdose rather than by the interactive potential of VR systems. In this manner, the film resembles Ken Russell's odyssey of drug-induced reversion *Altered States* (1980) more than any of the central works of the Cyberpunk genre.

The dystopian and apparently cautionary aspects of the film's treatment of virtual reality are, in this way, less a product of intention than their generic context. Despite its clear rejection of any Marinettian notion of progress and its apparent affinity to the dystopian characterisations of Gibson's writing, the film is ultimately less a representation or prediction of VR than a curdled cocktail of generic traditions and aggregated themes which refer back to their own traditions rather than foregrounding the commentaries on VR the film's auteurs have emphasised.

Rock Culture – Sound and Vision

> William Gibson writes while watching MTV. He's a recent addition to the canon of writers whose work rock'n'roll people read. ... But Gibson uses very little music in his work ... (it's) a kind of of offstage influence.[18]

Rock music, or perhaps more precisely, the cultural forms, lifestyles and preoccupations associated with it, have had a significant influence upon the cultural context, development and popularisation of cyberspace. Indeed, as numerous accounts have cited, the key DataGlove system designed for VPL by Tom Zimmerman was inspired by a popular mime practice. Zimmerman set out to create an 'air guitar' – the imaginary instrument rock fans 'play' whilst miming to the sound of their favourite rock performers – which was *actually playable*.[19] Even independent of this specific connection, music-associated youth cultural magazines such as the American *Rolling Stone* and *Mondo 2000* and the British *The Face* have, in particular, played a central role in publicising and popularising the cyberspace phenomenon. This in turn reflects the manner in which rock culture foreshadowed aspects of virtual reality experience through its own forms and traditions.

The *immersion* in sound and light offered to the user who dons glove and goggles and thereby enters another 'world' has parallels with a variety of popular music practices. One significant precursor of the audiovisual environments of cyberspace has been the integration of sound and vision in rock performance. Acts as diverse as the Grateful Dead (in the late 60s), Hawkwind (in the 70s) or Laurie Anderson (in the 80s) attempted to create integrated audiovisual performance experiences which can be seen to have anticipated aspects of current virtual reality programmes. Similarly, the integration of complex light shows with pre-recorded sounds at various dance events, including those momentous Acid House 'raves' of the late 80s, provided another precedent.

These cultural forms and their conventions fed into another form, music video, which – though a passive rather than interactive medium – has also prefigured aspects of cyberspace. Whatever the degree of specific influence of MTV and music video on Gibson's writing, a number of music videos (particularly those which feature human figures interacting with computer graphic sequences) can be seen to both prefigure, and of late *represent*, the visual environment and user-experience of cyberspace programmes. As I have argued elsewhere, a preoccupation with novel technical effects has dominated a significant strand of music video production over the last two decades.[20] This has led to the production of a series of videos which insert the performer(s) into the (virtual) electronic spaces generated by the effects equipment used. David Mallett's video for David Bowie's 1980 single *Ashes to Ashes* is a significant early example, placing Bowie and his retinue in a garish fantasy chromakey world. But more significantly, The Cars' *You Might Think*, a major 'hit' on MTV in early 1984, directly prefigures a number of cyberspace's current preoccupations. Through computer graphics and advanced matting, the video features scenes where the Cars' lead singer Ric Ocasek turns into creatures such as a human-headed fly and a giant ape. In the video's narrative he performs as if in possession of the scale and mobility of these creatures – the visual images alternating between his point of view and that of the video's other character, the attractive young female he persists in annoying.

The potential to experience mobility and perception from the point of view of another creature, a key conceptual motif in *You Might Think*, is precisely one of those uses of cyberspace singled out by early experimenters with the form. As Lanier has been proud to observe, 'around here at VPL you have people become different animals all the time.'[21] Similarly, Stephen Levy noted that one VPL researcher had 'logged considerable time as a lobster'.[22] For all the presumably profound implications of such a perceptual and experiential shift, it is significant to note that one early user of VPL's equipment – an unidentified Hollywood director – used the system to indulge in a *You Might Think* style fantasy. After requesting the creation of an (effectively) hundred-foot-tall Amazon goddess for his personalised programme, he then used the transformative facility to explore her physique from a fly's-eye view, repeatedly circling her nipples ...

While videos such as *You Might Think* can be seen to have prefigured aspects of cyberspace, others have sought to *represent* the experiences it offers. The earliest and most significant of these representations occurs in the video for Max Q's 1989 single *Monday Night By Satellite*. The video, made for Australian group Max Q (a collaborative venture between INXS singer Michael Hutchence and musician Ollie Olsen) was directed by Jeff Jaffers with special effects co-ordination by Karen Ansell. It presents a computer-generated world where the musicians float through spaces which constantly transform through fractal progressions. In one way the video simply conforms to a particular tradition of competitive high-tech imagery in the form but there is an additional significance to its style and representative address. Both Olsen and Jaffers are members of the Australian cyberspace and hackers group 'Melbourne Cybergate' founded by Paul Brown in early 1990. The video can thereby be read as a significant representation of the perceptions of those involved in the early phases of cyberspace's development and promotion, a localised cultural vanguard.

Considered in this context, the most notable aspect of the video is its banality. *Monday Night By Satellite* is escapist in the most literal sense of that term. Its scenario is one of entry into an hallucinatory space produced by computer electronics where the video's protagonists float, dazzled by evanescent illusions. The escapism of the video is compounded by composer Olsen's statements on his interest in virtual reality (and that other currently fashionable popular science topic, Chaos Theory) at the time of making the tape. His views conflate a traditional mystical desire for transcendence of the material with unreconstructed rock culture hedonism. As he stated in an interview:

I want to become comfortable in the fact that there is ultimately no knowledge at all. ... That's where I really attach myself to chaos theory. I'm interested in infinity, and I want to feel comfortable in it and not to have silly notions of gods and bombs and ozone layers and things like that.[23]

Leaving aside his rather confused characterisation of Chaos Theory, the statement is one of hopeless futility, of escape into illusion. In the video, cyberspace becomes a bolt-hole from material, political and ecological reality, those tiresome inhibitors of the mental voyager. At a time when various other rock musicians such as Sting, Chrissie Hynde, Peter Gabriel and Peter Garrett are becoming noted for their support of eco-political issues, cyberspace and 'Chaos' look a good way out.

Nevertheless, cyberspace has also attracted considerable attention from what might be seen as the more astute and politically informed rock faction too. Laurie Anderson, for instance, whose multimedia shows throughout the 80s demonstrated both a use and an intelligent engagement with complex technologies,[24] has expressed an interest. Intrigued by the technology, its possible cultural applications and the high-tech mystique surrounding the form, she has suggested a number of possible applications. One of these, mooted as a collaboration between herself, Peter Gabriel and Brian Eno, is 'to have each of the three artists do a song, performed in a world he or she would design' and have the other artists join them, with the audience looking 'at three large TV screens, each of which would show what each artist is seeing'[25] – a project which extends collaboration and improvisation into an interactive visual medium.

Despite the potential of such a project, Anderson has, however, been cautious about the current state of the form and its technology. In particular, she remains unsatisfied both by the visual resolution of current systems and by the manner in which the goggles' screens still function as viewing surfaces. As she said of her first encounter with the medium, 'I felt I was trapped in the surface of a TV screen.'[26] In contrast, John Barlow, of The Grateful Dead, has waxed enthusiastic about more traditionally 'psychedelic' uses of the technology. He has proposed that it would be exciting to put the band 'inside Virtual Reality during a show and then rear-project the scene inside Virtual Reality on a screen behind the band so the audience can watch them become creatures and stuff, playing their instruments'[27] – a scenario which presumably does not involve the more complex meditations on technology present in Anderson's work.

The first music video to use sequences actually generated by cyberspace systems was produced in 1990 for Stanley Jordan's single *What's Goin' On*. Made (inevitably) in collaboration with Lanier, the video performs a dual promotional function. It promotes the single (and Jordan himself) by associating them with the new 'hot' medium of cyberspace; and promotes cyberspace itself within the youth cultural context of music television. This latter aspect is emphasised by the manner in which the video represents its technology. In many ways it is almost a demonstration tape for cyberspace in which Jordan incidentally appears. Jordan has confirmed this aspect in interviews, describing how he wanted to publicise what he sees as 'the future of entertainment'.[28] The video consists of three principal sequences edited together and synched with the pre-recorded soundtrack. These comprise standard music performance footage, sequences of Jordan in the VPL labs donning visor and data glove and sequences of the video graphic environment experienced by Jordan whilst 'in' the cyberspace programme.

Despite the radical potential claimed for cyberspace systems, the graphics sequences represented in the (two-dimensional) video appear relatively orthodox. Matching Jordan's somewhat predictable request for a cyberspace programme of 'a space I could fly around in with lots of music toys',[29] the cyberspace sequences feature a vividly coloured room full of floating guitars and other instruments together with a graphic representation of Jordan himself. Although ingenious, they illustrate the limited capacity for an individual's experience of cyberspace to be represented on a one-dimensional screen – a problem which would presumably afflict Barlow's idea for cyberspace programmes for live Grateful Dead performances.

Although the potential to represent cyberspace experiences in music video appears limited, cyberspace technologies themselves suggest more ambitious forms of cultural production. Given the interest shown by musicians such as Anderson, Gabriel or Jerry Garcia, a scenario might be envisaged whereby audio releases were accompanied by promotional cyberspace software in much the same way as they are today by music videos. These programmes would allow the system-user to enter the particular 'world' designed for the audio track and to explore and interact with its virtual environment (within the limits of the programme). From a sales point of view, such programmes would, unlike music video, offer the user a multiplicity of interactive 'routes' and options. The market appeal of such programmes would presumably be further enhanced if the performers could be represented in cyberspace with a greater degree of fidelity than today's limited systems allow. The market appeal of any form which would allow its user to enter cyberspace and interact with stars like Madonna is obvious. We might even postulate another option, the availability of a multiplicity of versions of individual programmes, much as multiple versions (mixes, remixes, etc.) of individual music tracks are available today. These, selectively priced, could offer 'greater', or simply 'different', options for interaction. For the fan, the opportunity to enter a cyber-karaoke system where you could jam with the band of your dreams, would presumably be an irresistible prospect.

On a more radical level, Lanier has also hypothesised how cyberspace systems could profoundly extend the boundaries of musical creativity. Going beyond such developments as the 'air guitar' simulator or the 'virtual drum kit' system designed by NASA engineers, Lanier's vision is far more ambitious. In his imagination, future cyberspace systems would enable the user to improvise 'real things' such as cityscapes or whole 'virtual worlds'. Still at the hypothetical stage, Lanier has suggested these as cyberspace applications which can be activated, played and controlled through 'virtual objects' resembling musical instruments. As he explained to Stephen Levy:

> Okay, you're in virtual reality, right? And there's this virtual instrument on this virtual table. It's a funny instrument, maybe a bagpipe. You've never played it before. You pick it up and toot out a few notes. What happens initially is, there's one crooked, funny skyscraper, and a slum. But as you play it, all of a sudden a city spins out.[30]

Such a system would obviously constitute a new cultural form with rich possibilities, a whole new medium. As yet, it is unattainable, beyond the capacity of existing technologies. But before writing it off as wild fantasy, the product of an over-fertile imagination, it is worth noting Lanier's track record at turning the wildest dreams into (virtual) reality . . .

Psychedelia

> The closest analog to Virtual Reality in my experience is psychedelic, and, in fact cyberspace is already crawling with delighted acid heads.[31]

Well they outlawed LSD. It'll be interesting to see what they do with this.[32]

The characterisation of cyberspace as 'psychedelic' derives from a number of factors. The first of these concerns the cyberspace user's immersion in an interactive environment. Transcending traditional spectatorship or the limited interaction possible with computer games, the closest analogy to the cyberspace user's interaction with an (illusory) cybernetic 'world' has been seen as the hallucinatory experience of drug use. While this analogy does not stand up to sustained scrutiny, other aspects, such as the suspension of 'the real' in favour of disorientating fantasy worlds, and different perceptions of bodily capacity and control, have contributed to the comparison. The analogy has been strengthened by its discussion in popular cultural circles where its most significant uses have been perceived as either recreational escapism, or else as some more supposedly profound 'consciousness-expanding' experience.

The association of cyberspace with psychedelia and psychedelic counter-culture has strong parallels with the manner in which these have been associated with popular music culture. Closely related and mutually supportive in the 60s, they have converged at various other points since – most notably the late 80s with the popularity of both the drug Ecstasy and Acid House music. As writers such as Harry Shapiro have chronicled, popular music and drug culture have been closely associated since at least the turn of the century.[33] The 60s, however, saw a particularly concentrated – even 'programmatic' – liaison between the two. At centres such as Andy Warhol's Factory in New York City, Leary's Millbrook mansion in upstate New York, Ken Kesey's La Honda retreat in southern California and Leary-disciple Michael Hollingshead's World Psychedelic Centre in London, key musicians became acquainted with LSD and other drugs and subsequently produced music (and lyrics) which reflected this encounter. Bands such as the Beatles, Grateful Dead, Rolling Stones and Velvet Underground and musicians such as Eric Clapton and Donovan all became inducted into 'Psychedelic Culture' at these centres. Following the opening up, or 'democratisation' of LSD access via the series of 'Acid Test' happenings in California (where unlimited Kool Aid fruit juice spiked with LSD was available for a flat $1 fee), drug use also spread widely throughout youth culture as a recreational pursuit.

Various style magazines and cultural commentators noted a return to a hallucinogenic drug culture in the late 80s and attributed this to a pattern of cultural cyclicity. While it is probably inaccurate to characterise the late 80s as primarily a 'revival' or 'replay' of the late 60s, there was a degree of observable cyclicity of interests and preoccupations which led to a revival in the fortunes of *some* key 60s figures. In musical terms, The Grateful Dead are perhaps the most significant example. In their earlier incarnation as The Warlocks, the group had virtually been the 'house-band' of the mid-60s 'Acid Tests'. By the late 60s and early 70s, they had built a reputation for themselves with their extended 'psychedelic' and often drug-induced 'jams'. Generally adjudged to be at an artistic nadir in the early 70s, the group managed to sustain themselves until the late 80s when they became a major hit with a new generation. Their success may, at least in part, be attributed to the manner in which they have not simply pursued a nostalgia trip but also engaged with distinctly contemporary cultural preoccupations. Since the late 80s, they have been notable for their enthusiasm for cyberspace technologies and the allegedly 'consciousness altering' potential of their use. Lead vocalist and guitarist Jerry Garcia is often cited as a new convert to the form and lyricist John Barlow has also championed it in a number of articles.[34]

This revival in fortunes and interest has not only affected rock performers. Timothy Leary, advocate of LSD as a universal panacea and author of *The Politics of Ecstasy*, has also resurfaced, this time as an advocate of cyberspace. Indeed, he was a notably early convert, linking the 'ecstatic politics' of the 60s with the new technology by starring in a video promo made for the Autodesk company's Cyberia project in winter 1988. This time around he is back not just as a (sub)cultural guru but also as a businessman. Founder of Futique Inc., in his polemical articles he now also publicises his company's product.[35] Although not the first to advocate the exploration of LSD as a means of prompting the human creative and perceptual responses (this 'honour' falling to Oscar Janiger in the 50s[36]), Leary was perhaps the drug's most successful publicist. Beginning his campaign to publicise the mind-expanding potential of the drug in 1962 (when it was still legal in the United States), he developed a serious and studious approach to the drug's use for 'inner voyages' and enhanced meditation. Although he developed this in his much publicised *The Politics of Ecstasy*, his influence waned after the dissolution of the Millbrook centre, his drug-bust in 1965 and the massive popularity of LSD as a recreational drug rather than 'psychic aid'.

The explosion of interest in virtual reality has contributed to a revival of interest in such psychedelic pursuits. Companies are predicting that cyberspace systems will not only appeal to the youth market but also to the generation who grew up with 60s' psychedelic culture. As a spokesman for the British company Division emphasised, 'members of the old drug culture are now a bit older. They've got money to spend, and they want to spend it on virtual reality.'[37] Consumer interest has been stimulated by assertions about the positive social and consciousness-expanding effects of cyberspace. Many of these parallel those initially made for LSD as a utopian or 'civilising' drug. Paul Brown's assertion that a proto-cyberspace system he observed in operation in 1985 'acted as a catalyst for close spontaneous human interaction' in a manner which 'encounter-group therapists have been trying to create ... for decades',[38] for example, recalls much of the revolutionary rhetoric of Leary and his followers. In particular, it recalls 60s poet Allen Ginsberg's (psilocybin-inspired) notion that world peace would be possible if all world leaders would share the drug experience and change their perceptions and behaviour accordingly (or, as the slogan later had it, 'Turn On, Tune In, Drop Out').

Despite the consumption habits of many of Gibson's characters in the Cyberpunk novels, cyberspace has displaced drugs as a preoccupation for the majority of its advocates. Indeed, for many writers and early explorers, cyberspace is, at this stage at least, a 'safe' alternative to chemical use. As Lanier has observed, 'the idea of a technology coming along which has the fun of the Sixties' idea of what drugs were, along with the safety and insulation you have with computers, is a very seductive combination'.[39]

The pristine safety of this scenario is, however, unlikely to last. Whatever *actual* effect prolonged exposure to cyberspace systems may have, it is not too fanciful to assume that a generation of neurologists and psychologists will soon log and publicise the various states, conditions, syndromes and disorders likely to be diagnosed amongst early users. If established patterns are followed, this in turn will lead to moral panics, press campaigns and lobby groups against the medium. Indeed, there is an aspect to cyberspace which might yet provide moral panic groups with something approaching the ultimate horror scenario. The 'plug-in drug' of television which so preoccupied Marie Winn and other American behaviourists[40] is likely to fade as a social horror in favour of the more engrossing realms of virtual reality. Much of the rhetoric which was figurative about television is likely to be literally true of cyberspace. If there is any truth in the recurring claim

196

that it is actually in the interests of the dominant power group to let disadvantaged youth groups preoccupy and disable themselves with drug culture, a scenario might be conceived where the establishment's desire for social control will encourage cyberspace use to proliferate.

New Age Mysticism

> The first interview was in Boston during the (1989) SIGGRAPH Conference. Virtual Reality was the hot topic ... and by the time I caught him ... Jaron had been lionized into demi-divinity.[41]

> Are you ready to make a world? I call this course God 101.[42]

Euphoria over the revolutionary nature of cyberspace technology has often been expressed in decidedly 'mystical' tones echoing the 'spiritual' concerns of 60s hippie psychedelia and converging with aspects of those beliefs and practices which have come to be known as 'New Age'. This convergence is of course a somewhat awkward one. Cyberspace is premised on aspects which seem initially antithetical to the New Age sensibility. Instead of making individuals more in touch with their 'inner harmonies' and the 'resonance' of the universe, cyberspace users are instead inserted into a cybernetic virtual reality within which our bodies have only a virtual existence. The pertinence of cyberspace to the New Age sensibility lies in its perceived capacity to complement and extend the spiritual aspects of meditation and 'spiritual development'. In one fell swoop, cyberspace systems are seen to reconcile what Lewis Mumford described as that divide between 'Utilitarian' (mechanistic) and 'Romantic' (humanist) sensibilities which has typified Western culture since – at least – the Industrial Revolution.[43] The reified domain of cyberspace is posed as an electronic realm where both designers and users can combine rational, imaginative and creative impulses in a sphere untrammelled by the commodification, market economy and general responsibilities of day-to-day living.

This perception reflects the millenarian aspects of the term 'New Age' itself. Its world order is posed as fundamentally post-materialist and it promises to fill the perceived spiritual void of Western society. New Age is, however, nothing if not contradictory. In particular, New

Age is big business. In both the US and the West in general, books, paraphernalia (crystals, jewellery etc.), services (such as flotation tanks) and devices (such as synchro-energisers) are all highly lucrative products. The New Age market encompasses both the middle-aged established-income generation who grew up in the 60s and younger people meeting it for the first time.

As a movement and as a marketing phenomenon, New Age relies heavily on the promotion of particular individuals as product champions, fashion initiators, pace-setters, rhetoricians and, perhaps most crucially, gurus. So pronounced is the guru-orientation of the movement that some of the key individuals involved in its popularisation, most notably actress Shirley MacLaine, have had 'gurudom' thrust upon them. MacLaine's ideas about the 'inner technology' of the body have even informed some academic discussions of human–computer interfacing.[44]

Jaron Lanier, most often cast as the 'inventor' of cyberspace technology, has also emerged as its guru. Unlike those theoreticians who have achieved celebrity status by pronouncing on the revolutionary implications of new technologies (MacLuhan, Toffler, Virilio etc.), Lanier is distinctive by virtue of his practical involvement with the medium he theorises about. He also inhabits a different historical moment and has benefited from a different process of image-making and promotion. To use a term appropriated by 60s rock culture, one consciously acted out by Jim Morrison, Lanier appears and behaves as a 'shaman' – a man of magic and mystery. Lanier's public persona also resembles that of Leary in his early career when, as Harry Shapiro emphasised:

A religious fervour had gripped him; religious imagery informed all he felt about LSD. He was a priest of the God Acid; there was a message to preach, souls to be saved, bibles and tracts to be written.[45]

The religious aspects of Lanier's image go beyond his conviction and fervour. His public persona draws on one of the most powerful strands of American imagery, Christian religion. With a biography stressing how he emerged 'out of the desert', and with his unkempt Marleyesque dreadlocks, he evokes an image of the ascetic prophet – a latter-day John the Baptist striding out of the deserts of New Mexico, mumbling cryptic truths and possessed by apocalyptic visions. This image has been significant in his promotion. The *Wall Street Journal*'s major feature on Lanier[46] was accompanied, not by 'state of the art' computer graphics but by a black and white portrait done in medieval woodcut-style, suggesting Lanier as an old-style charismatic prophet or heretic. The 'cool' world of science and cybernetics is presented as infused with a quasi-religious fervour without the revised theism which has also infused the world of 'New Physics'. Virtual reality itself is the 'transcendent beyond' in Lanier's vision.

Playing with such imagery is of course playing with fire. Whatever Lanier's status as a youth cultural 'guru', his pronouncements are manifestly heretical. They lay him open to religious characterisation not only as a 'false prophet' but, presumably, as a servant of Satan (a classic case of karmic return . . .). Chief among his sins is his attempting to 'play God'. Describing his work at VPL he has said, 'We put together worlds real fast here. We put together worlds in an hour or two. And it has to become a few seconds.'[47] In this light, the anecdote with which John Barlow prefaces his extended interview with Lanier, in what is perhaps *the* key New (Cyber) Age publication *Mondo 2000*, has a deeper resonance:

> I remember it very clearly. It looked like this. Jaron Lanier, whom I had never seen before, was walking across the central lawn of the Hebrew girls' camp in the Santa Cruz Mountains where the Hackers Conference is held. He was a diverting sight in the rays of the late afternoon sun. . . . The only trouble with this pellucid memory is that Jaron was not at Hackers. . . . This phantom remembrance is an example of something which comes up a lot these days. I call it *jamais vu*, the vivid memory of an event that never happened. And, given what Jaron's work is doing, irregularities will soon afflict more than the admittedly brain-damaged like myself.[48]

Barlow creates a superhuman status for Lanier, as a sage or guru capable of manifesting himself in various places and times, resembling the shadowy figures of cyberspace who pop in and out of various realities – virtual or otherwise – in the fictional Cyberpunk genre. Whatever the precise characterisation, Barlow's description goes beyond the complimentary prose of a captivated critic and instead reflects a sense of awe at a figure whose work and prophecies are perceived to herald a 'new age' of culture and consciousness.

The millenarian sensibility evident here is obviously of a different order from the pessimistic Armageddonism of the Christian New Right. Its optimism fits far more clearly with New Age utopianism which, amongst other things, predicts that the next generation will be born with strong psychic powers, able to conceive, communicate and commune with nature and mankind in new 'deeper' ways. Marrying psychedelic rhetoric with New Age thought, Barlow's prose proposes Lanier and cyberspace as revolutionising consciousness by breaking open the everyday 'collective hallucination we call reality' – a spiritual 'making strange', the ultimate deep *verfremdungseffekt*. Barlow's phraseology is playfully ironic here, making Gibson's characterisation of cyberspace as a 'consensual hallucination' reflect back on everyday reality as just another consensual order. It is this which is the cornerstone of the New Age euphoria over cyberspace, a move beyond the automaton aspects which mystics such as Gurdjieff and Ouspensky perceived to dominate existence, towards a 'purer' thought realm where the materiality of the body can be left behind. In this manner, however dressed up, we have the reductum of the enthusiasm for cyberspace which musician Ollie Olsen summarised earlier: its potential to be a bolt-hole from reality.

New Orders

This chapter has aimed to demonstrate how cyberspace technologies and virtual reality have been promoted, popularised, and to a large extent constituted within a number of popular cultural discourses. These have provided the form with both a profile and consumer demand in advance of its availability. As previous sections detail, Lanier has been a pivotal figure in this. His pronouncements and persona have provided valuable publicity for the companies involved in developing and marketing the technology. Lest it be forgotten in the hyperbole, however, all the agencies currently involved in producing and promoting cyberspace, including Lanier's own VPL, are either commercial, governmental-military or otherwise academic institutions funded by industry or government bodies. As a medium which appeals to various markets (consumer electronic, rock culture, New Age etc.), the commercial outlook for cyberspace looks rosy. Ironically, while much cyberspace rhetoric has been premised on the New Age aspects of its techno-futurist aesthetic, the major investment and development of the medium look likely to emanate from existing companies like Nintendo, chiefly known for marketing games based on violent, and often military, themes. The visual style and scenarios of these games closely resemble those of the computer-assisted military sensing and simulation systems which came to public attention during the 1991 Gulf War. Indeed such is their convergence with existing military technologies that a number of observers referred to the Gulf conflict (and the manner in which it was represented via the world media) as a 'Nintendo War'.[49]

While cyberspace may be significantly different from previous cultural media, its programmes, virtual realities and user experiences are just as firmly rooted in contemporary capitalism as any other form of contemporary culture. Those who have promoted it as 'revolutionary' have neglected to consider the possibilities of transcending established cultural forms and conventions with technologies and cultural practices originated from within that selfsame culture. Nowhere is this avoidance clearer than in the manner in which Lanier has advocated cyberspace as an innately peaceful medium whilst lamenting the violent nature of currently available glove technology games. Lanier's sadness is blatantly 'unworldly', since this development was patently obvious to anyone aware of the history and economic basis of the computer games industry. Indeed, given the likely industrial contexts of cyberspace's future development, there may well be other potentially alarming uses of cyberspace systems. Consider, for instance, the manner in which cyberspace users might encounter advertisements. Gibson has suggested that the 'commercial breaks' in cyberspace might be akin to 'freebasing TV ads', might be 'like having pure, uncut advertising injected directly into the brain'[50] – a scenario presumably more attractive to the radical capitalist than to the New Age guru.

Instead of emerging from a somehow 'innocent' cybernetic realm, cyberspace systems and their virtual experiences have been produced by contemporary capitalism and reflect its cultural forms and paradigms. This is not to underestimate the potential of the form, however; it undoubtedly constitutes an exciting advance in audiovisually interactive and 'environmental' systems. The medium of cyberspace and the virtual realities which will come to be constituted within it, have much to offer artists and cultural practitioners. There may yet even be profound communicative and philosophic engagements with the form in ways which we can now only begin to grasp. Whatever these might be, however, cyberspace will clearly not inaugurate a New Age of consciousness through its technology alone nor through the capacity of its programmers to conjure fantasy worlds – interactive or otherwise.

NOTES

1. James Foley, 'Interfaces for Advanced Computing', *Scientific American*, October 1987, p. 86.
2. Kevin Robins, *Into the Image – Visual Technologies and Vision Cultures*, mimeo, Centre for Urban and Regional Development Studies, Newcastle University, Newcastle upon Tyne, 1991, p. 12.
3. Ibid. pp. 12–13.
4. Richard Guilliatt, 'SF and the tales of a new romancer', *The Sunday Herald* (Australia), 17 December 1989, p. 37.
5. Paul Brown, 'Metamedia and Cyberspace: Advanced Computers and the Future of Art', in Philip Hayward (ed.), *Culture, Technology and Creativity* (London: John Libbey/Arts Council, 1990), p. 227.
6. Timothy Leary, 'The Communication Revolutions of the Twentieth Century', *Tension* no. 23, October–November 1990, p. 19.
7. Paul Brown, 'Metamedia and Cyberspace', p. 238.
8. Fredric Jameson, 'Introduction', in his *Postmodernism or the Cultural Logic of Late Capitalism* (Durham: Duke University Press, 1991), p. ix, footnote 1.
9. Leary, 'The Communications Revolution', p. 19.
10. Leary, cited in Guilliatt, 'SF and the tales of a new romancer'.
11. Leary, cited in Guilliatt, 'SF and the tales of a new romancer'.
12. William Gibson, in Jim McClellan, 'From Here to Reality', *The Face* vol. 2 no. 15, December 1989, p. 70.
13. Brett Leonard in (unattributed) interview transcript in August Entertainment's 'Production Notes' for *The Lawnmower Man* (1992).
14. ibid.
15. ibid.
16. ibid.
17. ibid.
18. John Williams, 'Musical Notes', *The Face* vol. 2 no. 27, p. 117.
19. Successful in this initial endeavour, one of the first projects Lanier and Zimmerman developed was a Jimi Hendrix 'simulator'!
20. See Philip Hayward, 'Industrial Light and Magic – Style, Technology and Special Effects in the Music Video and Music Television', in Philip Hayward (ed.), *Culture, Technology and Creativity*, pp. 124–48.
21. Jaron Lanier, in Stephen Levy, 'Brave New World', *Rolling Stone* (Australian edition), no. 448, October 1990, p. 92.
22. Levy, ibid.
23. Ollie Olsen, in Ute Junker, 'Ollie Olsen', *Ots*, 18 April 1990, p. 31.
24. For a discussion of this aspect of her work see Andrew Murphie, 'Negotiating *Presence* – Performance and New Technologies' in Philip Hayward (ed.), *Culture, Technology and Creativity*, pp. 209–26.
25. According to Peter Schwartz, technical advisor to Peter Gabriel, in Stephen Levy, 'Brave New World', p. 95.

26. Laurie Anderson, cited by Stephen Levy, ibid.
27. John Barlow, 'Life in the Data Cloud', *Mondo 2000* no. 2, Summer 1990, p. 50.
28. Stanley Jordan, cited in Melinda Newman, 'Stanley Jordan Embraces Virtual Reality', *Billboard* vol. 102 no. 27, 7 July 1990, p. 53.
29. Ibid.
30. Jaron Lanier, in Stephen Levy, 'Brave New World', p. 95.
31. John Barlow, 'Being In Nothingness – Virtual Reality and the Pioneers of Cyberspace', *Mondo 2000* no. 2, Summer 1990, p. 41.
32. Jerry Garcia (The Grateful Dead), in John Barlow, ibid. p. 41.
33. Harry Shapiro, *Waiting for the Man – The Story of Drugs and Popular Music* (London: Quartet, 1988).
34. See, for instance, his perceptive survey 'Being In Nothingness – Virtual Reality and the Pioneers of Cyberspace' and his somewhat less critical interview with Lanier 'Life in the Datacloud' – both in *Mondo 2000* no. 2, summer 1990.
35. In the penultimate section of his article 'The Communications Revolutions of the Twentieth Century', in the Australian magazine *Tension* no. 23, October–November 1990, pp. 16–19, Leary states 'My own group, Futique Inc., is developing educational courseware (DisKourses) and Mind Movies. These are multi-lingual, multi-media interactive programs in which users "jack into cyberspace and perform books and direct film scripts". Gibson's incredible fantasy future is already "up and running" and soon to be outdated.'
36. Amongst his volunteer guinea-pigs were 'jazz eccentric' Lord Buckley, conductor André Previn and actor Jack Nicholson (who later wrote the screenplay for the film *The Trip* (1966), based on his experiences with Janiger).
37. Division spokesman, in Dorian Silver, 'Reality is Getting More *Unreal* Daily – Cyberspace', *The Face* vol. 2 no. 27, December 1990, p. 96.
38. Paul Brown, 'Metamedia and Cyberspace' p. 236.
39. Jaron Lanier, in Stephen Levy, 'Brave New World', p. 95.
40. See, for instance, Marie Winn, *The Plug-in Drug* (New York: Viking Press, 1977).
41. John Barlow, 'Life in the Datacloud', p. 44.
42. Jaron Lanier, in Stephen Levy, 'Brave New World', p. 95.
43. Lewis Mumford, *The Future of Technics and Civilization* (London: Freedom Press, 1986), pp. 34–6.
44. Indeed, so seriously is MacLaine taken in some (American) circles that scientific and technical papers cite the influence of her work. In her 1990 paper presented at the Australian Computer Graphics Association's 'Ausgraph 90' event, Paras Kaul of California State University proceeded to argue the case for 'a greater sophistication' in sound/image relations in computer graphics, 'based on the research of Shirley MacLaine, expressed in her book, *Going Within* [where] each of the seven nerve centers of the body has its own vibratory level of energy which resonates to a corresponding note on the musical scale' – *Ausgraph 90 Proceedings*, p. 25.
45. Harry Shapiro, 'Waiting for the Man', pp. 131–2.

46. Entitled 'A Kind of Electronic LSD?' referred to by Stephen Levy, 'Brave New World', p. 95.
47. Jaron Lanier, in John Barlow, 'Life in the Datacloud', p. 50.
48. John Barlow, 'Being in Nothingness', p. 44.
49. See, for instance, Christopher Dickey, 'Eyeballing the Nintendo Apocalypse', *Rolling Stone* (Australian edition), no. 456, April 1991, pp. 52–3.
50. William Gibson in Jim McClellan, 'From Here to Reality', p. 73.

INDEX

206

209

46   09